"The Roswell case is the most important UFO case of all time because it is from here that all decisions were made. It was the first of the cover-ups, the first attempt at misdirection, and one of the most important events in human history. It is where creatures from another world were first seen by creatures from Earth. That we still argue about the reality of this case today is simply unbelievable."

—Kevin D. Randle, Ph.D., coauthor of *UFO Crash At Roswell* and *The Truth About the UFO Crash At Roswell*

"No two men have done more to drag the truth about Roswell out of the shadows and to expose the outrageous cover-up which has been droning on for 60 years now than Tom Carey and Don Schmitt. If the cover-up is ever going to have a stake driven through it and the Roswell case resolved once and for all, it will most likely be Tom and Don who will do it. Their prolific contributions to Ufology constitute not only a bodrock of truth we can all be proud of, but demonstrate what dedication and sacrifice above and beyond the call of duty can produce. Their new book is another milostone in the deconstruction of the Roswell cover-up."

—Jeff Rense, nationally syndicated talk show host

"The mystery surrounding this crash has never been adequately explained—not by the independent investigators, and not by the U.S. government."

—Bill Richardson, governor of New Mexico, in the foreword to *The Roswell Dig Diaries*, a Sci Fi Channel Book

"Truly, something extraordinary crashed outside of Roswell, N.M. in July 1947."

—CBS News/48 Hours

"I am almost completely convinced that the object that crashed near Roswell was composed of materials not common on Earth."

—Major General Kenner F. Herford, USAF (retired)

"Roswell has long been a point of great interest to me.... When I asked General [Curtis] LeMay for permission to see it [the Roswell wreckage stored at Wright Patterson Air Force Base in Dayton, Ohio] he hit the ceiling and admonished me, *Not only no, but hell no!! And if you ask again, I'll have you court-martialed!* "

—U.S. Senator Barry M. Goldwater, Major General U.S. Air Force (deceased)

"...something big did happen at Roswell."

—Unnamed GAO investigator, as told to investigative columnist Jack Anderson, in "The Air Force Tried to Lead Everyone Astray on the Roswell Incident" with Michael Binstein, the *Albuquerque Journal*, June 1, 1995

WITNESS TO ROSWELL

Unmasking the 60-Year Cover-Up

Thomas J. Carey
and
Donald R. Schmitt

New Page Books
A division of The Career Press, Inc.
Franklin Lakes, NJ

WITNESS TO ROSWELL
EDITED AND TYPESET BY KARA REYNOLDS
Cover design by Lu Rossman/Digi Dog Design
Printed in the U.S.A. by Book-mart Press

To order this title, please call toll-free 1-800-CAREER-1 (NJ and Canada: 201-848-0310) to order using VISA or MasterCard, or for further information on books from Career Press.

The Career Press, Inc., 3 Tice Road, PO Box 687,
Franklin Lakes, NJ 07417
www.careerpress.com
www.newpagebooks.com

Library of Congress Cataloging-in-Publication Data

Carey, Thomas J., 1940-
    Witness to Roswell : unmasking the 60-year cover-up / by Thomas J. Carey and Donald R. Schmitt.
        p. cm.
    Includes bibliographical references and index.
    ISBN-13: 978-1-56414-943-5
    ISBN-10: 1-56414-943-9
        1. Unidentified flying objects—Sightings and encounters—New Mexico—Roswell. 2. Government information—United States. 3. Conspiracies—United States. I. Schmitt, Donald R. II. Title.

TL789.5.N6C37 2007
001.94209789'43--dc22

                                                                    2006103001

We just want the facts, ma'am.

—Sgt. Joe Friday, Detective Division, L.A.P.D.

Record enough facts, and the answer will fall to you like a ripe fruit.

—Franz Boaz, American anthropologist

Dedication

To my beloved wife of 39 years, Doreen, not only for coming up with the title of this book, but also for her emotional support and encouragement in allowing me to pursue my "hobby" all these years. —TJC

To my loving wife, Marie, who inspires me to go beyond the second star to the right, and then straight on 'til morning. —DRS

Acknowledgements

This work is intended to inform those among you, the interested public, who desire to know the truth behind a truly extraordinary event that occurred 60 years ago, as of this writing. A cover-up of the true nature of this event by elements of the United States Military was immediately instituted, and still survives, leaking but essentially intact, to this very day.

The dedicated, proactive Roswell investigative team of Tom Carey and Don Schmitt remains committed to ferreting out and reporting to you the ultimate truth of the so-called Roswell Incident by developing and following every clue, lead, or hint, no matter how small or where it may take us. To that end, this work represents the first major publication of the Carey/Schmitt investigative team—a down-payment to history—since it was formed in 1998, and will offer up new information and interpretations regarding the Roswell events stemming from our still-continuing, intensive investigation into this remarkable case of apparent alien visitation.

We would like to thank all of the witnesses, as well as others with source information who have come forward, many with great reluctance and some with fear for their own well-being, and agreed to talk to us "on the record" about those long-ago events. Regrettably, because Father Time waits for no one, many of these have since passed away. Without their courage and cooperation, we could not have moved this case forward beyond previous works on the subject, and this publication would not have been possible. Special thanks must go to Julie Shuster, herself the daughter of a key player in the 1947 Roswell events, and her staff at the International UFO Museum and Research Center in Roswell, New Mexico for their enduring assistance and support. The IUFOM&RC has truly become our base of operations when we are in Roswell. Thanks must also go to Nathan Twining, Jr. (whose father, the late Air Force General Nathan Twining, was in the thick of this story from start to finish), for his support, encouragement, and friendship, and the folks at the Sci Fi Channel in New York City for their continued interest in and support of our efforts on this subject. Specific thanks must also go to Roswell photographer Jack Rodden, who has provided us with several key leads and helped us gain access to especially reluctant witnesses, and to Roswell archaeologist Pat Flanary, whose knowledge of the Roswell region has been of immense help, especially in our search for the final Roswell crash site. And finally, special thanks must go to nuclear physicist Stanton Friedman for paving the way and providing us with witnesses to further our investigation.

We also thank:

Mr. and Mrs. Paul Harden of Socorro, N.M. for personally assisting us with our continuing investigation of the Plains of San Agustin.

Robert Durant for his thoughtfully kind words, encouragement, and professional assistance through the years.

Gloria Hawker, for her assistance in facilitating interviews for the authors with reluctant witnesses, especially Elias "Eli" Benjamin.

And lastly, a very special thank-you to Kevin Randle, not only for his groundbreaking work and steadfast position on Roswell, but also for his continuing service to our country.

Contents

Foreword
By Paul Davids

I cannot overemphasize the importance to me of the book you now hold in your hands—one of the most coherent, logical, thorough, and levelheaded works yet written about a subject of colossal importance. The lessons that we, as Americans, have to learn from the tragedy, travesty, mystery, and sheer wonder of the "Roswell Incident" are too many to list. Bottom line: None of us would wish that an incident like this, with potential historic implications for our nation and for mankind, would ever be handled this way again by the government, the military, or the press. In my opinion, to say that we have been lied to and are still being fed an official lie about this subject is a gross understatement. And it saddens me. However, in spite of all the official disinformation we the public have been fed about Roswell for the past 60 years, one very good thing resulted from the renewed attention about this UFO case during the Clinton administration in the 1990s (a good thing that has seldom or never been mentioned, and for which there has been no official follow-up): Former Secretary of the Air Force Sheila E. Widnall, who signed off on a report (*Roswell: Case Closed*) that I consider a setback in the search for the truth in every respect, must nevertheless must be thanked and appreciated for the one positive and prescient action she took. Secretary Widnall issued an order freeing all former servicemen of any secrecy restrictions that may have prevented them from telling what they know about the 1947 Roswell Incident. No longer would they have to fear recrimination, loss of pension, or even prison for violating any "oath of secrecy" forced upon them by the military long ago.

This action expanded the potential witness pool. Thomas J. Carey and Donald R. Schmitt are the only Roswell researchers of whom I am aware who seized the opportunity like energetic prosecutors. There were many former uniformed personnel who, up until that time, had refused to talk out of fear. The authors of this book were able to elicit a great deal of new testimony from many older servicemen—there is much here that you have not heard before, as a result of the work of Carey and Schmitt, and of the one specific action by Sheila Widnall. Every word and scrap and parcel of the new testimony contained herein further demolishes the government's new official stories designed to close the Roswell investigation with the "Mogul Balloon" and "Crash Dummy" explanations. All the new testimony is consistent with the fact that an extraterrestrial spaceship of unknown origin crashed near the small New Mexico town of Roswell in 1947 with aliens aboard, and the government concealed it from America and the world, much as Lieutenant Colonel Phillip Corso claimed was the case in his historic 1997 book, *The Day After Roswell*. Yes, you read that correctly—I used the word *fact*. I can no longer doubt the extraterrestrial explanation, and neither will you or any other reasonable person, after absorbing the breadth and detail of the documented testimony in this book.

For those of you new to the subject of Roswell (and there can't be many people left in that category, can there?) this book will take you straight to the key issues and testimony of the case. And for those of you who have so many books about Roswell in your libraries that they are practically falling off the shelves, what you will find here is coherence, organization, thoroughness—and best of all, massive amounts of continuing testimony relevant to the case. The new testimony and developments take us far beyond the original Donald R. Schmitt book on this subject, written in 1991 with Kevin Randle (*UFO Crash at Roswell*), all the way up to today. You will find much that is new, especially in the witnesses who at long last came forward, freed from their security oaths to provide information and testimony meant not to embellish the case, but to clarify it and fill in the missing details. You will learn why the authors now believe that key whistle-blower Major Jesse A. Marcel was one of the actual witnesses to alien bodies, and why the shocking treatment of rancher Mack Brazel, which is substantiated by many witnesses, so thoroughly contradicts all of the government's official stories by which the Air Force and Pentagon have come to label the Roswell Incident a "myth" and declare it CASE CLOSED.

Ladies and gentlemen of the press, of the military, and of the government—and former Secretary of the Air Force, Sheila Widnall—the case is *not closed*. I am shell-shocked to now know, beyond any reasonable doubt whatsoever, that the so-called conspiracy theorists who have sounded the alarm about our government's UFO cover-up have been absolutely correct. The skeptics be damned. Or better yet, may the skeptics read on and be awakened.

By way of background, in 1989 I optioned the motion picture rights to a 17-page outline that Donald R. Schmitt coauthored, and which he was then busy turning into his first book about Roswell. It was a meager check: $25, which he split with his coauthor. In a way, the size of the check reflected not only my very limited development funds back then, but also our assessment of our prospects—the outline had already been turned down by many publishers—and our option deal was soon followed by rejections from almost every TV network and major motion picture studio, all of which wrote curt rejection letters explaining the lack of interest, sometimes offering opinions about why such a film had little chance of ever being made, or should never be made. However, four years later, none of those networks or studios seemed to remember that they had spurned the project, as many asked me, "How come you never brought that project to us?" (Believe me, I had!)

In 1993, that $25 option deal based on Don Schmitt's writing had grown into a high-budget cable TV movie called *Roswell* (also known as *Roswell: The UFO Coverup*), starring Kyle MacLachlan, Martin Sheen, and country singer Dwight Yoakam. The film was nominated for a Golden Globe Award for Best Motion Picture for Television of 1994. We didn't win, but the mere nomination was historic, because the Hollywood Foreign Press Association was applauding a film declaring that there is a UFO cover-up and that we have been lied to about this subject by government suits with straight faces for half a century.

Tom Shales, *Washington Post* staff writer, wrote a stunning review, with comments such as, "You don't have to be Oliver Stone to find such a conspiracy entirely plausible..." and, "Even if you don't believe in UFOs, you can certainly believe that the military establishment could behave this way." He also wrote that the film "lingers hauntingly in the mind long after the closing credits have scrolled away." Alan Rich of *Variety* also offered praise, stating that director Jeremy Kagan paced the story convincingly, but he also felt that the film effectively raised suspicions about the American military's use of disinformation on the U.S. public.

It is now 13 years since the debut of the film, and it is no exaggeration to say that its impact on our culture is still felt. It helped launch an industry of Roswell-related books and documentary programs, and even a TV series. It awakened millions of people to the likelihood that we have been visited by beings from other worlds, and that the government has no interest whatsoever in telling us.

Walter Goodman, writing for the *New York Times*, loved the film but didn't believe it. He stated that for most of its 90 minutes, our film "maintained an engrossing course," but he concluded with the obvious puzzlement that is most often addressed by those unfamiliar with the facts by stating, "What prevents this professionally fashioned hokum from being a high flier is the annoying question of how a cover-up that involved hundreds or thousands of people could have been maintained for 30 years or even 30 seconds in this expose-prone society." Goodman, quite obviously, is not taking into consideration the extent of the cover-up that led to the creation of the first atomic bomb. The nation did not know for years that thousands of personnel were holed up in Los Alamos, New Mexico, creating a monster that would change the world. Appropriately, I am now in Los Alamos as I write this foreword, because a stage play I wrote is soon to open here. The contention of Tom Carey and Don Schmitt is that the Roswell Incident, like Los Alamos and the development of the atomic bomb, changed the world, and that we, the public, have not been granted the privilege of being told. There are officials among us who do not wonder any longer whether other intelligent life exists on worlds other than Earth; they have long known that the answer is yes. And this has complicated their lives in ways that they refuse or are forbidden to discuss.

And what about the spaceships from other worlds that conduct reconnaissance here on Earth and sometimes make contact with both civilians and government? Officially, they do not exist—but of course they *do* exist. Astronauts Edgar Mitchell (who walked on the Moon) and the late Gordon Cooper have stated that they exist. But the *New York Times* has not been listening, and the president appears to be deaf. Or at least he isn't talking. But he is in good company—the company of every former president, some of whom (such as Lyndon Johnson, Gerald Ford, Jimmy Carter, and Bill Clinton) wanted answers about UFOs before they became president and urged government disclosure. However, upon becoming president, they lost their vocal cords when it came to this issue.

This book will answer to your satisfaction the question posed by the *New York Times* in its review of our film. In fact, this book is the closest to the truth about the Roswell Incident you will ever stumble upon, until that ever-mythical and distant Day of Disclosure dawns. What you have been seeking is the true story, the facts, the reality that the government withholds from you and that the network news (with help from anchormen such as the late Peter Jennings) has twisted and morphed into a mush of falsehoods, precooked and prepackaged for dumbed-down viewers. And in this book, I think you have found what you are seeking. Also, fortunately, the book has been footnoted to the extreme, so you can track and inquire and investigate the sources of every statement you are being asked to accept.

Don Schmitt has paid his dues, and the same is true of his coauthor, Tom Carey. Together they have devoted over a quarter of a century solely to study of the Roswell Incident. You are about to enter a zone of distilled facts, culled from witness testimony, sworn or simply sincere. In the old TV detective show, *Dragnet*, Sergeant Joe Friday always asked for, "Just the facts, ma'am." You are about to get just the facts. And the facts make liars out of a lot of otherwise respectable people. But sometimes people in high places do not lie: The former defense minister of Canada, the honorable Paul Hellyer, was not lying when he stated on camera recently that the UFO cover-up is a fact and that governments have been secretly studying advanced extraterrestrial technologies for many years. And Vice President Dick Cheney was not lying when he stated, essentially, that if he had ever been briefed about UFOs it would surely have been classified, and he would not therefore be at liberty to discuss it. But as this is written, he is the vice president. Presumably, he and his administration have had the power to change course on this issue. But neither he nor "they" nor their predecessors have chosen to do so. Long after we are gone, history will pass judgment on the wisdom of those decisions. I personally think history will condemn those decisions harshly.

So who am I to be telling you this and to be making such assertions? I am just a movie producer, but a movie producer with a certain tenacity and conviction. Unfortunately, what I say and think does not count for a lot of people in the "real world" because movie producers so often deal with fiction. But I am nevertheless a film producer who is the son of a famous historian from Georgetown University (the late Dr. Jules Davids) who was closely associated with two presidents, both as a ghost writer (for JFK) and as a professor (to young Bill Clinton). I have heard and learned many things in my many years. And all that I have heard and learned leads me to believe that Tom Carey and Don Schmitt are absolutely correct. I no longer see any possibility that they are wrong, or that the official government stories about UFOs are correct.

This book is just in time for the 60th anniversary of the Roswell Incident, which will be widely remembered in New Mexico in the summer of 2007. A revolution in thinking about UFOs is about to overtake us all.

And so I urge you, by all means…read on!

—Paul Davids, Executive Producer of *Roswell*,
the Showtime Original Movie
January, 2007

Preface

How do we define a mystery? To the good people of New Mexico and many others involved in what we have termed "the ultimate cold case file," it can be defined in a single word—Roswell. At the dawn of the 21st century, Roswell has become synonymous with one of the most important events of all time. For that fact alone, it deserves to be researched and investigated until there is nothing left to investigate, or until a final conclusion is reached that is acceptable to most reasonable minds. The authors believe that the latter option has already been achieved.

To demonstrate this fact, we will build a case for you, focusing first on the legal framework and parameters by which the case must be judged. In its way, Roswell has proven to be as painstaking a case to develop and present—spanning 60 years—as any court case that has ever been decided. It is the case for an amazing event and the extreme measures that the military authorities took to suppress it. As with any jury, your time and attention are needed to follow the witness evidence. You might find it difficult at times, but it will become evident that another word summarizes this entire event: cover-up.

Understanding the case requires us to understand the times in which it occurred. We have to return to an America just two years after victory in her greatest war, when the military was held in perhaps the highest esteem ever by its citizens. We have to return to a time when the predicted post-war depression wasn't happening after all; when the last shreds of Eastern Europe's independence were being torn away with the descent of the "Iron Curtain," and the Cold War was becoming really chilly; when a single Paris fashion designer would decree all hemlines down; a time before air-conditioning (except in movie theaters) when city dwellers slept in parks to escape the summer heat; and when the press had a real tradition of filling the hot-weather news stories with hopes, fads, and wonders. It was a time before television, when radio was the chief means of in-home news and entertainment. Roy Rogers married Dale Evans, and the Brooklyn Dodgers' Jackie Robinson had just broken Major League Baseball's color barrier. The Big Band Era was all but over, but rock 'n' roll was still years away, and popular music reflected the uncertain-but-hopeful outlook of a victorious nation, as charted in *Billboard*'s top 10 songs for the week of July 6, 1947:

1. "Chi Baba, Chi Baba"—Perry Como
2. "Peg O' My Heart"—Jerry Murad & The Harmonicats
3. "I Wonder, I Wonder, I Wonder"—Eddy Howard
4. "Peg O' My Heart"—The Three Suns
5. "Temptation"—Red Ingle & The Natural Seven w/vocal by Jo Stafford
6. "Peg O' My Heart"—Art Lund
7. "That's My Desire"—Sammy Kay Orchestra w/vocal by Don Cornell
8. "Across The Alley From The Alamo"—The Mills Brothers
8. (Tie) "I Wonder, I Wonder, I Wonder"—Guy Lombardo & His Royal Canadians w/vocals by Don Rodney and The Lombardo Trio
9. "Peg O' My Heart"—Buddy Clark
10. "That's My Desire"—Frankie Laine
10. (Tie) "Peg O' My Heart"—Clark Dennis

During the two weeks encompassing the last week of June and the first week July 1947, newspapers across the country carried accounts describing the arrival of *flying saucers*. Witnesses throughout the country would describe flying "discs" and other assorted, metallic flying objects that defied conventional explanation. Military pilots were placed on 24-hour alert, and radar operators were on 24-hour standby—all looking skyward and hoping that whatever was invading our airspace was not a new threat to our national security that might lead to another war.

The state of New Mexico in 1947 was the most sensitive and highly guarded area in our country, if not the entire world. Not only was there ongoing atomic research at Los Alamos where the first atomic bomb was developed, but there was also the testing of captured German V-2 rockets taking place just to the south at White Sands near Alamogordo. Not far from Alamogordo was also Trinity Site, where the world's first atomic bomb was detonated. And at Roswell itself was the headquarters of the 509th Bomb Group, the only atomic strike force in the world at the time. It was the 509th that just two years before had dropped the two atomic bombs on Hiroshima and Nagasaki to end World War II. Little did they know that they would also become involved in one of the most significant, most historic events of all time—the crash of an unknown object.

In the late evening of July 3, 1947, a severe thunder and lightning storm raked central New Mexico. During the height of the storm, local ranchers would later describe hearing a loud explosion that did not sound like the other thunderclaps. Civilians would arrive at the site first. Some would attempt to report it to the local sheriff. Others would later describe what they saw, but they would wait many years before finally admitting to their closest family members and friends facts that still defy all reasonable and conventional explanation. As you will read, these people, members of America's "Greatest Generation," believed that they witnessed, up-close and personal, the remains of an interplanetary vehicle of unknown origin—a crashed flying saucer.

Introduction

Through the years that we have been investigating the Roswell Incident, two questions that we are often asked are, "With so many other reported UFO cases, now running into the tens of thousands, why have you concentrated on this one to the exclusion of others worthy of further investigation?" and, "Why continue to investigate a [now] 60-year-old case?" The reasons are several, and we will attempt to share some of these with you now.

Most researchers became interested in the subject of UFOs when they were children or very young adults, and we are no exceptions. There was something about the notion that intelligent life might exist elsewhere in the universe—and might actually be visiting us—that piqued our imaginations. This interest has persisted into adulthood and has in fact intensified over the years, especially with the recent discoveries of 200 or so planets outside our own solar system. More recently still is the discovery of an Earth-like planet in another star system in our galactic "neighborhood."

The vast majority of scientists and academicians believe that, statistically at least, other life must surely exist elsewhere in the vast universe. The divide arises, however, when the question of whether intelligent, extraterrestrial life forms have ever visited the planet Earth is asked (in other words, have "they" been able to get *here* from *there*?). Serious UFO researchers believe that there exists an overwhelming body of evidence to support the notion of alien visitation, and polls of the general public at large tend to reinforce this belief. However, "academic-types" believe that, not only has this not happened, but it is also impossible. This belief is not the result of stringent research into the subject or a conclusion derived from a reading of UFO literature; it is nothing more or less than a belief based upon the old axiom, "It can't be, therefore it isn't." The closest they come to a "scientific" explanation is to mutter something about the vast distances that would be involved in any interstellar travel. The late Cornell astronomer, Carl Sagan, who took the standard, safe academic position regarding UFOs—namely that they don't exist—nevertheless believed that there were at least 1 million evolved intelligences in our own Milky Way galaxy alone! We believe that life in the universe, just as on Earth, is the norm and not the exception. Just as Jeff Goldblum's character predicted to a dismissive audience in *Jurassic Park*, "Life finds a way."

The discerning reader will see that this debate revolves around the question and nature of "proof." With regard to the UFO phenomenon, what constitutes *proof* of alien visitation? Unfortunately, most reported UFO sightings involve solitary witnesses reporting "lights in the sky," who do not advance knowledge and are, quite frankly, uninteresting to veteran researchers. Daylight sightings of structured craft are more interesting, especially when reported by multiple witnesses, but again these do not lead us anywhere as far as "proof" of alien visitation is concerned. Interesting stories? Yes. Proof of anything? No. Physical trace cases in which some aspect of the environment has allegedly been disturbed by a UFO (for example, broken tree limbs, oil-like stains and depressions in the ground, "radiation" burns and the like) are interesting but inconclusive, because the observed "physical traces" allegedly left by the UFOs could just as easily be the result of a more prosaic process. Alleged UFO crashes, on the other hand, offer the *possibility* of recoverable artifacts from another world, be they a ship, parts of a ship, or crew members. UFO investigators having a "nuts and bolts" mentality naturally gravitate to this end of the UFO spectrum, as opposed to, say, the abduction phenomenon.

To cut to the chase, the Roswell case offers the best chance that we have at making the case for extraterrestrial visitation by recovering an incontrovertible alien artifact. What we apparently have here is an interplanetary craft of unknown origin having been blown into a million little pieces over a sheep pasture in Corona (central New Mexico) during an intense thunder and lightning storm. Before the military arrived, countless local ranchers and their children visited the site. At a companion site approximately 15 to 20 miles away, closer to Roswell, the remainder of the craft and its unlucky crew met their ultimate fate. This site was also discovered and visited by a number of civilians before the military arrived to secure it. During the clean-up of the crash sites and the subsequent recovery operations that included the boxing-up of the wreckage for shipment, scores of military personnel had access to crash artifacts. Human nature being what it is, it is entirely conceivable—no, likely—that artifacts were taken by civilians and surreptitiously lifted by various military personnel as souvenirs. This was in fact the case, according to many of the firsthand accounts we have on record.

The wreckage/debris from the Roswell crash is most often described as consisting of several different types. The most numerous were palm-sized and smaller pieces of wreckage of very thin and light, but extremely strong, pieces of "foil" similar to the aluminum foil found in a pack of cigarettes (highly unusual for its time because of its strength, but nothing overtly otherworldly in its appearance). There were other types of wreckage found, all characterized by extreme light weight and strength. There were even small "I-beams" that looked like balsa wood struts with strange symbols embossed along the inner face. Instead of "alien writing," Roswell skeptics, debunkers, and the U.S. Air Force all maintain that the witnesses are mistaken about the ultra-light, super-strong materials, and that the I-beam symbols are nothing more than flowery Scotch tape they say was used to reinforce the balsa wood sticks supporting the radar kites back in 1947. The point is that if we are fortunate enough to recover any of these types of artifacts, their provenance would not be immediately recognizable and accepted as extraterrestrial until they were analyzed by reputable metallurgists. Results and conclusions would have to be drawn, and reports written. Presumably, an announcement of the findings would then be made to the press. In fact, this scenario has already taken place—several times—but results suggesting an extraterrestrial origin for alleged ET artifacts have been dismissed with charges that the analyses were inadequate or biased, and therefore inconclusive or unacceptable.

There is, however, one type of wreckage from the Roswell crash described by witnesses that would be *immediately* recognizable as something truly extraordinary without having to be first sent away for analysis. We refer to it simply as the "Holy Grail of Roswell"—the recovery of a piece of *memory metal*. It has been described as being fairly numerous (in small pieces, of course) at the Foster ranch debris-field site near Corona. Witnesses have stated that a piece of it was extremely thin and light—the color of aluminum—and that one could crumple a piece of it up in one's hand and then lay it on a flat surface, where it would quickly un-crumple itself into its original flat, pristine condition, without evidence of a crease. It also could not be scratched, cut, burned, or permanently deformed in any way. We did not have anything exhibiting those properties in 1947, and we still do not have anything similar to that today. This is the type of

Roswell wreckage our investigation is actively searching for. We have several leads in this direction that we are currently pursuing.

The more mundane reasons that we like this case are that it has everything an investigator would want: alleged government secrecy, cover-ups and misconduct, a large witness pool upon which to draw, historical context and continuity, potential artifacts as well as alien bodies, and finally—the case is just plain exciting in its implications. It has held Carey's undying attention for almost 17 years and Schmitt's for almost 20.

The answer to the question as to why we are *still* investigating a 60-year-old case is twofold. The first is that, although we believe there is evidence to support an extraterrestrial conclusion for the Roswell Incident, major media outlets such as the *New York Times* and *The History Channel* have uncritically bought the Air Force's balloon explanation for the Roswell events; therefore, we are attempting to develop overwhelming evidence for an alternative conclusion to the 1947 Roswell events that even the *New York Times* cannot ignore. The other reason is that our investigation is racing against the clock as witnesses pass away at an increasingly rapid pace. At some point, there will be no more firsthand eyewitnesses to the Roswell events left. Time is of the essence.

1
The Ultimate Cold Case File

Crime shows have proven to be a very popular and hardy staple for TV producers and viewers alike for decades. Shows such as *Man Against Crime, Gangbusters*, and *Dragnet* from the early days of TV, through the more sophisticated *Peter Gunn, Richard Diamond Private Detective*, and *Perry Mason* of the late 1950s and 1960s, to *Kojak, Columbo*, and *Hill Street Blues*, right down to today's ultra-legalistic *Law and Order* and super high-tech *CSI: Crime Scene Investigation*. Though separated in time culturally, stylistically, and technologically, all share one common theme—the search for truth.

In early July of 1947, *something* crashed to Earth in the high desert (higher than 2,000 feet) of eastern New Mexico during one of those severe thunder and lightning storms that occurs in the region every year during monsoon season. A few days later, the U.S. Army Air Forces (as the U.S. Air Force was called until later that year) electrified a nation and the world by issuing a press release announcing that its 509th Bomb Group at the Roswell Army Air Field (RAAF), located just south of the sleepy New Mexico town of Roswell, had "captured" a flying saucer that had crashed nearby. Within hours, however, a press conference was hastily convened at Eighth Air Force Headquarters in Fort Worth, Texas (the command to which the 509th Bomb Group was attached), to announce that it was all a big mistake. The *flying saucer* was nothing more than a misidentified *weather balloon*! The press immediately lost interest, and the story quickly died. Outside of the occasional rumor, the story was then forgotten and remained buried for the next 30 years. Then, in 1978, the intelligence officer of the 509th Bomb Group at the time of the incident broke the silence by publicly stating that what crashed outside of Roswell in 1947 was no weather balloon, but something "not of this Earth."

A few interested UFO investigators took note and undertook a civilian investigation of the case. By the early 1990s, several books had been written on the subject, all favoring an extraterrestrial conclusion, and the case was prominently featured on the popular TV show *Unsolved Mysteries,* which also strongly suggested an extraterrestrial answer for the mystery. As public awareness of the case grew, pressure mounted for some form of official restatement by our government concerning its position on the matter. This occurred in 1994 when the Air Force admitted that it had in fact lied in 1947 with its weather balloon explanation, but it was now telling the truth with its *third* explanation for Roswell: What crashed was now a high-flying contraption composed of multiple balloons, multiple radar targets, and a listening device belonging to a special project—Project Mogul—that fell to Earth near Roswell. Although the project's purpose—to detect sound waves from the anticipated detonation of the Soviet Union's first atomic bomb by employing high altitude, balloon-borne, acoustic sensors—was Top Secret, its off-the-shelf components were not. Far from it—the prosaic rubber balloons, tinfoil radar targets, and balsa wood struts used in the project were of the *exact same types* that were used in most weather balloons and radar targets of the time—materials that any 6-year-old would have no trouble identifying! Then, in 1997—the 50th anniversary of the Roswell crash—the Air Force brazenly offered up its *fourth* explanation, this one to try to deal with the long-held rumors and eyewitness accounts of diminutive (3 1/2 to 4 foot tall) "alien bodies" that were also alleged to have been recovered from the Roswell crash. Known as the "dummy explanation" for obvious reasons, the Air Force spokesman was met with derisive howls of laughter from members of the press when he attributed such claims to the Air Force's use of full-size (6 foot tall) mannequins in several projects involving high-altitude parachute drops that were conducted in New Mexico *in the 1950s* in preparation for our country's manned space program. To explain away the 10-year time disparity, the Air Force claimed that the witnesses were unwitting victims of a mental processing affliction known as "time compression," whereby recollections of past events tend to contract the time frames in which they took place as a person ages. Thus, those who claimed to have seen alien bodies from the Roswell crash in 1947 were really remembering a chance encounter with crash-test dummies that they somehow stumbled upon while searching for rattlesnakes out in the desert in 1959! Project Mogul and "dummies-from-above" continue to be the Air Force's "explanation" for the Roswell crash.

The search for truth in the real world of trying to solve cases ideally involves a twofold investigation of pertinent facts: (1) the search for incriminating, physical evidence, from old-fashioned fingerprints on the murder weapon to the currently trendy and "infallible" DNA evidence at the crime scene (in other words, forensics), coupled with (2) relevant and credible eyewitness testimony. When presented to a jury in a logical and coherent manner, this investigative combination constitutes "proof" as we know it, and has, with notable exceptions, stood the test of time in proving to be a case-winner. In the absence of direct physical evidence, the prosecution will attempt to build a circumstantial case against a defendant based solely upon witness testimony as the proof—yes, witness testimony in and of itself is considered *evidence*, and if sufficiently convincing, *proof*—in every courtroom across the land, and has indeed sent many a defendant to the electric chair. This fact must be stated up front because of constant complaints by skeptics and debunkers of the so-called Roswell Incident[1] who appear not to know or respect the legal standing of witness testimony, by downplaying it or ignoring it altogether when it comes to the subject of UFOs, and especially Roswell. Regarding the latter, the standard line goes that because there exists no incontrovertible *physical evidence* to support the case for an alleged crash of a UFO near the town of Roswell, N.M. in 1947, it did not happen. Case closed.

Unfortunately, not every criminal or civil investigation results in an outcome involving a prosecution or other resolution, often due to a lack of evidence to move the case forward to an indictment or charge. When this impasse persists over a period of time, a case becomes what is euphemistically known as a "cold case file." Today, there are thousands of such cases stuffing overburdened police file cabinets in every jurisdiction, most of which unfortunately will never be solved.

A recently popular TV show, *Cold Case Files*, has taken up the theme of trying to solve old, seemingly unsolvable cases that have languished for years. Although these are fictionalized accounts, many of the show's weekly offerings are based upon real-life cases that have lain dormant, on the average, for 10 or 20 years. What we find interesting about this show are the parallels between the investigative tools employed by the show's Cold Case Investigative Unit in trying to investigate an aged case, and our experience in investigating the Roswell case. The parameters are remarkably similar, but with a few notable differences. The *Cold Case* investigators still have at their disposal as potential targets of investigation a combination of still-available, fertile sources of case evidence such as: (1) physical evidence just waiting to be uncovered and subjected to forensics, (2) key, finger-pointing documents readily available on microfiche at local repositories, and especially (3) still-living, easily located witnesses willing, however reluctantly, to belatedly spill their guts. The happy result of all this activity is usually another cold case file scoped, investigated, and solved—all in one hour's time!

Considering the fact that we have a combined total of 35 years of investigative experience dedicated solely to uncovering the truth of the Roswell Incident, and the fact that the case still remains unsolved, or at least unproven in a majority of the public's mind 60 years after the event, we see the Roswell Incident as the ultimate cold case file. Most of the original investigators who were once active on the case during the 1980s and 1990s have left the field and will only engage again if something worth their additional effort drops into their laps. We remain the only proactive investigative researchers still working the Roswell case.

Although there have been several pieces of metal submitted to various UFO investigators through the years purported to have come from the Roswell flying saucer, upon analysis none were found to be sufficiently exotic in terms of their constituent elements or construction to be considered unequivocally as coming from another world. In one particular instance, the subject piece of metal was exotic indeed, but upon inspection, turned out to be nothing more exotic than a piece of Japanese jewelry! Meanwhile, our search for physical evidence—the Holy Grail of the Roswell case—continues.

Document-type evidence in the Roswell case consists mostly of the newspaper accounts from 1947 announcing the "capture" of a flying saucer near Roswell, followed quickly by a retraction of that story in the guise of a "misidentified weather balloon" that stood as the explanation for the next 30 years. Because of the timing of the original press releases, newspapers in the eastern United States carried both versions of the story on the same day (July 9, 1947), while most newspapers in the western time zones carried the flying saucer story one day (July 8, 1947) and the weather balloon retraction story on the following day (July 9, 1947). At a minimum, the newspaper accounts verified the fact that *something* did in fact crash near Roswell in early July of 1947, and key participants in the event were named. Just *what* crashed became (and still is) the issue.

Since the mid-1980s various government documents, alleged by some Roswell investigators to be genuine, have surfaced that would seem to verify the truth of the crash and recovery of an extraterrestrial spaceship and its crew in southeastern New Mexico in 1947. Referred to collectively as the MJ-12 Documents, they highlight some of the problems associated with "documents-as-proof" that are frequently encountered in UFO-related research: lack of provenance for the document(s) in question, and a lack of agreement among researchers regarding the genuineness of a document. Tracing a document back to a UFO investigator with an agenda and no farther does not constitute adequate provenance. We must know who the ultimate originator of the document in question was in order to properly research and verify its context and background. Without its provenance thus established, a document should immediately become suspect as being fraudulent, especially if the original of the document is unavailable. To make matters worse, UFO researchers cannot agree on the importance that should be attached to apparent discrepancies when they are found in such documents. The finder of the discrepancy—whether in the form of the incorrect date format, a misplaced comma, or a questionable signature—will discount the entire document as fraudulent, whereas the advocates of the document will attempt to downplay the discrepancies as minor matters signifying nothing, in order to save its hoped-for document-as-proof status. The point here is that without standing and general agreement regarding its import, a document as proof of anything is worthless.

In 1993, the Government Accounting Office (GAO), which is the investigative arm of Congress, at the request of the late New Mexico congressman, Stephen Schiff, undertook a search of all relevant government agencies (the Department of Defense, the CIA, the Air Force, and so on) for documents relating to the 1947 Roswell Incident, for the purpose of establishing a paper trail of events from the appropriate time period. The results of the search were published by the GAO in 1995, and instead of clarifying things served only to muddy the waters even more.[2] No additional documents were turned up by any of the agencies tasked by the GAO beyond those very few documents that were already known, but a bigger surprise came when it was discovered that *all* documents, such as teletype messages, telexes, radiograms, letters, invoices, and other records emanating from the Roswell Army Air Field (as the late Walker Air Force Base was known in 1947) covering the general time frame of the Roswell Incident had been destroyed years before *without explanation or apparent authority.* To Roswell investigators such as ourselves, already convinced of a massive government cover-up of this case, there can be no innocent explanation for this. To skeptics of the Roswell Incident, well, it was just one of those things signifying nothing.

One final introductory note regarding documents as they relate to the Roswell investigation has to do with two documents whose provenance is *not* an issue. The first is an FBI memo dated July 8, 1947 that was written by the FBI's agent in Dallas, Texas to their office in Cincinnati, Ohio shortly after the Eighth Air Force's commanding officer, General Roger Ramey, held a press conference in his Fort Worth office and announced to the world that the flying saucer recovered at Roswell a few days earlier was nothing more than a misidentified weather balloon. The memo suggested that a lie had been perpetrated upon the public at the staged press conference, and that the flight transporting the Roswell wreckage from Fort Worth Army Air Field (where it stopped after leaving the RAAF) to Wright Field in Dayton, Ohio had not been cancelled, as Gen. Ramey had dramatically declared to the press. The second document is referred to by many as the "smoking gun" of the Roswell case. It is a telex that was held in the hand of the architect of the Roswell cover-up himself, Gen. Roger Ramey, during his aforementioned press conference, which seems to tell a different story than the one he was giving to the press.

Several key witnesses to the Roswell events of 1947 unfortunately passed away long before the case appeared on the radar of UFO investigators. The sheriff of Chaves County, George M. Wilcox, for which Roswell is the county seat and who was used by our military to assist them in the cover-up, passed away in 1961; the Corona sheep rancher, William W. "Mack" Brazel, who first discovered his pasture filled with strange wreckage—and something else—and thereby was responsible for starting the entire Roswell chain of events, died in 1963, the same year as Gen. Ramey; the commanding officer of the RAAF in 1947, Colonel William H. Blanchard, died of a heart attack at his desk in the Pentagon in 1965 as a four-star general and vice chief of staff of the Air Force; and Major Jesse A. Marcel, the intelligence officer under Col. Blanchard at the Roswell base in 1947, passed away in 1986, but not before breaking his 30-year silence in 1978 regarding an event to which he bore witness and believed to his dying day originated "not from this Earth," thereby igniting a controversy that is still with us today.

The Department of Veterans' Affairs estimates that veterans of World War II, whose numbers include most of those involved in the Roswell Incident, are leaving us at a rate of about 1,500 per day. And as any insurance actuary will tell you, that statistic will swell at an ever-increasing rate with the passage of time. For this reason, we have gone beyond racing the undertaker and are dangerously close to the finish line with our investigation. (It is sobering indeed to note that the youngest known participant in the 1947 Roswell events, a then 7-year-old boy named Dee Proctor, passed away last year at the age of 66.) And of those who are still with us, many have succumbed to the ravages of old age, such as Alzheimer's, Parkinson's, and so on, and cannot now be interviewed. As a result, we find ourselves increasingly interviewing the children and grandchildren of the actual participants, and an alarming number of *these* are starting to pass on as well. We estimate that, of the military personnel who were stationed in Roswell in 1947, *at least* 90 percent are now unavailable to us because of death or infirmity. These same statistics also hold true for the civilian population living in and around Roswell in 1947. It is due to the complete lack of verifiable physical evidence, the dearth of acceptable documentation, and mostly to the ever-decreasing nature of the witness pool after the passage of 60 years that we refer to Roswell as the ultimate cold case file.

Although we believe that crimes were committed by our military against civilians in Roswell and Corona during its heavy-handed suppression and cover-up of the Roswell Incident, no charges were brought at the time, and the Statute of Limitations has long ago run out. The case still remains, however, an active historical mystery left to us from the 20th century to solve. Even allowing for the given limitations facing the Roswell investigation, we have amassed what we believe is overwhelming evidence to sustain an extraterrestrial conclusion for the Roswell events of 1947, enough to prevail in any court case against the U.S. Air Force and its balloon explanation. Any such hypothetical court action would involve a simple "preponderance of the evidence" standard of proof (used in civil cases) as opposed to the higher standard of "beyond a reasonable doubt" (used in criminal cases) to render a verdict. The truth be told, the Air Force's case for Roswell is so water thin (there is no physical evidence, pertinent documents, or credible witnesses, living or dead, to connect a balloon event to the Roswell Incident) that it would also be a loser in court—beyond a reasonable doubt.

In science, where the bottom line is also the search for truth, Ockham's Law of Parsimony, a.k.a. Ockham's Razor, is used to decide among competing hypotheses the one that best explains the observed data. It holds that, with all other factors being equal, the simplest hypothesis that explains the most observed data is the best, and must prevail. Thus employed, it serves as a tool for eliminating competing-but-lacking theories, hypotheses, and explanations from others being considered. In the Roswell case, competing hypotheses as to what might have crashed in 1947 (a V-2 rocket, an experimental rocket plane or jet aircraft, a propeller-driven Chance Vought "Flying Flapjack," a Northrup "Flying Wing," a Japanese "Fugo" balloon-bomb, or an errant atomic bomb) have all been investigated and eliminated. That leaves us with two remaining, competing hypotheses: the Air Force's high-altitude Project Mogul and time-compressed memories of anthropomorphic dummies-from-the-sky[3] vs. a crash of a bonafide UFO—a *flying saucer* in 1947 terms—along with its unfortunate crew, which is favored by most civilian researchers. Which is the bogus hypothesis?

The Chance Vought "Flying Flapjack" was being developed in 1947, but was confined to the state of Connecticut.

Photo printed with permission from Steve Ginter.

Without conclusive physical evidence and/or accepted documents to decide the case one way or the other, the Roswell Incident is of necessity a "witness case." (It should be pointed out, however, that we are continuing a proactive search for all three types of evidence.) On the "anti-Roswell" side of the debate, the Air Force can offer *not a single, credible eyewitness* to a balloon event at any of the three Roswell crash locations identified by us or during the subsequent recovery operation. There is not a shred of evidence—nothing—to connect a wayward Project Mogul balloon-train to what crashed in Mack Brazel's sheep pasture in July of 1947; time-compressed dummies-from-the-sky as the answer for the purported recovery of "little bodies" from the crash is so far-fetched that no one, save a few stolid mainstays of the so-called mainstream media[4] who normally do not accept *anything* that our military says at face-value, has taken it seriously—not even Roswell skeptics.

On the "pro-Roswell" side of the debate, we can offer scores of credible eyewitnesses, military and civilian, out of a total witness pool to date of several hundred first-, second-, and third-hand witnesses to an *extraterrestrial* event that we know today as the Roswell Incident. None of these knows the entire story of what occurred, as each knows only what he or she witnessed or took part in. It has been our task to piece together, like a jigsaw puzzle, these moment-in-time snapshots into a larger picture of what took place so long ago. Because of the wealth of credible witness testimony that we have secured in our investigation of the 1947 Roswell crash (we have witnesses along the entire timeline of events—from the discovery and recovery of the UFO and its crew at the crash sites, their initial transport to the base at Roswell where a preliminary autopsy was attempted, the flight to Fort Worth where the cover-up began, and the flight to their final destination at Wright Field), we have been able to formulate a coherent chronicle for a case of apparent alien visitation. For this reason, applying a healthy dose of Ockham's Razor to the known facts of the Roswell Incident *must* result in a rejection of the Air Force's current explanation as bogus.

2

Myth or Reality
The Undeniable Truths

Contemporary folklorists, such as Dr. Thomas E. Bullard from the University of Indiana, have long maintained that most legends are derived from some basis of factual occurrence. Cult figures are often composites of true-life individuals, and classic fictional stories typically evolve around genuine historical events and people.[1] But we maintain that the attempt to reduce an actual real-life experience to the level of mythology is further proof of the ongoing cover-up of Roswell. This was no more evident than in the ABC primetime special on UFOs in 2005, when the host, the late Peter Jennings, referred to the "myth of Roswell" no less than five times in his introductory statement.[2]

The word *myth* is bandied about as a total dismissal of all relevant facts, and as intended, relegates the novice to the stature of believing in Santa Claus. The agenda becomes quite clear: The comparison of Roswell to mythology is intended to complete the damage control left unfinished by Project Mogul and the wooden crash dummies. Plainly stated, we contend that this most recent tactic on the part of the federal government is, in reality, explanation *number five*: The Roswell incident never happened. It's all folklore created by the UFO buffs, a number of so-called witness opportunists, and the very city of Roswell itself to create a tourist attraction.

Just check any of the recent rebuttals from Roswell debunkers, and the word *myth* has become the new *official* solution to the 60-year-old mystery. Their mission: to destroy the Roswell Incident and anyone who dares associate with it. The obvious question we should all ask is why, after 60 years, is there still a need to disprove the existence of Santa Claus? If they remain so secure in their tacit dismissal of all available facts concerning the event, why are they promulgating the next official explanation? Is it

Colonel William Blanchard.

Photo printed with permission from the U.S. Air Force.

any wonder that before he passed away, Congressman Steven Schiff accused the U.S. Air Force of a "massive ongoing cover-up"?[3]

During the ABC special, Peter Jennings expounded, "There are no credible witnesses." There is absolutely no doubt on our part that he never entertained the thought of actually interviewing such individuals. So how can he possibly make such a blanket statement, unless someone else put those words in his mouth? We certainly respected Mr. Jennings's usual high standards of journalistic integrity.

Through the course of our own investigation, we have amassed a continuously growing roster of more than 600 people directly or indirectly associated with the events at Roswell, who support the first account—that initial claim of the flying saucer recovery. That such testimony would be summarily dismissed by skeptics and initiate mythological status based on its historic record is an insult to reality and the eventual disclosure of the truth.

We ask you to consider the following:

1. On Tuesday, July 8, 1947, 11 a.m. Mountain Time (MT), Roswell Army Air Field commanding officer Colonel William Blanchard announced the recovery of a flying disk. It is important to note that Blanchard was the officer entrusted with oversight of the first atomic-bomb strike force in the world, based at the RAAF. This was two and a half days after Washington, D.C. was alerted to the crash that would initiate their orchestration of Blanchard's press release.

2. Later that same day, at approximately 4:30 p.m. Central Standard Time (CST), General Roger Ramey, the commander of the Eighth Air Force and Blanchard's supervising officer, presented to the press an alternate story: He claimed the Army had recovered a rawin target device suspended by a Neoprene rubber balloon. ("Rawin" is a method of determining wind speed and direction by using radar or radio waves to track a balloon carrying either a radar-sensitive target or radio transponder.)

3. Mack Brazel, the ranch foreman who first discovered the debris field, was abducted and detained by the U.S. Army Air Forces for four or five days while cleanup operations continued at the site. Brazel was denied access to a phone, was given an Army physical, and was subjected to rigorous questioning and intimidation while under arrest at the RAAF.

Within hours of the initial press release that a flying saucer had been recovered, General Roger Ramey held a press conference in his office in Fort Worth to announce that a mistake had been made. It was a weather balloon.

Photo printed with permission from the 1947 RAAF Yearbook.

4. Extreme security measures were exercised at Brazel's ranch and separate related locations. Armed guards encircled the primary areas, a second cordon was placed around its outer perimeter, riflemen were stationed on the surrounding hills, and MPs (Military Police) were posted on outlying roads that led to these immediate areas.

5. Special, unscheduled flights arrived from Washington, D.C., with additional units arriving from White Sands AAFB in Alamogordo, N.M., Fort Bliss in El Paso, Texas, and Kirtland AAFB in Albuquerque. Unscheduled flights from Roswell transported wreckage or remains to Fort Worth, Texas, Patterson Field in Dayton, Ohio, Andrews AAFB in Washington, D.C., and the Los Alamos National Laboratory, via truck from Kirtland.

6. Senator Dennis Chavez, chairman of the Senate Appropriations Committee, phoned Walter Whitmore Sr., majority owner of radio station KGFL in Roswell, to strongly advise him to do as he was instructed by the Federal Communications Commission (FCC) in an earlier call and not broadcast a wire-recorded interview with Mack Brazel.

7. An FBI telex dated July 8, 1947, at 6:17 p.m. CST from the bureau's Dallas office disputed Gen. Ramey's announcement to the press that the special flight transporting wreckage to Wright Field had been canceled, as well as Ramey's explanation of a balloon and foil radar target.

8. On July 9, 1947, U.S. military officials searched news offices in Roswell, Albuquerque, and Santa Fe to retrieve copies of the original press release or any other related documentation that was contrary to the weather balloon explanation. The recorded interview of Mack Brazel was also confiscated from the home of Walt Whitmore Sr.

9. Six witnesses have testified to seeing Brazel escorted through Roswell under military guard as he was taken to *The Roswell Daily Record* and *Morning Dispatch* newspapers and KGFL and KSWS radio stations to personally retract his claim of discovering the remains of a flying saucer.

10. Multiple firsthand military and civilian witnesses who actually saw the crash have testified to that effect.

11. Multiple firsthand military and civilian witnesses have testified about separate locations, including a debris field, body site, and final impact site.

12. More than two dozen witnesses, both military and civilian, agree on the unconventional characteristics of the wreckage. Both types of witnesses have described "memory" materials as well as fiber optics associated with the crash.

13. Multiple firsthand military and civilian witnesses have given sworn testimony regarding bodies recovered from the crash.

14. The late Senator Barry Goldwater, also a brigadier general, USAFR, after personally hearing details from his close friend William Blanchard concerning Roswell in the early 1960s, tried in vain to gain access to the files through high-ranking officers in Washington. In a letter dated July 26, 1994, he stated that his request for Roswell information from the chairman of the Joint Chiefs, Gen. Curtis Lemay, was "the only cussing-out he ever gave me."[4]

15. In 1993, the late Congressman Steven Schiff sent three separate letters to then Secretary of Defense Les Aspen requesting specific information and access to all files concerning the Roswell Incident of 1947. All three letters went unanswered. Similar requests also went unanswered from the White House, the Pentagon, and all branches of the military, as well as the FBI, CIA, and NSA.

16. A growing number of military and civilian witnesses are providing deathbed testimony, all admissible in a court of law, confessing to direct knowledge about "nonhuman" bodies recovered at Roswell in 1947. None—we repeat, none—have given one admission about a weather balloon.

17. A growing number of witnesses, both military and civilian, are now stating that there was indeed a *survivor* of the crash.

18. Finally, the most shocking revelation to date is that the U.S. military resorted to physical threats against American civilian witnesses. Children were terrorized in their homes and parents were warned that their children would be killed if they ever spoke one word about the true nature of the event. What possible secrets could children possess about a secret weather balloon project? In fact, many had actually handled pieces from the crash, and a smattering had seen the bodies. At the very least, many had overheard their parents' reaction when discussing the crash.

In May of 2006 we were approached by Eric Haven, a researcher for the Discovery Channel's popular TV program *Myth Busters*. Typically, they would have encouraged us to provide source material to present the pro-UFO position so they in turn would attempt to disprove it. We're sure they were caught completely off guard when we suggested a new twist on their show's premise: What if we were to have a special-effects team from Hollywood create an exact replica of the Mogul balloon, launch it, and then bring it down on the very spot where Brazel supposedly discovered the real thing almost 60 years before? Our challenge to them was to see just how unconventional such a device looks on the ground when its right in front of you and you can actually pick it up and hold it in your hands. In other words, let's start with the premise that *the Mogul Balloon was the real myth*. As expected, we never heard from Mr. Haven or anyone associated with the show again; we proposed to burst the *wrong* balloon.

The Corona Debris Field
Much Ado About Something

Based on all supporting information regarding the Mogul Balloon explanation, this must have been an extremely isolated occurrence. After all, for something as mundane as a weather balloon, how could it generate all the excitement it evidently did? And indeed if this happened to be a specific Mogul launch gone awry, which project directors would later categorize as *missing*, how was it that so many people would become involved in just the immediate ranchland surrounding the debris field location? How was it that so many civilians were able to find remnants of a Top Secret project while the authorities, who now claim they *were* looking for it, could not? And how is it that none of them describe the remains of any type of balloon device, Top Secret or not?

Anyone who has ever taken the time to travel to this remote territory immediately observes the immense size of the ranches themselves. One would also learn that in 1947, this area of New Mexico had little if any electricity—in other words, no TV or radio; a total lack of outside communication. It is fascinating to note that this particular region didn't even receive phone service until 1986! This is harsh, high desert country by any definition—brutally hot in the summer and frigidly cold each winter. Prevailing winds are cause for constant soil erosion, and much of the land is baron and stark. Rattlesnakes, tarantulas, scorpions, and Gila monsters all share a space with the local human population. Monsoon rains typically arrive each July and August, causing gravel and dirt roads to wash out and become impassible. Even today, four-wheel-drive vehicles are required transportation through much of the region. Broken axles, drive shafts, and flat tires are the norm. The land has basically remained the same throughout the centuries and is famous for the Lincoln County range wars, which followed the War Between the States. Billy the Kid, Pat Garret, and John Chisum rode the same territory that Mack Brazel and all his neighbors did in 1947. It still continues to amaze us how the most ardent of skeptics, regardless of never speaking to a single witness, think that residing in or passing through Albuquerque fully qualifies them to make an educated opinion on ranching the high country of central New Mexico.

This road sign on Route 285 in Lincoln County, N.M. attests to the remoteness of the region even today.

Photo courtesy of Tom Carey, 2001.

That is why we intend to demonstrate to the reader all of the ancillary activity surrounding this incident in the Corona ranch region, which *did not involve Mack Brazel or his family*. Why would so many adults and young people travel in pickup trucks or ride on horseback up to 75 miles on dirt roads to witness a downed weather balloon every one of them had stumbled across so many times before? Even today, there is an old water holding tank that remains as direct testimony to many decades past—it is over-flowing with rotting weather balloons gathered up by young and old alike from one end of the ranch to the other. Any responsible rancher will tell you that there is absolutely no way that Mack Brazel would allow the remains of any type of discarded wreckage, Mogul included, to be left lying out in that open pasture. You see, cattle and sheep are like goats. They'll eat anything in their path, and all that Neoprene rubber from cluster balloons in a Mogul device could suffocate the poor animals. Keeping the herds alive and productive was the primary function of the ranch supervisor, and there is no reason to doubt that Brazel was good at his job. But this situation was much different. There was so much of the stuff, and nowhere was there an instrument package or even a name tag to be found directing the bearer to whom and where to report the find (as would be expected with weather research balloons, particularly the Mogul balloons, which had their own "Reward Notice" from New York University). And besides, the "damn stuff" scared the sheep away from the pasture anyway.[1]

Where it all began. The debris field site where Mack Brazel found pieces of strange wreckage, starting a chain of events known today as the Roswell Incident.

Photo courtesy of Tom Carey, 2006.

Also keep in mind that this was before the military was ever alerted to the find, and days before the Army would issue the now famous press release about the capture of a flying saucer. In fact, it was *three or four days* earlier.

So who are these other witnesses the Air Force now refuses to acknowledge? Who are these other people who were drawn to see a whole pasture full of super-strong material that snapped back after being bent? And what happened to them as a result of seeing too much?

The very first outside witness just happened to be with Mack Brazel the very morning he discovered the wreckage. We have confirmed from numerous sources that this young boy would often spend weekends with Mack learning to be a good ranch hand. He was the 7-year-old son of Mack's nearest neighbors, Floyd and Loretta Proctor. His name was Timothy, but his family and friends called him "Dee" after his middle initial. After Mack returned him home with a sampling of the wreckage, it became evident that as soon as he had the chance, he got right back on his horse and gathered up a number of friends and headed back to explore the wild story all the adults were talking about. There appears to have been a young girl who accompanied the "cowboys." A few have mentioned her by name, but she still refuses to talk to this day.

Such would also become the fate of Dee. Whatever else he witnessed, according to his mother, Loretta, in days to come, he would return home and behave as though something or somebody had severely frightened him. And from that moment on, nobody, including his family, could get him to utter another word about the adventure. An adventure that, by all accounts, tormented Dee for the rest of his life. True, many years later he would dismiss the entire affair and chuckle that he wasn't even born at that time—which got quite a reaction from his mother. But he would finally share a glimpse of the true story with her in 1994 when she was suffering from a life-threatening blood clot in her neck. Dee decided to pick up his mother and take her for a drive—not to the site everyone already knew about, but rather atop a ridge some 2 1/2 miles to the east. Even then he parsed his words carefully, but he wanted her to know just in case. "Here is where Mack found something else," he confessed. His mother couldn't get her own son to admit anything further. And he never did. Dee Proctor died of a heart attack in January of 2006.[2]

One of the other young men whom we believe was with the others was the son of a local hired hand. He went by the name of Jack but his correct name was Sydney Wright. It was in 1998 that Jack would finally

The Dee Proctor body site.
Photo courtesy of Tom Carey, 2003.

disclose what may also have been the cause of Dee Proctor's lifetime of silence. Jack admitted that he, the two sons of rancher Thomas Edington, and one of rancher Truman Pierce's daughters somehow managed to get to "the other location."[3] It was there that they witnessed something that none of them expected.[4] Later, this would most certainly play into the military abduction of Mack Brazel.

There can be no doubt that Brazel made every effort to enlist the advice of many of his neighbors. Ranchers such as Clint Sultemeier, curious enough about the story, would drive over to the Foster ranch (of which Brazel was the custodian) and actually retrieve a number of souvenirs. Sultemeier mistakenly thought he was smart by hiding his collection where nobody would think of looking. But officials would soon be retrieving *all* the evidence and let nothing stand in their way in doing so.[5]

Within the next two days after the crash, others who owned surrounding ranches would go out of their way to check out the story about "pieces of a flying saucer." Budd Eppers and Truman Pierce would arrive on the scene.[6] Glaze Sacra would load a number of "weightless" pieces of metal into his pickup and head discreetly home.[7] Danny Boswell's parents, who owned a ranch 25 miles to the east, drove 45 minutes to see for themselves what everyone was talking about.[8]

Just what everyone was talking about were not pieces of a Mogul weather balloon. Rather, eyewitness descriptions were consistent about nearly indestructible characteristics, fiber optics, I-beams, and the pieces that amazed them beyond all others—the "stuff that would flow like water after you wadded it up in your hands."[9] In any event, the evidence remained scattered across the open range of the Foster ranch as prevailing winds continued to whisk it more and more to the southeast for *three full days* before Mack Brazel would finally complete his weekly chores and make the 75-mile trek to Roswell and report the fantastic discovery to the authorities. But not before he had exhausted every attempt to get every last word of advice he could. Besides the Proctors and Sultemeiers, he took samples of the debris to his uncle Hollis Wilson, and perplexed patrons at Wade's Bar in Corona would hand fragments from one end of the bar to the other, each one attempting to cut or burn the pieces.

The town of Corona today, including Wade's Bar, where Mack Brazel showed around pieces of debris.

Photo courtesy of Tom Carey, 2000.

From there he would show the owners as well as customers at the Corona General Store. It seemed as though no one had any solution to what crashed out on that arroyo. From all known accounts it would seem that everyone remained as puzzled as the next person. Portions of the unknown object eventually found their way to the annual Fourth of July rodeo an hour to the south in Capitan. Holiday revelers recalled memory metal being flashed around the festivities. It seemed as though everyone was aware of the crash, *except the authorities!*

Finally, the frustrated Brazel would run into his friend, state police officer Robert Scroggins. At last, someone with an official background who might be able to shed some light on the entire mystery. But no, the experienced officer had never seen anything like it either. The best he could offer was an alternative plan of action: He was heading home to Hobbs, which was east of Roswell. He would take a larger section of the memory material and report it to the military in Roswell. Yet, Scroggins couldn't help but wonder, "If it was military, why weren't they looking for it? And if it wasn't ours, then whose was it?"[10]

Still, Brazel remained undeterred and became more and more agitated as to under whose purview the wreckage remained. Someone was responsible for nearly a mile-long swath of the stuff, and he couldn't get the sheep to cross through the area to get to water. And so he was left with no alternative but make the long drive down to Roswell and report it himself. After all, maybe some of his neighbors might be right about the reward for a genuine "flying saucer," and he did have ranch business to attend to anyway. So, Brazel made the tedious journey to Roswell first thing Sunday morning, July 6. Little did his friends and neighbors suspect that Brazel would be getting into the territory of military regulations and restrictions that would alter his and his family's very perception of patriotic duty. Brazel was about to experience a dark side of his country he had never imagined.[11]

No sooner had word hit the community of Roswell about all the "strange goings-on" up at "some ranch north of town," than others saw an opportunity for possible fame and fortune. Charlie Schmid, who lived just north of town, jumped right on his motorcycle and headed out into the desert. "I had no idea what to expect, but it sounded like the thing to do at the time," mused Schmid. "I somehow managed to skirt around enough fence lines, sinkholes, and livestock, and arrived at the outer rim of all that metal. I picked up a few pieces along the fence. They had funny writing on them and seemed real strong. I thought it had to be some big secret test by the army, so when I heard an engine approaching I just took off. It was definitely no weather balloon."[12]

Paul Price and his older brother also heard about the crash of a "flying saucer" north of town. "We knew most of the ranchers, so it wasn't long before we got to the right spot. There were so many parts for as far as you could see. Some of the pieces just snapped back in your hands when you bent them." Price was asked if he and his brother retrieved any of the pieces. "I have nothing more to say about it," he replied.[13]

At sunrise on Monday, July 7, Major Jesse Marcel and Captain Sheridan Cavitt, two intelligence officers from the RAAF, would arrive on the scene. Brazel and the two men had just spent the night at the old Hines house after the rancher brought them there the evening before. They would spend the better part of the day examining, collecting, loading, and containing what they couldn't fit into two vehicles. Marcel would send Cavitt on ahead to report directly to Colonel Blanchard back at the base. The major would check over the area one last time and head out later. All testimony from firsthand witnesses maintains that debris still covered an area the size of a football field by the end of the day on Monday. More troops would be needed.

It was here that Maj. Marcel, Capt. Cavitt, and Mack Brazel spent the evening of July 6 eating a can of cold pork 'n beans for dinner. The cattle shed in the background is where Brazel stored some of the larger pieces of the wreckage. The Hines house still remains today, but the cattle shed does not.

Photo courtesy of Tom Carey, 1994.

A full-scale cleanup operation would then commence with 50 to 60 troops the very next morning.[14] One of the young sons of a hired hand from the Richards ranch, which adjoined the Foster ranch from the south, spied with a couple of other boys from a distant hill.

His name was Trinidad "Trini" Chavez. "There were soldiers lined up and picking up all this material," he said. "Trucks and jeeps surrounded the area. We saw men with rifles get out of one of the trucks, well we figured we saw enough." Young Dan Richards had already recovered a few of the memory material pieces, and unknown to Trini at the time, his dad had as well. Alas, it was too late for Trini to take a piece of the wreckage himself. "Too many damn soldiers," Trini said.[15] Later that day, after dark, witnesses would report observing trucks with large spotlights heading in earnest to the "other location."[16]

It would appear that the military extended their cordon of the area to not only the immediate debris field, but also the ranch proper, the main ranch house, and the outlying roads. Budd Payne, another rancher in the Corona area, found out the hard way by merely chasing a stray steer onto the Foster ranch—no sooner than he rode onto the property, a jeep carrying MPs roared over a ridgeline and bore down on him. Payne, who would later become a county judge, was physically accosted and forced off the ranch. He was ordered not to set one foot on that parcel of land until their work was completed. Years later, at Payne's constant encouragement, Brazel would show him the precise location, "which caused all that commotion."[17]

Now, the military was fully aware of all the civilian curiosity. They had to account for each piece, and they suspected everyone—*including children*! Ranchers were forced to inform on one another. Ranch houses were and ransacked. The wooden floors of livestock sheds were pried lose plank by plank and underground cold storage fruit cellars were emptied of all their contents. Glass jars were scattered, broken on the ground.[18]

American citizens were threatened into submission by agents of the U.S. government. Not a single shred of evidence could be left behind, though some would later claim that a piece of the memory material was kept in the safe at the pumping station a mile away.[19] Troops spent more than two days picking up every last trace in the pasture, finishing with industrial vacuum cleaners.[20] All that would remain were the gouge and the tire tracks that crisscrossed the rocky terrain. Just as the ground had been stripped naked of all its secrets, so had the local residents.

A vast assortment of physical proof was recovered from more civilians than we will ever know. Some may have temporarily slipped through their official grasp, but though we have had numerous false alarms, no such evidence has surfaced and no one is talking. Stories about home and vehicle break-ins abound even up to the 1980s, and so do the mysterious disappearances of actual debris. Rancher L.D. Sparks described how just a few years after the original incident, Dan Richards had him toss a thin piece of foil-like material in the air as he fired a rifle at it. "Shot after shot just ricocheted off of it," Sparks claimed. "I would crumble the piece into a ball and watch in amazement as it would unfold as it floated through the air."[21]

Unfortunately, we'll never know what became of his proof. Richards was killed in a single vehicle accident shortly thereafter. And true, it is very conceivable that the long chain of caves that surrounds his parents' ranch house may have been too large a haystack even for the military, such as it remains for present researchers. Deep in the bowels of the old Richards ranch, buried treasure may still lie yet to be discovered.

Everything was *forced* to return to normal. "You are not to say another word about the incident" became an all too common catch phrase throughout the Corona high desert region. It seems unlikely that an event that captivated the nation—albeit for just a few hours—could be a simple weather balloon device, affecting the personal lives of so many and leaving them cold and cynical about their government. What tactics were utilized to insure the full cooperation of all the civilians who saw and knew too much? Roswell photographer Jack Rodden did business with many of the ranchers from the Corona area. One of the ranchers told him that his three kids had come home one day, at the time of the incident, frightened to death and refusing to talk about what they had seen. Rodden pressed the issue and was told by the old-timer that the kids had gotten too close to something, and someone in the military had scared them badly.[22] Other parents emotionally recounted how their young children were never the same. "When they returned home they looked as though they had seen a ghost!" "They were frightened, shocked, and grew increasingly paranoid," spoke a number of the residents. About what? A Mogul weather balloon? Observing a field peppered with strange wreckage? Or was it what a handful of them regrettably saw at the "other location"? Was the military forced to take them aside and put some additional fear of God into them? Almost all of them to this day refuse to talk about it—even with their families.[23]

Many years later, Sydney "Jack" Wright would lament how he grew up overnight from the image that has haunted him all these years: "There were bodies, small bodies with big heads and eyes. And Mack was there too. We couldn't get away from there fast enough."[24]

4

They're Not Human!

From the very beginning of the Roswell investigation by civilian researchers more than two decades ago and until quite recently, the role played in the Roswell Incident by the sheep rancher who started it all, Mack Brazel, had pretty much remained unchanged. As will be covered in detail later in the book, sometime during the first week of July, 1947, in the course of his duties as the foreman of the J.B Foster ranch, located 33.2 miles southeast of Corona, he discovered a pasture full of pieces of strange, silvery wreckage the morning after a severe thunder and lightning storm during which he thought he had heard an explosion. After consulting with neighbors and relatives about his find, and being told about a possible $3,000 reward offered by a newspaper for pieces of a "flying saucer,"[1] he took their advice and drove the 75 miles in his ancient pickup to Roswell.[2]

Mack Brazel, 1951.

Photo printed with permission from Joe Brazel.

Upon his arrival in Roswell, Brazel reported his find to the sheriff's office, but could not seem to get Sheriff George Wilcox interested enough to do anything about it. Brazel even showed him some samples of the wreckage he had brought with him, but to no avail. Fortunately for Wilcox, whose eyes had glazed over, he then received a phone call from a young announcer from Roswell radio station KGFL named Frank Joyce, who was looking for any local tidbits of news that he might put on the air—not a minute too soon for a thankful Wilcox as he passed Brazel off to Joyce with, "Well, there's somebody here right now with a story you might be interested in." So Wilcox handed Brazel the phone. After some back and forth between the two, Joyce suggested to Brazel that he should contact the air base in town, and hung up.

KGFL Roswell announcer and United Press "stringer," Frank Joyce, in 1947.

Photo printed with permission from Frank Joyce.

We knew that two days later, on July 8, 1947, the *Roswell Daily Record* carried a banner headline heard 'round the world: "RAAF Captures Flying Saucer on Ranch Roswell Region," which was retracted the next day, when the Army Air Forces claimed that the flying saucer wreckage was really just the misidentified remains of a weather balloon. We also knew from family members and friends that during this period Mack Brazel had been taken into custody and detained at the RAAF for the better part of a week or more. He also seemed to have changed his story from that of the previous day, as evidenced by a front-page interview article that appeared in the July 9, 1947 *Roswell Daily Record*, wherein he described his find in terms consistent with a rubber weather balloon and a tinfoil radar target. At that point, the press lost interest in the story, and Brazel was allowed to go home a few days later, a bitter man at having been treated so badly by his country just for having done what he saw as his patriotic duty.

There were several things about Brazel's account that always bothered us. One was the persistent claim by some of his neighbors that, shortly after he was released from the clutches of the military, he was somehow able to purchase a brand-new pickup truck and then leave his Foster ranch employment entirely to start his own business in Alamogordo, N.M., which was closer to his home in Tularosa. Not bad for someone barely scratching out a living off the land and known for not having two nickels to rub together. In short, it had all the earmarks of a bribe to us. Another mystery was the fact that the military took Brazel into custody for a week or more and basically worked him over. Upon his release, Brazel bitterly told his family that he felt as if he had been in jail, and that he would never again report anything to our government, "unless it was an atomic bomb." We could not understand why the military would go to such lengths with Brazel, as it had done with no other witness, if he had only discovered pieces of wreckage—no matter how strange. Surely he could have been convinced in short order that it was from a secret project or some such cover story, and Brazel could have gone on his way a happy camper. Something was missing, it seemed to us, in Brazel's story.

The first hint at an answer to our questions was provided in a series of Roswell update articles by William Moore in the early and mid-1980s, before Moore left the Roswell case. He had located and interviewed KGFL announcer Frank Joyce. By that time, Joyce had left Roswell and had become a well-known radio and TV personality at KOB in Albuquerque. Joyce told Moore that he had had not one, but *four* conversations with Brazel. We knew about the first one between Brazel and Joyce on the telephone, but the other contacts were new information.

In May of 1998, we paid a visit to Frank Joyce in his Albuquerque home. He had recently retired from KOB and from public life and seemed to be in a talkative mood. He recalled for us that he had never spoken to anyone about his 1947 Roswell experiences for the first 20 years after the event. When he finally did start to talk about it, he always stated that there was more to his story, but that he did not want to talk about it at the time. Now, post-retirement, he was feeling different about things. He told us that he was going to tell us something he had never told anyone, and started us off on a cautionary note: "Don't stop me once I get started, or I might realize what I am doing and shut up." We were only too happy to oblige. The following is our reconstruction of Frank Joyce's account of his initial conversation with Mack Brazel on the afternoon of July 6, 1947, shortly after Brazel had arrived in Roswell to report his discovery, as revealed to us for the first time by Frank Joyce.[3]

BRAZEL: [angrily] *Who's gonna clean all that stuff up? That's what I wanna know. I need someone out there to clean it up.*

JOYCE: *What stuff? What are you talking about?*

BRAZEL: [somberly] *Don't know. Don't know what it is. Maybe it's from one of them 'flying saucer' things.*

JOYCE: *Oh, really? Then you should call the air base. They are responsible for everything that flies in the air. They should be able to help you or tell you what it is.*

BRAZEL: [At this point, according to Joyce, Brazel really started "losing it."] *Oh, God, Oh, my God. What am I gonna do? It's horrible. Horrible. Just horrible.*

JOYCE: *What's that? What's horrible? What are you talking about?*

BRAZEL: *The stench. Just awful.*

JOYCE: *Stench? From what? What are you talking about?*

BRAZEL: *They're dead.*

JOYCE: *Who? Who's dead?*

BRAZEL: *Little people.* [Now barely audible.] *Unforunate little creatures....*

JOYCE: [At this point, Joyce thought to himself, "This is crazy!" He decided to play the role of Devil's Advocate to a story he did not believe.] *What the...? Where? Where did you find them?*

BRAZEL: *Someplace else.*

JOYCE: *Well, you know, the military is always firing rockets and experimenting with monkeys and things. So, maybe...*

BRAZEL: [shouting now] ***God dammit! They're not monkeys, and* THEY'RE NOT HUMAN!!** [With that, Brazel angrily slammed down the phone to end the conversation.]

KGFL had every intention of broadcasting the story of the century, which is why its staff escorted Brazel to the home of the station's owner, Walt Whitmore Sr., and recorded Brazel's testimony late in the evening of Monday, July 7, 1947. At least, that was the plan—until the U.S. Army took custody of Brazel and the KGFL wire recording, and removed both to Roswell Army Air Field south of town.

Efforts continued the next morning to disseminate preliminary news information to the local townspeople. But Washington was watching. Early in the morning on July 8, George "Jud" Roberts, minority owner at the station, received a long-distance phone call from T.J. Slowie, the executive secretary of the FCC, who warned him that the matter involved national security. Should KGFL air any portion of Brazel's interview or issue any information regarding it, it would lose its broadcasting license.[4]

As if that weren't enough to squelch the story, another call to KGFL came from Washington a few minutes

Frank Joyce, the day he revealed "the rest of the story" regarding his interviews with Mack Brazel.

Photo courtesy of Tom Carey, 1998.

later. It was from U.S. Senator Dennis Chavez, who strongly suggested that KGFL do exactly as the FCC had cautioned.[5] When station executives asked for his help, he indicated that the decision was out of his hands. The station immediately complied with the FCC's order.[6]

While the officially sanctioned intimidation of a news source in Roswell was underway, another situation was developing at KOAT Radio in Albuquerque, an affiliate of both ABC and Mutual networks at that time. Secretary Lydia Sleppy remembers vividly the frantic phone call she received from John McBoyle, general manager and part owner of sister station KSWS in Roswell, which had to rely on KOAT to transmit to the Associated Press wire service. "Lydia, get ready for a scoop!" McBoyle excitedly said. "We want to get this on the wire right away. Listen to this! A *flying saucer* has crashed....No, I'm not joking. It crashed near Roswell!"

Sleppy urgently asked program director and acting station manager Karl Lambertz to witness her reception of the story and its transmission. Using the teletype, Sleppy alerted ABC News headquarters in Hollywood to expect a "high bulletin" story. Lambertz looked on as she initiated the connection. "It's a big crumpled dishpan..." McBoyle—hardly containing himself—continued over the phone, "...and get this. They're saying something about little men being on board."

Before Sleppy could type out a mere couple of sentences, a bell rang on the teletype machine, indicating an outside interruption. McBoyle, meanwhile, started to converse with someone in the background and the discussion became more intense as it went along. Moments later he nervously told Sleppy, "Wait a minute, I'll get back to you....Wait....I'll get right back."[7]

He did not. The very next moment, the teletype came back on line and printed out the following order:

> **ATTENTION ALBUQUERQUE: DO NOT TRANSMIT, REPEAT, DO NOT TRANSMIT THIS MESSAGE. STOP COMMUNICATION IMMEDIATELY. NATIONAL SECURITY MATTER.**

In stunned disbelief, Sleppy observed that the message was from the FBI. No further attempt was made to transmit McBoyle's amazing story in any shape or form.[8]

At a later time, Sleppy was speaking with McBoyle and broached the subject of the strange series of events. The veteran reporter's response shocked her: "Forget about it. You never heard it. Look, you're not supposed to know. Don't talk about it to anyone." Another time, he mentioned to Sleppy that he had observed a plane take off from the RAAF on route to Wright Field with wreckage on board, but was unable to get near it because of all the armed guards posted in the area.[9]

Lydia Sleppy would wait 25 years before breaking her silence. For his part, McBoyle returned to ranching in Idaho, and disregarding any and all exhortations from his wife, son, and daughter, refused to discuss the matter. "I don't remember," is all he would say to us before he died, thus taking the true story about the "crumpled dishpan" with him to his grave in 1991.[10]

Unfortunately, "they" soon got to Mack Brazel as well, and the next time Frank Joyce saw the rancher, he didn't have the same things to say. When the military escorted Brazel to KGFL, Brazel sat down at the microphone and retracted his original story. The unusual material that Brazel had carried with him in two boxes all the way from his ranch to Roswell was now, "nothing more than a weather balloon," according to Brazel. Taking Brazel out of the broadcast booth during a music break, Joyce followed the older man out into the front lobby of the radio station. "That's not the story you told me before," Joyce bluntly told Brazel. The rancher stuck to his new story while growing more agitated. Brazel could see by the look on his face that Joyce was rapidly losing respect for him. Brazel then said, "They told me it would go hard on me if I didn't do what they said." Presumably, Brazel had been warned of the dire consequences—not to the nation, but to Brazel and his family—if he said anything that conflicted with the Army Air Forces' new, official story. At that point, Joyce noticed the uniformed men standing just outside the glass door entrance. The reporter made one last attempt to get the truth. "What about the 'little green men' you told me about the other day?"

The rancher paused as he walked over to the door and put his hand on the doorknob. Turning toward Joyce, he casually said in a soft-spoken, matter-of-fact voice, "They weren't green," and out he went.[11]

5

Afraid They Would Shoot at Us

Robin Adair, a photographer with the Associated Press (AP), received a phone call from the main office in New York on Tuesday, July 8, 1947, telling him to get to Roswell, New Mexico immediately, "even if it meant leasing a plane," for the journey from El Paso, Texas.[1]

Fully briefed on the situation just to the northwest, Adair felt it wise to try getting some aerial shots before landing in Roswell. He instructed his pilot to fly the plane north toward Lincoln County. He told us:

> We didn't do a bit of good by it. We couldn't get any [pictures]. Even then, the place was surrounded by policemen and FBI people. They wouldn't let us get within three-quarters of a mile of the place. We were afraid they would shoot at us. We did take a plane up there, but we couldn't land anywhere around it [the debris field on the Foster ranch]. We got as close as we could and we wanted to get lower....They [the military officers on the ground] just waved....You couldn't tell if they were waving us off or just politely telling us to get the hell away from there.[2]

From the air, Adair managed to observe all of the activity at what was later determined to be the debris field. Many troops, vehicles, and MPs covered the large open field. Some areas also appeared to be scorched. Even from the altitude they were flying, the photographer could make out what he called the "gouge." He remarked, "You couldn't see too good from the air....Apparently, the way it cut into [the ground], whatever hit the ground wasn't wood or something soft. It looked like it was metal." His lasting impression was that it had descended, impacted the ground, and then ascended back into the air.[3]

Heading south to Roswell, he observed that the terrain became more rugged and canyon-like. Still, he and the pilot continued to look for any type of military activity below. Adair said that he saw two recovery sites. "One of them wasn't very distinct. The other was [more easily seen]."

After landing at the old municipal airstrip west of Roswell, Adair linked up with reporter Jason Kellahin. Kellahin had also received a call from the New York office and had driven down from Albuquerque. That evening, the team went to the offices of the *Roswell Daily Record*, where Adair proceeded to set up the equipment to transmit wire messages back to Albuquerque.

The two planned to interview rancher Mack Brazel, who was now retracting his original story, though he continued to insist that what he saw was not any type of weather balloon.[4] Adair snapped the cowboy's picture—cowboy hat and all. The photo and Kellahin's story were tediously wired back to the New York office. Transmitting the pictures was considered so important, or maybe such a novelty, that the *Record* ran a story on the front page of the July 9 edition along with a photo of both Adair and Kellahin. The photo taken of Brazel during this session—a head shot of the wary Brazel wearing his cowboy hat pulled back slightly—was the first wire photo ever sent from Roswell by any news organization.[5]

Brazel's name and face would be household items, however briefly, by the end of the next day. Brazel told the journalists that he had found the debris almost a month earlier, on June 14, while doing his chores on the ranch. His wife Margaret, daughter Bessie, and son Vernon were with him on the ranch at the time. In that interview (published in the July 9 edition of the *Roswell Daily Record*) Brazel claimed that the wreckage he found consisted of rubber, tinfoil, tape, and wooden sticks that were all confined to a rather small area. The story ended with Brazel saying that he had found weather balloons on two previous occasions, but that this object did not resemble any of those. "I am sure that what I found was not any weather observation balloon," he said.[6]

According to *Record* editor at the time, Paul McEvoy, the military officers then escorted the rancher out of the news office immediately upon the conclusion of the interview. While they were walking toward the waiting staff car, two of Brazel's neighbors, Floyd Proctor and Lyman Strickland, passed by. Both men were surprised when their friend walked right past them without acknowledging them in any way. Proctor would later say that the military was keeping Brazel on a "short leash."[7] Three other neighbors—Leonard "Pete" Porter, who lived on the ranch just south of Brazel's, and ranchers Bill Jenkins and L.D. Sparks—reported that they saw Brazel "surrounded" by military personnel in downtown Roswell. They said the Brazel kept his eyes down and pretended he didn't notice them.

6

Harassed Rancher Sorry He Told
The Aftermath of a Balloon Recovery:
The True Story

What is generally perceived by the novice is that after Mack Brazel turned most of the country on its ear with the story of the millennium, the "higher-ups" returned the world to reason and sanity with the most logical explanation they could muster. The press went for the bait, accepted the old switcheroo, and the poor, ignorant rancher went back to Corona a humbled man. Our national security was not an issue; rather, it was our overreaction to the fanciful claims of some wide-eyed intelligence officer at some military base in some one-horse town called Roswell. And as General Ramey intimated, only those who over-imbibe see such things. Unfortunately, for those who tend to distrust officialdom on just about every issue but this one, the story does not end here. And sadly for Mack Brazel and those dear to him, it was only the beginning.

But first we will need to retrace just exactly what chain of events took place from the moment Brazel rightly or wrongly attempted to perform his civic duty by going to the authorities and report the crash of something beyond the realm of explanation. For all of his trouble, he became caught up in a web of malfeasance and cover-up that altered his life and that of his family even up to today. We will discover that in the government's world of sinister suppression and egregious intimidation one does not just walk away unscathed after a Mogul balloon recovery. As singer/actor Dwight Yoakam, in his portrayal of Mack Brazel in the highly acclaimed movie *Roswell* defiantly responded to his interrogators, "...unless you're expecting some surprise balloon attack."[1]

There is absolutely no evidence that Mack Brazel *ever* spent an entire day driving all the way to Roswell, New Mexico to report any type of weather balloon device—except for the one time on Sunday, July 6, 1947. This is a matter of indisputable fact. Certainly, all of the eyewitness testimony

presented in this tome provides a wealth of circumstantial evidence argu-
ing that Brazel was not alarmed over a mere balloon or anything else so
prosaic. To the contrary, all of his actions and those of his neighbors suggest something truly out of the ordinary, which would eventually lead
Brazel to fill up a couple of cardboard boxes with a selection of some of
the debris and head off to Roswell to an ignominy that would haunt him
for the rest of his life.

It is true that whatever Brazel brought to the attention of Chaves
County Sheriff George Wilcox impressed him enough that he immediately
dispatched two of his deputies from Roswell to it check out. What clearly
elevated the entire affair to a national level of interest was the fateful
phone conversation with KGFL's Frank Joyce. At that moment, the press
learned of the whole dramatic affair, and if not for the military interven-
tion, this book would be 60 years late, and obsolete. To Joyce's everlasting
regret, the very worst piece of advice he provided the unfortunate rancher
was to report the crash to the RAAF. No strangers to Top Secret tests in
their immediate area, Joyce and the Sheriff Wilcox thought, what else
could it be?

Picture the following situation: It is a holiday weekend, some rancher
wanders into your town with an outlandish story about wreckage from a
flying saucer strewn across the desert floor. Next, the local media gets
wind of the story, and in short order the most elite unit of the U.S. military, in charge of our one and only nuclear bomb wing, is alerted to look
into it. The rancher has quite a tall tale, but there's more: He has brought
in physical proof. Case in point: There would have been absolutely nothing about the physical remains of a Mogul balloon that would have suggested it was part of a Top Secret project. Should we then assume that if
the "evidence" were simply remnants from a weather balloon—Neoprene
rubber, wooden sticks, flimsy reflective foil, masking tape, and bailing
twine—that not only the head of intelligence from the base, Major Marcel,
but also the head of the CIC, Capt. Cavitt, would have been ordered by
the base commander, Col. Blanchard, to make the long drive back with
the rancher and personally investigate it? Marcel, in the event it is one of
ours, and Cavitt, if it is one of "theirs." Neither man questioned his superior officer after examining the assortment of debris just brought into the
sheriff's office.

Ever since Brazel tipped off the radio station, Joyce's boss, Walt
Whitmore Sr., wanted to get his hands on the main source. At some time
on Monday, July 7, while the two intelligence officers went about their

assigned mission, Whitmore arranged for someone to grab Brazel at the ranch and bring him back down to Roswell. By that time Whitmore surmised that the cowboy was about to become a heavily sought-after man. But where to hide him? Why, Whitmore's home—what better place? That very evening the station minority owner and newsman, "Jud" Roberts, conducted a wire-recorded interview with Brazel. Having already signed off broadcasting for the day, KGFL would have to wait until morning to break the biggest story in the history of the network.[2]

Roswell radio station KGFL as it looked in the 1940s.

Photo printed with permission from Mrs. Walter Whitmore, Jr.

Unfortunately, time was not in their favor, and Brazel was quickly becoming a fugitive. Marcel and Cavitt were about to report back to headquarters. And for some unknown reason, Marcel had sent Cavitt long ahead of him to report back to Blanchard. According to Marcel, they couldn't identify the material.

As part of the Army's urgent attempt to get control of the entire situation, they grabbed Brazel and his recorded testimony first thing the next morning. It was now Tuesday, July 8—just hours before posting the famous press release. It was all so contrived and calculated. As Brazel was thoroughly interrogated at the base, Marcel was ordered to report to "higher officials," and Blanchard was about to announce that he was conveniently going on leave *after* the holiday weekend. Now, with all of the principles out of the picture, the stage was set for it all to be rationalized away. By late that afternoon Gen. Ramey denigrated Blanchard, Marcel, and some "old west cowboy" who was probably just looking for attention. "It's just a weather balloon!"[3]

Clearly, the story should have ended there—especially for Mack Brazel. But we would be remiss not to consider why the military found it necessary to take him early the next day to the *Roswell Daily Record* to recant the entire sordid tale. Surely Ramey's *official* explanation should have trumped that of any lowly civilian. Or was it part of a full-scale damage control program to further promulgate the government's stand on flying saucers—a preemptive strike so to speak. Too many people, including the press, knew the true story. And up until the Fort Worth press conference, nobody was talking about any weather balloon—except for Gen. Ramey. Should we believe that Brazel voluntarily made himself into a public spectacle? He had just spent the past *five days* trying to simply get someone to explain and clean up all that mess on a ranch he was hired to supervise. Everyone offered advice, but no one had any answers—not his neighbors, the state police, the sheriff's department, intelligence officers at the base, nor its own commander. No one. Yet the Army was still compelled to hold on to Brazel and escort him with MPs to all the media outlets throughout Roswell *the day after the balloon explanation.*[4] And when they completed their derisive manipulation of the media, what did they do with the ranch foreman? They returned him back to the base for another *three days!* It is quite evident that this civil abuse of Brazel was due to the fact that he had witnessed more than just unusual wreckage. He had seen more—something that could hardly be explained away as a mundane weather balloon, or even an experimental vehicle made of some new exotic material.

During this disruption, Brazel had no hired hands to complete the ranch's chores. Cattle and sheep had to be fed and watered, and horses needed tending. The troops assigned to the special cleanup operation were oblivious to such trivial concerns, but Brazel's two older sons, after hearing about his disappearance, made their way to take over the ranch affairs.[5] Unfortunately, son Paul made the error of arriving first—during the military's occupation. Paul was a rancher in Texas at that time and traveled some

Mack Brazel standing between his two oldest sons, Paul (left) and Bill (right). This picture was taken in the mid-1950s when when Mack was working as a security officer.

Photo printed with permission from Mrs. Fawn Fritz.

distance to help out his father—or at least try. To our frustration, as with so many others who saw too much, Paul would never discuss the situation with us. He always told us he had absolutely nothing to say. Finally, just before he passed away from cancer in 1995, he confessed one important concern as a rancher to his nephew Joe: "You know what always riled me even up to this day?" he asked. "Every time I tried to get to the main ranch house [10 miles from the debris field] to water the horses in all that summer heat, the damn Army forced me off the ranch. I tried again the next day and they still threw me off the property. I was sure they did nothing for any of the animals."[6]

Bill would fare somewhat better when he and his wife Shirley showed up from their home in Albuquerque just as the troops headed back to Roswell with all the remaining evidence.[7] They quickly went about the task of returning things back to normal. But such was not the case for his father when he unexpectedly showed up just as mysteriously as he had disappeared. Word was that he was flown back in a small plane. No apologies, no regrets for all of the mental and physical mishandling.[8] He was bitter and humiliated, and his good-natured spirit was broken, seldom to be seen again. Daughter Bessie would be taken aside by her dad and warned, "Don't believe everything you read about me in the papers. The government is going to use me to keep something secret!"[9] His son Bill would press him. "It's better that you don't know," Mack told him. Bill would persist. Cutting him off completely, his dad would slam the door: "You don't want to know."[10]

At this juncture we need to reiterate: Would all this have been necessary if the precept of a weather balloon was sufficient? Let's assume for the moment that it was still part of a Top Secret project—say, Mogul. Remember, the authorities were not looking for any missing test launch. No chase planes were patrolling the area. And still Brazel was subjected to the following violations of his civil rights:

1. Being physically abducted by the U.S. Army from the private residence of Walt Whitmore, along with a First Amendment violation for the confiscation of the wire recording from the media.

Bill Brazel and his wife, Shirley, newly-weds in 1947.

Photo printed with permission from Joe Brazel.

2. Being physically detained at the RAAF for up to five days at the base "guest house" for questioning. He could identify all his neighbors, yes, but what could Brazel possibly tell them about a Top Secret Mogul balloon? There is absolutely no evidence that he was ever accused of being a spy for a foreign government.

3. Being confined at the Roswell base for five full days without the benefit of due process. In fact, he was not permitted to make *any* phone calls—not even to his wife.

4. Being forced to undergo a full Army physical examination— for being exposed to balloon parts? Or was it a full-body search for the same? Brazel would later complain that he felt very degraded over this indignity. He would later complain upon his return home that he was kept up all hours of the night and asked the same questions over and over again. It has been suggested, based on the testimony of newsman Frank Joyce, who claimed similar treatment by the authorities, that Brazel was isolated on the final day of confinement, and subjected to subtle brainwashing in a final attempt to silence him.[11]

In summation, it is abundantly clear that whatever Mack Brazel saw, it *was* definitely a threat to our national security. At least the Army's actions to pressure and coerce him into submission smack of strong-armed tactics generally reserved for captured enemies of the state—hardly the treatment of an erroneous man. The question persists: Does a Mogul weather balloon merit such measures?

For those who still insist on believing the official explanation, Mogul was officially declassified in 1972, but the primary objective was already clearly known in 1947. Mogul eventually became just another obsolete government test that had outlasted its usefulness. And still, the Brazels remained suspect and under surveillance by agents of the U.S. government— possibly another reason for Mack's total silence about the incident.

True to his word, whether out of loyalty to his country or just fear and deep concern for the safety and well-being of his family, Brazel never did talk. In fact, he went out of his way to avoid any conversation about this bleak time in his life. Hired workers such as Ernest Lueras remember just how much Mack's demeanor had changed: "There was one particular time I rode along with him down to Tularosa [from Corona, three hours],"

Lueras said. "This was right after he got into all that trouble with the Army. He didn't say anything. I tried to strike up a conversation. Not a word was said for the entire time I was with him. They [the military] really messed him up."[12]

"My dad was never the same," expressed Bill with a look of melancholy in his face.

Possibly driven by lack of resolution, his son continued to seek out some answers, eventually salvaging enough evidence to fill a cigar box. After heavy rains, Bill knew enough to return and check for any failings from the military cleanup. But this time there would be no drive to Roswell.

Bill's daughter Fawn remembered how the sheep still refused to graze at the site. "This went on for about *five years*! I was there when my dad would attempt to lure them back by placing feed right in the middle of the pasture. They would have sooner starved. It just didn't matter, something was still spooking them. We never saw anything like it."[13] All of this would be a harbinger of things to come.

It was something he regretted for the rest of his life—the day in 1949 when Bill turned over the cigar box to a Captain Armstrong and three NCOs,[14] the very next morning after he simply acknowledged "finding a few scraps" at Wade's Bar the evening before.[15] Whether out of shame or fear, Bill always described the encounter as rather straightforward and routine, but Fawn, to her everlasting horror, witnessed much more. While her father was leading the military intruders to the pasture, others, on a more circuitous mission, arrived at the ranch house. "There were six soldiers, who came right into the house. They pulled drawers from dressers, emptied closets, and proceeded to pry up floorboards in Dad's bedroom. They completely trashed the house." It looked to be more of a warning than any methodical search. "From the house they went to the cattle shed and started to slit open each feedbag and let it pour over the ground," Fawn said. "They even emptied a water holding tank." They didn't say a word, and as fast as they had stormed the ranch, they fled like thieves leaving the location pillaged and violated. "Did anyone in authority even offer to pay for all the damage?" we asked. The pain was still evident in Fawn's response: "How could this happen? How could this ever happen in this country? It was beyond belief. They made Dad swear not to say anything. First it was Granddad, then Dad." Who would be next?[16]

The late Bill Brazel, wheelchair-bound in this 1998 picture with Don Schmitt.

Photo courtesy of Tom Carey.

The obvious issue here has to do with the urgency with which the military acted. Keep in mind that Project Mogul was a Top Secret program— *the project, not the materials!* Once again, the elements that composed a Mogul device were conventional and identifiable to everyone. And when it is broken up and scattered on the ground in front of you there is nothing Top Secret about it. A cigar box of balloon scraps would hardly warrant such an official reaction. Bill Brazel was not in possession of Mogul secret documents; all he ever admitted to was discovering pieces from the debris field, which the military wishfully assumed had been sufficiently vacuumed. Evidently, they were wrong. Clearly, the military was in desperate search for something much more sensitive than balloon fragments. And most shocking of all, this entire incident happened *two years after the original crash*, which portends the true seriousness of this situation, and explains why the Brazels were still being watched.

Months after returning home in 1960 after serving in the Navy, Mack's youngest son Vernon would disappear. Mack himself would die from a massive heart attack in 1963. Bill's son (Mack's grandson), William R. Brazel, was shot to death while hunting with two companions in 1964, and one other hunter was also killed by a second bullet. State police concluded that *both* were shot accidentally. Is it any wonder that Mack Brazel was sorry he ever told anyone back in 1947?

Former real estate salesman Howard Scoggin of Las Cruces, N.M. described a 1959 encounter with Mack Brazel. Scoggin had gone to a local restaurant for lunch with a friend who pointed out Brazel sitting alone at another table. Against his friend's better advice, Scoggin got up and approached the unsuspecting Brazel and asked him about the 1947 incident. Without saying a word, the rancher clenched his fist tightly, grimaced, and slowly rose out of his chair. Fearing for his personal safety, the surprised and now wary Scoggin backed away while Brazel slowly stalked past him and out of the restaurant, leaving his food on the table. "It was like watching one of those werewolf movies when Lon Chaney turns into the hairy monster," recalled Scoggin.[17]

KGFL minority owner Bob Wolf just happened to run into Mack at a festival in Corona mere months before he died. It was some years since the aging cowboy had passed through the area, so Wolf took advantage of the opportunity and brought up 1947 while exchanging social niceties. Brazel's entire attitude immediately changed. "He looked as though he had seen a ghost," described Wolf. "Those people will kill you if I tell you what I know!" said the rancher. He stormed away and unobtrusively slipped out from the gathering. Wolf would never see him again.[18]

On only one occasion would Fawn ever overhear her grandfather comment about the incident. "It was not uncommon for granddad to come riding up to the ranch house with an injured lamb cradled in his lap," she told us. "He treated all people and animals with respect and kindness. That is why it didn't surprise me when he softly spoke of 'those poor unfortunate creatures' back in 1947." But just as quickly he cautioned, "It wasn't anything anyone would ever want to see. Thank God you didn't!"[19]

7

Nothing Made on This Earth

It is now 60 years after the event, and it is still unclear whether Major Marcel knew that the mangled remains of a weather balloon and radar kite were part of the secured cargo he escorted aboard a B-29 bomber to a meeting with General Roger Ramey in Fort Worth, Texas. One thing, however, is certain: Until the day he died in May of 1986, Marcel swore that what he personally recovered in the desert north of Roswell was not what was displayed for *Fort Worth Star-Telegram* news photographer James B. Johnson in Gen. Ramey's office on July 8, 1947. And, as if to add insult to injury, after Marcel was instructed to pose with the substituted weather device, Ramey also ordered the major not to say a word to any of the press waiting outside the room.[1]

As the chief intelligence officer of the 509th Bomb Group at Roswell Army Air Field, Marcel likely found it strange that he was all but completely eliminated from the press conference that followed his photo op. Marcel was kept in seclusion for the next 24 hours; he finally was allowed to return to Roswell on the evening of Wednesday, July 9. The B-29 that carried Marcel from Fort Worth back to Roswell was nicknamed *Straight Flush* and bore the tail number 447301. It was piloted by Captain Frederick Ewing.[2]

Maj. Marcel returned to his home in Roswell just one day after he had displayed some of the true wreckage to his wife, Vi (short for Viaud), and son, Jesse Jr. Upon his return, Marcel informed both of them that he was no longer able to talk about it with them. But that didn't prevent him from trying to get some answers back at the Roswell base.[3]

The very next morning, Marcel arrived at his office and confronted the officer who had accompanied him to the Foster ranch with Mack Brazel to first investigate the crash—the head of counterintelligence for the Counter Intelligence Corps (CIC), Captain Sheridan Cavitt.

> "I want to see the report of what all happened here while I was in Fort Worth," Marcel demanded.
>
> "What report?" Cavitt responded. "I don't know what you're talking about."
>
> "I outrank you," the major snapped back.
>
> "I take my orders from Washington," Cavitt said bluntly. "If you don't like it, you can take it up with them."

On that brusque note, the CIC officer put an abrupt end to the debate.[4]

It should be pointed out that CIC NCO (noncommissioned officer) Lewis "Bill" Rickett was also present at the heated exchange. To him, the preceding discussion was most out of character for both men; the Marcels and the Cavitts were good friends.[5] Furthermore, the captain's wife, Mary Cavitt, told a most interesting story. According to her, within a few nights of Jesse's return from his special flight to Fort Worth, the two couples got together for their weekly game of bridge. But this night was different. The wives remained in the main room while the two husbands toiled over the stove in the kitchen. As Mary described, "The men turned up the heat as high as it would go, and it still had no effect."[6] That's because the focus of their efforts was no simple pot of boiling water—it was a piece of the *real* crash debris. Mrs. Cavitt claimed this rather astonishing scenario ended when, "Cav [her husband] reminded Jess that the material was classified 'Top Secret' and he had better get rid of it." According to her, "The two men went out onto the patio," with the nigh-indestructible material. Moments later, when they returned, it was gone. "It never came up again." Loyalty and security oaths had prevailed.[7]

During a radio telephone interview with KOAT in Albuquerque in 1985, Marcel ended his recollections by adding this caveat, "I haven't told everything." One would think that the head of intelligence at Roswell would have been privy to all details regarding the incident. True, he was removed from the scene for the better part of two days during the most crucial part of the recovery operation, but if indeed there were bodies involved, how could Marcel not have known the truth? Even today, his son Jesse Jr. maintains that his father never uttered a word about such things. Others might disagree.

Major Jesse A. Marcel, the intelligence officer of the elite 509th Bomb Group at the RAAF, dispatched to inspect the wreckage on the Foster ranch. He believed that the wreckage was from an extraterrestrial spaceship.

Photo printed with permission from the 1947 RAAF Yearbook.

Our investigation has concluded that Maj. Marcel *had* to know about the alien bodies that were recovered from the crash—not second-hand by hearing about them from others in the chain of command, but firsthand from actually seeing them himself. If you accept that Mack Brazel found alien bodies *someplace else* on his ranch (detailed in Chapter 6), as he told the KGFL radio announcer when he first came into Roswell on Sunday, July 6—which we do—then you have to believe that Brazel not only told Maj. Marcel and Capt. Cavitt about the bodies, but also showed them to the officers when they followed Brazel out to his ranch in Lincoln County to look at the wreckage on July 6, 7, and 8. That this may have been the case is suggested in an interview that we conducted with former Technical Sergeant Herschel Grice in 2002. Grice was a ground maintenance crew chief in the 715th Bomb Squadron on the Roswell base in 1947. He was also a member of Marcel's intelligence team working within the 715th. Grice said that he knew Marcel well and that Marcel was a good officer and a "straight-arrow" as a person. He also said that Marcel once told him about seeing the alien bodies. Grice couldn't remember any of the details other than to say that Marcel had referred to them as, "white, rubbery figures."[8]

Sue Marcel Methane is a family member of the Houma, Louisiana Marcels, from where Jesse Marcel hailed, and to where he returned when he left the Air Force. In discussing her famous relative with us in a telephone interview in 2002, she said that she had a chance to talk to him shortly before his death in 1986. She did not recall how or why the conversation turned to the subject of the Roswell Incident, but it did. Methane said that the one thing that stuck with her from that conversation was his description of the dead aliens. "He reffered to them as 'white powdery figures.' I can't picture them, but that's what he called them."

Marcel At-a-Glance

- Major Jesse A. Marcel—in charge of Army Air Forces security and intelligence briefings at Kwajelein Base in the Pacific (command center for Operation Crossroads, which test fired two atomic bombs).

- Maj. Marcel—recipient of three commendations including one from Gen. Ramey.

- Maj. Marcel—head intelligence officer, A-2, of a select squadron of people in charge of the atomic bomb back in 1947.

- Maj. Marcel—who remained the head of intelligence at Roswell for another year and was then promoted to lieutenant colonel in the Air Force Reserve with recommendations from both Blanchard and Ramey.

- Maj. Marcel—who was then transferred to Washington, D.C., where he was made the SAC chief of a foreign technology intelligence division.

- Maj. Marcel—who at the Pentagon's insistence, was assigned to the Top Secret Special Weapons Project.

- Maj. Marcel—scapegoat, whom the U.S. Army would have us believe was so incompetent that he couldn't identify the rubber, wooden sticks, foil, tape, and string that comprised a very common weather device.

Military scoffers have suggested that the reason Marcel was never publicly reprimanded or even demoted for attempting such a canard was to avoid attracting any additional embarrassment to the already humiliated

Army. But this was far from an isolated internal affair. No one can credibly prove that Marcel, with the willing assistance of the public information officer, Walter Haut, cavalierly put out a press release, without outside knowledge or permission. All of which we are asked to just chalk up to poor judgment and overreaction on the part of two overly zealous officers?

Col. Blanchard and the brass all the way to Washington had wreckage in their possession since the day rancher Mack Brazel brought it into town—*two full days before the announcement went out*! Every action Marcel took in the entire Roswell affair was following the orders of his superiors. The RAAF publicly stated *they* had a flying saucer in their possession— not Marcel. And after the public spectacle subsided, clearly the higher-ups were much more confident with Marcel than the general public. But then again, the public accepted the balloon story. Apparently, the military knew otherwise.

During the last few years of Marcel's life, as he gradually struggled more and more with emphysema, he bravely tried to tell the world the truth about what he saw and handled out on that patch of desert property so many years before. "It was nothing we had ever seen before," Marcel stated on the record. "It was not an aircraft of any kind; that I am sure of. We didn't know what it was. It was *nothing made on this Earth*."⁹

8

The Senator and the Aliens
"Get Me the Hell Out of Here!"

On Monday, July 7, 1947, New Mexico's newly elected, 32-year-old lieutenant governor, Joseph "Little Joe" Montoya was in the sleepy desert town of Roswell. There are no written records that will confirm the exact whereabouts of Little Joe that day,[1] but thanks to the long-term memories of a few *Montoyistas* (young political supporters of Montoya), we know for a fact that Montoya was in Roswell. And the town of Roswell—especially the air base just to the south—was anything but sleepy that day.

The brothers, Ruben and Pete Anaya, who would become lifelong friends of Joe Montoya, lived next door to one another on Albuquerque St. in the south end of Roswell in 1947. Both were active in local Democratic politics, and both were card-carrying Montoyistas. Though U.S. Senator Dennis Chavez was the highest-ranking elected

Joseph "Little Joe" Montoya, New Mexico's lt. governor in 1947. He later rose to prominence as a respected U.S. congressman and senator.

Photo printed with permission from the U.S. Senate Historical Office.

Hispanic politician in New Mexico at the time, many in the state's Hispanic community felt that Chavez had become too "establishment" from his years in Washington, and as a result, did not adequately represent their interests and concerns. "Little Joe," as they affectionately referred to the then lieutenant governor, was their man, and the rest is history. Almost.

It is not entirely clear how Joseph Montoya came to be on base at the Roswell Army Air Field on the exact day and moment that wreckage from the downed UFO began arriving there. Also arriving was the first set of "little bodies," including a possible survivor from the crash site just north of town. The site had been accidentally discovered 35 miles northwest of Roswell in Chaves County earlier that day by a group of civilian archaeologists who telephoned the sheriff's office and fire department in Roswell from a service station in the nearby hamlet of Mesa. This site was closer to Roswell than the debris-field site in Lincoln County that the RAAF's Maj. Jesse Marcel and Capt. Sheridan Cavitt had gone to the previous day with sheep rancher Mack Brazel. Marcel and Cavitt were at this time still in the field, and had not yet returned to Roswell.

New Mexico Senator Dennis Chavez, brought in by the Air Force to help silence Roswell civilians.

Photo printed with permission from the U.S. Senate Historical Office.

The central depository for the retrieval operation, including the bodies, was Hangar P-3 (today known as Building 84) located along the flight line at the east end of the base proper. One account has Montoya being called to the base from Roswell, as the highest-ranking state official in the area at the time, to view the wreckage and the bodies. The other account, the most likely scenario, told to us by the Anaya brothers, put Montoya on the base with other public officials for a regularly scheduled special event—the dedication of a new airplane. After the dedication, according to the late Ruben Anaya, Montoya went over to the hangar area to greet some local, civilian Montoyistas who were working there and who wanted to meet him. He arrived in the vicinity of Hangar P-3 just as the first military vehicles were bearing down with wreckage and bodies from the crash site north of town. What then ensued was something that would cause Montoya to admonish his friends to never say anything at the threat of being called liars, something that would bring Senator Chavez and Chaves County Sheriff George Wilcox into the case to enforce the secret, and something that Montoya's family refuses to discuss by claiming that he was not involved.

Hangar P-3 today (Building 84).

Photo courtesy of Tom Carey.

Our investigation was first made aware of Ruben and Pete Anaya in 1991 during a book signing in Roswell for the then recently released *UFO Crash at Roswell* when Ruben Anaya's daughter introduced her father to coauthors Kevin Randle and Don Schmitt. It was in a number of interviews that we had with Ruben Anaya, Pete Anaya, and Pete's wife Mary in 1991, 1992, 1994, and 2002, that we learned the details of Joseph Montoya's 1947 extraordinary encounter. Ruben Anaya was also interviewed separately in 1993 by anti-Roswell researcher, the late Karl T. Pflock, for his

2001 book, *Roswell: Inconvenient Facts and the Will to Believe*. The Anayas were also interviewed in 1997 by British researcher Tim Shawcross for his book of the same year, *The Roswell File*. The following narrative of the 1947 events involving Joseph Montoya represents a synthesis of the details gleaned from these interviews.

The first inkling that Ruben Anaya had that something was amiss was a panicked knock at his front door. It was his father informing him that Joe Montoya had just called him (neither Ruben nor Pete Anaya had a telephone) from the base to tell him to get Ruben to come out to the base as quickly as possible. Ruben Anaya went to his father's house and returned the call to find out what Montoya needed. Anaya recalled that Montoya sounded, "real excited" and "panicky-sounding" over the phone, "like he had seen a fire or something." Talking as fast as he could in Spanish, Montoya told Anaya, "I'm at the big hangar. Get your car, Ruben, and pick me up. Get me the hell out of here! Hurry!" Returning home with alacrity, Ruben Anaya went next door to his brother's house to confer with Pete Anaya, who had been chatting with two fellow Montoyistas,

The water tower where the Anaya brothers picked up a shaken Joseph Montoya after his close encounter at the "big hangar"—still standing in the background.

Photo courtesy of Tom Carey, 2003.

Moses Burrola and Ralph Chaes. All four then piled into Ruben's car and headed for the base.

The Anaya car had no difficulty in passing through the main gate at the RAAF because Ruben worked on the base as a cook at the Officers' Club, and as a recently discharged WWII veteran, was also a member of the NCO Club. Because of these affiliations, his car had an official base sticker prominently displayed, which the guards at the main gate recognized, so they waved the car on through. The base also had not yet gotten its act together in dealing with this unprecedented emergency, and therefore had not yet gone into "lockdown mode." Not wanting to be seen in this situation by anyone who would recognize him, Montoya had told Anaya not to drive near the base headquarters located in the center of the base because there were too many people there. Following these instructions, the Anayas finally arrived at the large water tower that still looms ominously over Hangar P-3, but could go no further, as their route was blocked. It was then they noticed the burgeoning excitement around the hangar, and that there were MPs as well as some city police controlling the entrance to it. Just then, the side door of the hangar opened and out sprinted Little Joe Montoya, "...like a bat out of hell," according to Ruben Anaya. Montoya quickly got into the back seat of the car and exhorted, "Come on, let's go. Let's get the hell out of here!" Ruben Anaya noticed that Montoya was very pale, "...like he had seen a ghost or something," and was shaking uncontrollably. Anaya concluded that something must have frightened his friend severely. "He was very, very scared," Anaya would tell us years later. Pete Anaya would also attest to Montoya's strangely frightened appearance that day. Ruben then asked Montoya if he wanted to be driven to the Nickson Hotel, where Montoya normally stayed when he was in Roswell, but Montoya instead responded, "No. Just take me to your house. I need a drink bad." On the ride back, Montoya, at least initially, was still in a state of high excitement and anxiety as he kept shaking and twitching while rocking back and forth and muttering to himself, "They weren't human! They weren't human!" Later, he just sat quietly, glumly staring out the window during the remainder of the drive back to town.

When they arrived at Pete Anaya's house, Montoya collapsed in a heap on the sofa. He was handed a small glass of scotch, which he quickly downed, but with no apparent effect. Montoya wanted something else. He was then given a bottle of Jim Beam, three-quarters full, which he then drank straight from the bottle in three big gulps, "boom, boom, boom," as

Ruben would later describe it. They told Montoya to take it easy. "No, I've got to calm myself down. You are not going to believe what I've just seen. If you ever tell anyone, I'll call you a damned liar."

Still excited, Montoya launched into his account. "We don't know what it is," Montoya allowed. "There was a flying saucer. They say it moves like a platter—a plane without wings. Not a helicopter." Ruben Anaya revealed to us that when Montoya got excited, he tended to speak in Spanish; therefore, his "close encounter" was described to them mostly in Spanish—*un plato muy grande con una machina en la media* ("a big saucer with a machine in the middle"). "I don't know where it's from. It could be from the moon. We don't know what it is."

We don't know if Montoya actually saw the craft or was simply told about it by crews returning from the crash site. We suspect that it was the latter, because the recovery had just commenced and other eyewitnesses only described seeing pieces of wreckage being brought into the hangar at this time—not an intact vessel—along with something else. Montoya seemed to confirm this himself a little later by stating that he had seen wreckage being brought into the hangar when he was there, but that there was nothing that resembled an intact ship, just pieces of metal he didn't get close enough to examine.

Montoya wasn't finished. He then told the Anayas that he had also seen "four little men." He described how small they were, along with the stunning fact that "one was alive!"[2] There is a question as to the exact number of "little men" Montoya said he saw that day. Pete Anaya confirmed his brother's belief that Montoya had said there were four, but Pete's wife, who had been an interested bystander in the living room, thought he had mentioned only two. We believe that the correct total under discussion is four—three dead, and one alive. Montoya described the beings as, "short, only coming up to my chest." Ruben Anaya added that, "Montoya stood up as best he could and held his hand up to his chest with his palm facing down to indicate how tall they were. Montoya was a little guy himself, which would mean that they were about 3 1/2 feet tall." Continuing with Montoya's description, "[They were] skinny with big eyes shaped like tear-drops. [The] mouth was real small, like a knife-cut across a piece of wood, and they had large heads."

He then described for the Anayas the scene inside the hangar. Each of the little men, including the one that was alive, was stretched out on a table brought over from the mess hall and set up for that purpose. "I knew that one was alive, because I could hear it moaning." Montoya said that it was moving with its knees up on the table, and that these, plus one hand, were also moving. "They were so skinny that they didn't look human," Montoya told them. As with the wreckage, Montoya could not get as close to the little men as he would have liked, this time due to the press of doctors and technicians around the tables. He got close enough, however, to see that their skin was a pale white and that they had no hair. Each wore a silvery, tight-fitting, one-piece flight suit. "From what I could see, they had four long, thin fingers [on each hand]. They had large [for their size], bald heads. I wasn't close enough to see what color their eyes were, but they were larger than normal." Just prior to his dash from the hangar, Montoya said that the little men were taken over to the base hospital. Exhausted from his ordeal, and exasperated at Ruben Anaya for asking so many questions, Montoya had reached the end of his tether. "I tell you, they're not from this world!" Upon hearing this, Ruben Anaya recalled, "We thought, 'This guy, he's out of whack.' That's when I shut up."

After finishing the recounting of his day's "not from this world" activities, Montoya finally began to relax. He lay back on the sofa and fell asleep, but it was a fitful sleep. He kept jerking and twitching himself awake, as if he was under a great deal of stress. After a while, he woke up and asked Ruben Anaya to call his brother Tom Montoya, who worked at the Nickson Hotel in downtown Roswell where he was staying, to come over and pick him up. Anaya, after placing the call from his father's house, arrived back about the same time that a car driven by another Montoyista, Fred Willard, was pulling up to his brother Pete's house (Tom was unable to leave his duties at the hotel, and had called Willard to go to the Anayas' in his stead). Montoya came out of the house, and Willard got out and helped him into the car. The group of loyal Montoyistas just stood there in a state of semi-shock, watching in awed silence, as the car sped away.

The following morning, Ruben and Pete Anaya drove to the Nickson Hotel to check on the lieutenant governor. A now more composed Montoya gave the brothers a little update as to what was going on: "Confidentially, they shipped everything to Texas, and those little guys are in the hospital." Montoya then reiterated for the Anayas his admonishment of the previous day, that if they talked to anyone about what happened at the base the day before, he would call them liars. With that, the Anayas left and went home. That evening, the Anayas had an unexpected visitor. Because the two Anaya brothers and their families lived next to each other, a tired and stressed Sheriff George Wilcox was thankful to have a "twofer" on his hands. The Anayas had no idea why the Chaves County sheriff's car would be stopping in front of Pete Anaya's house. Both families went outside and met Sheriff Wilcox on the front lawn. Wilcox had a message for them. Unknown to the Anayas, Wilcox had delivered the same message to certain other civilians in Roswell that day at the behest of the Army Air Forces. He told the Anayas in no uncertain terms that if they talked to anyone about what the lieutenant governor had told them, everybody, including the children, would be killed![3] After delivering his civil-rights-violating threat, Wilcox returned to his cruiser and drove off, leaving the stunned and outraged Anayas to contemplate their fate. On several subsequent occasions, Ruben Anaya said that he, his brother, and Moses Burrola did in fact try to discuss the episode with Montoya, who was by this time talking about much more than just calling them liars. "It's too dangerous to talk about. The FBI will do away with you," he said. Could that be what Wilcox meant? Anaya wasn't sure, but the warning was again clear. In a later discussion, Montoya repeated the warning: "If you talk about it, someone, maybe not the FBI, but someone in the government will get you."

A different appeal was tried on the Montoyistas by Joseph Montoya's longtime New Mexico adversary, Senator Dennis Chavez. Sometime after Montoya's experience in the hangar, as Ruben Anaya recalled it, Senator Chavez summoned him, his brother Pete, Moses Burrola, and Ralph Chaes to the Nickson Hotel where he was staying to discuss something. After preliminaries, Chavez bluntly told them, "Joe Montoya is a damn liar! He didn't see anything. It was a secret project, and it could hurt us with Russia and Germany if word of it got out."

By the decade of the 1970s, when Joseph Montoya was a sitting U.S. senator, the "UFO crisis" of those early days had long passed. UFO sightings were still being reported, to be sure, but the Air Force was officially out of the UFO business, having closed its Project Blue Book in 1969.[4] And, out of fear of ridicule, there was no longer any talk of "crashed saucers" or "little green men." It was in this milieu that John Anaya, the son of Pete and Mary Anaya, joined the staff of Senator Montoya in Washington, D.C. We had an opportunity to talk to John Anaya at his parents' home in September 2002 when we were videotaping his parents for our Sci Fi Channel documentary, *The Roswell Crash: Startling New Evidence.* We asked him if he had known Little Joe Montoya. "Yes, I knew him well," he said. "I worked for him for 10 years." We went right to it and followed up the first question with, "Did you ever ask him about what your parents are testifying about today?" "Yes, I did," he said. "I asked him if it was true. He said that it was, but that if I ever told anyone, he would deny it."

Ruben Anaya passed away in 2002. Moses Burrola died many years ago, but before he passed, he told his wife about that unforgettable day in July of 1947 when Little Joe Montoya came to Roswell. She confirmed for us that her late husband had indeed known Montoya and had been good friends with the Anayas. She could not remember any details of that day, however, only that something very unusual had happened. Ralph Chaes was never located or interviewed and is presumed to be long gone. In 2004, we received a tip from someone who called the International UFO Museum & Research Center (IUFOM&RC) in Roswell suggesting that we talk to a Roswell resident by the name of William "Bill" Glenn, the owner of Glenn's Furniture in Roswell. The caller said that Glenn had been Joe Montoya's personal pilot back in 1947 and might know something. Schmitt followed up on the lead by talking to Glenn, who informed Schmitt that he wasn't Montoya's pilot until much later, and that Montoya's pilot in 1947 was a fellow by the name of Fred Willard, who was still alive and living in Roswell. According to Glenn, Willard had been Montoya's driver, pilot, and all-around coordinator of Montoya's itinerary whenever Montoya was in Roswell.

We had always assumed that it was the Anaya brothers who had driven Montoya to the Nickson Hotel or back to the base to catch a flight after leaving Pete Anaya's house. And Karl Pflock, in his 2001 book, stated that it was Montoya's brother, Tom, who had picked him up and drove him back to the Nickson. Before approaching Willard, we ran this new information by Pete Anaya, as Fred Willard's name was new to us and had never come up in any of the previous discussions with the Anayas about Joseph Montoya. "Yes. It *was* Fred Willard. I had forgotten, but it was Fred who came and got Montoya that day." We then approached a friend of ours, Bruce Rhodes, who works at the UFO Museum in Roswell, and who was by coincidence a friend of Willard's, to try to arrange a meeting. Rhodes suggested that, because Willard was known to have his morning coffee the same time every day at the midtown Denny's restaurant located not far from the UFO Museum, we could probably meet there. We gave Rhodes the go-ahead to set up a meeting.

As we waited with Bruce Rhodes in our booth at Denny's for Fred Willard to show, it crossed our minds that maybe he wouldn't. After all, it wouldn't be a first. Rhodes had told Willard only that we were going to ask him some general questions about the Roswell Incident, whether he knew anything about it or not. Joseph Montoya's name had not been mentioned as a possible topic of discussion. Sometimes that was enough, in our experience, to cause the Roswell-related affliction, *cold-feet-itis*. "Here he comes," said Rhodes, who waved him over to join us.

After exchanging pleasantries and a few softball questions about Roswell and the 1947 incident, we got down to business—in a pleasant way, of course. Willard acknowledged that he had been Montoya's coordinator and personal driver whenever Montoya was in Roswell, and that he later became Montoya's personal pilot, as well. Most importantly, he acknowledged being Montoya's driver in 1947. As our questioning began focusing on his relationship with Joseph Montoya, we noticed that Willard was becoming noticeably agitated and less and less talkative. We then dropped the big one on him and asked if knew anything about Montoya's "close encounter" out at the base in 1947. "No, I don't. Never heard that one." "He never told you about it? You were his driver in 1947. Wasn't it you who picked him up at Pete Anaya's house and drove him back to the Nickson after his episode out at the hangar?" At this line of questioning, Willard's entire demeanor began to change. He began to appear unstable in his chair. His lower lip began to quiver uncontrollably, and his right hand started to tremble as he tried to stir his coffee. His face turned visibly pale as he lowered his head to avoid our eyes by staring at his coffee cup. We were looking at someone whose life appeared to be passing right before him (and us) as we sat there. Willard never answered the questions or spoke coherently again that day. We left the restaurant feeling truly sorry for him, but also feeling that our questions had indeed been answered.

9

The Making of a Cover-Up

Mack Brazel delivered a box of recovered material to Roswell's sheriff's office, which confounded them as much as it had him, so Sheriff George Wilcox and Chief Deputy Tommy Thompson decided to contact the Roswell Army Air Field. Tuesday, July 8: Two days after the military received the Brazel material, which, according to Colonel Thomas DuBose, General Ramey had been "immediately" ordered by his superiors to ship to Washington, D.C.[1] Blanchard's statement simply said, "The disc was picked up at the rancher's home. It was inspected at the Roswell Army Air Field and subsequently loaned by Maj. Marcel to higher headquarters." To the media, that made perfect sense. Col. Blanchard was taking orders from his own boss and superior in the chain of command: Brig. Gen. Roger M. Ramey, commanding officer of the Eighth Air Force at Carswell AAF in Fort Worth, Texas.

Colonel Thomas DuBose, General Ramey's chief of staff in 1947.

Photo printed with permission from the U.S. Air Force.

It should be pointed out here that for this very purpose of maintaining open communications with the media, the military has public information officers (PIOs). At Fort Worth that person was Major Charles A. Cashon, whose job was to deal with the press. Ramey's own chief of staff, Col. DuBose, would state that one of the very reasons for substituting the weather balloon in the first place was to "get the press off the general's back." DuBose also emphasized that the substituted balloon "couldn't have come from Fort Worth. We didn't launch balloons!"[2] This should cast doubt on Ramey's personal experience with such devices. So it would seem more like a preemptive attempt by the general to *personally* make sure the press got it right.

The architects of the Roswell cover-up in front of the B-29 *Dave's Dream*; from left to right: Col. William Blanchard, Gen. Roger Ramey, Secretary of War Robert Patterson, SAC commander Gen. George Kenney, Deputy SAC commander Clements McMullen, and Capt. Eddie Rickenbacker (who was not part of the cover-up).

Photo reprinted from the RAAF newspaper *The Atomic Blast*, with permission from the U.S. Air Force.

It was just a year earlier that Gen. Ramey demonstrated his abilities at spin doctoring. He was in charge of the flight crews at the Bikini Atoll Atomic Bomb test. Following the dropping of the first bomb there, Ramey informed the press that it "was a complete and unqualified success." In reality, his specially picked crew was completely off target and destroyed most of the scientific value of the test.[3] The media accepted the general's assessment. But would they buy his explanation for what was found outside of Roswell a year later?

Consider the following inconsistencies in the records of events immediately following the announcement of the flying saucer recovery.

- Within an hour of the press release, science reporter Dick Pearce of the *San Francisco Examiner* called Blanchard's "higher headquarters" and talked personally with Gen. Ramey. The general told him the object resembled a weather balloon and radar reflector, similar to, Pearce noted, "the ones they sent up every day in Oakland."

- *The New York Times* likewise claimed that the story began to change "within an hour" of the press release.

- *The Washington Post* reported that Ramey informed the Pentagon press office that "the object was in his office" at that very moment; in fact, he hadn't yet seen it. Shortly afterward, he placed another call to the Pentagon press office and said the object was made of tinfoil and wood and was *25 feet across.*

- Ramey then informed another newspaper, *New York P.M.*, that the recovered wreckage looked "like the remains of a target and weather balloon," and was under "high security." Similar quotes appeared in various United Press articles.

- Other newspapers quoted Gen. Ramey as saying he "knew it was a weather balloon from the very beginning."

- Maj. Marcel, traveling on orders from Gen Ramey, arrived in Fort Worth on a special nonscheduled flight from Roswell AAF at approximately 5 p.m. CST with the "flying disc."

Every one of the previously cited interviews with or statements from Gen. Ramey took place *3 to 5 hours before* the B-29 aircraft carrying Maj. Marcel and the "flying disk" landed in Fort Worth. Once Maj. Marcel reported to the general's office, the famous weather-balloon press conference began in earnest.

10

"Some Things Shouldn't Be Discussed, Sergeant!"

*Well, what they brought back, they had this big old 18-wheeler that they brought back from the crash site. Now today, I just laugh at 'em, 'cause they say it was a weather balloon, you know, a **weather balloon**! And I say, "How come they have an 18-wheeler out there haulin' a balloon around?"* —Edward Harrison, Corporal of Security, 1027th AMS, 509th Bomb Group, RAAF (Roswell, N.M., 1947)

Tuesday morning, July 8, 1947, broke sunny and bright very early in southeastern New Mexico, as usual. Other than the weather, which would remain sunny but turn oppressively hot by noontime, there was something going on that was anything but usual to the anxious townsfolk of Roswell. They had been seeing more than their share of strange "things" in the skies overhead, termed *flying saucers* by the press, for the past few weeks, and now there was talk of a crash of one of them north of town. There was also talk of "little bodies" being found.

Patricia Rice of Garland, Texas owned the Alley Bookstore in Roswell with her husband, who also taught at the New Mexico Military Institute in 1947. She had heard about the crash the day before from her niece, Janet Rice. As she related her remembrances of that time to our investigation, "I can say without much exaggeration that the news of the crash got around that town of 25,000 people in about 25 minutes!"[1] Rumors were running rampant at local watering holes such as the Bank Bar in downtown Roswell, where servicemen from the base often went during off-duty hours to mix with other servicemen and with the residents of Roswell. One former serviceman who was stationed at Roswell AAF in 1947 said that the town mood at this time was "anxious...perhaps *scared* would better describe it."[2] And so far, the Roswell air base had said nothing, and the

Staff Sergeant George Houck.

Photo printed with permission from the 1947 RAAF Yearbook.

local media—the *Morning Dispatch* and *Roswell Daily Record* newspapers, as well as KGFL and KSWS, the local radio stations—had said nothing. Unnoticed that morning, except by a few RAAF airmen who had gone to the base chow hall for the 5 a.m. early-bird breakfast, was the 18-wheel "low-boy" parked outside. Staff Sergeant George D. Houck of the 603rd Air Engineering Squadron had checked it out of Squadron T (the base motor pool) a few minutes earlier, and before heading north, stopped at the chow hall for the early-bird. Similar to many other married RAAF airmen at the time, Houck was living in temporary base housing at the former WWII German prisoner-of-war camp located near Artesia, just south of Roswell. Houck ate alone that morning, and after finishing, put his tray in the "clipper" and quickly left.

At midmorning, with the morning staff meeting over, Colonel William Blanchard, commanding officer of not only the 509th Bomb Group, but also the Roswell air base itself, summoned the base PIO, 1st Lieutenant Walter Haut, into his office and told him to issue a press release for dissemination to the local media. The release, which began, "The many rumors regarding the flying disc became a reality yesterday when the intelligence office of the 509th Bomb Group of the Eighth Air Force, Roswell Army Air Field, was fortunate enough to gain possession of a disc..." was then hand-delivered by Haut to the four Roswell media outlets around noontime.[3] But it would be another three hours before the "shot-heard-'round-the-world" headline, "RAAF Captures Flying Saucer on Ranch in Roswell Region," hit the newsstands.

It was too late in the day for the Roswell *Morning Dispatch*, which would have to wait until the following day, July 9, to weigh in on the burgeoning Roswell "crashed saucer" story. Instead, by default, it would be the afternoon newspaper, the *Roswell Daily Record*, which would make history that day. Richard Talbert, a *Roswell Daily Record* paperboy in the summer of 1947, recalled for us a day in early July 1947 when he had just picked up his batch of the *Record*. It was somewhere between 3 p.m. and 3:30 p.m. as near as Talbert could recall. He was plying his trade in the vicinity of the *Roswell Daily Record* building at 4th and Main streets in downtown Roswell along with a number of other paperboys, when he looked up and saw something he had never seen before in his young life. Heading south down Main Street was a military convoy composed of one large, 18-wheel, low-boy or flatbed trailer protected by an escort of Jeeps in front of and behind it, each carrying a contingent of armed MPs. But it was the trailer—or what was on it—that really caught Talbert's attention that day. "The low-boy had a tarp on it, and there was something under the tarp. Whatever was under there appeared to be oval-shaped. I don't recall now how I did it, but I was able to get a quick look under the tarp. I think it must not have been securely tied down on one end, or it just came loose, and it flapped up briefly as it went past me. Anyway, I saw a silver, oval-shaped *something* that was approximately 4 to 5 feet wide by about 12 feet long and 5 to 7 feet high. It had a dome on it, but it was damaged because it was cut off at one end."[4] Bob Rich was also a paperboy that summer and saw the convoy pass "right though the center of town" that day.[5]

Paul McFerrin was a Roswell preteen in 1947 who was out with friends, Floyd and Lloyd Carter and Charlie Webb, that afternoon. "This was right at the time of the flying saucer incident," McFerrin said, "about a week or so after a very severe lightning storm that lasted two days. We were walking down Main Street when we saw this big, military flatbed transporting an egg-shaped object through town, obviously heading for the base. The flatbed trailer had a tarp over the object but you could pretty much tell what shape the object underneath was. It was escorted by MPs in Jeeps who were holding machine guns. Everybody in town knew about the crash."[6] A few miles farther south, Jobie MacPherson was in the middle of completing a roofing job for his employer, Lynn Everman Construction Co., when he spotted the convoy. "It was coming from the north heading toward the base and went right past me. Jeeps and a flatbed truck. I could see mangled metal sticking out on the flatbed and something else that had a conical shape to it, like a pod or something."[7]

In 1947, Private First Class (PFC) Rolland Menagh was a 20-year-old MP in the 390th Air Service Squadron (ASS) of the 509th Bomb Group stationed at the Roswell Army Air Field. Unlike the MPs of the 1395th Military Police Company at the RAAF, who were used for general base security under the command of base Provost Marshal Major Edwin Easley, the MPs of the 390th ASS, under the command of Maj. Richard Darden, held higher security clearances, which were required for guarding the Silverplates—the atomic bomb-carrying B-29s. When the UFO impact site was discovered north of town by civilians on the morning of July 7, MPs of both the 390th and 1395th were rushed to the scene to secure it. MPs of the 1395th were posted along the western edge of Highway 285 from Roswell in the south all the way to the hamlet of Ramon in the north in order to prevent civilians from reaching the crash site 5 miles west of the highway. The MPs of the 1395th also composed the outer ring of armed guards circling the crash site. MPs of the 390th formed an inner ring of armed guards circling the crashed UFO and its occupants. Because they would have been close enough to see the crash scene up close and per-sonal, the higher security clearances possessed by the MPs of the 390th were required for this task.

Menagh would later go on to become a security specialist for the Air Force Office of Special Investigations (AFOSI) after the Air Force became a separate branch of the armed forces. He passed away in 1996 at the age of 70, but our investigation located and interviewed Rolland Menagh, Jr. in 2005. He confirmed his father's presence at Roswell AAF in 1947 as well as his participation in the UFO recovery operation north of Roswell. "My father first told us about it in the 1960s," he said. "He was an MP who guarded the UFO crash site north of Roswell. He saw the ship, which he described as being round or egg-shaped and seamless." Menagh, Jr. said that his father did not see any bodies, but his brother Michael thought their father had told them there were *three* dead bodies:

> He said that the spaceship was loaded onto an 18-wheeler with a tarp covering it and then driven right through the center of town down to the air base. My father said that he

had accompanied it in a Jeep all the way from the crash site to a hangar at the base where it was deposited. Afterwards, he was sworn to secrecy, and when he left the Air Force, he was reminded about the episode and told to, 'Keep quiet, or else!' Later, in retirement, he periodically received visits from military-types in dark suits over the years who were obviously keeping tabs on him.[8]

Earl V. Fulford, now 81 years old, was in July of 1947 a staff sergeant with a Top Secret clearance in the 603rd Air Engineering Squadron (AES) at the RAAF. He had arrived at Roswell in 1946 upon re-enlisting in the Army Air Corps after spending WWII in the U.S. Navy. He worked as an aircraft mechanic and forklift operator in the hangar located next to Hangar P-3, which was the center of the UFO crash-retrieval operation. One of the main tasks of the 603rd was the overhauling of the B-29's temperamental Wright Cyclone engines. Because each engine of the four-engine, Boeing B-29, "Superfortress" bomber had to be overhauled every 65 hours due to its tendency to overheat and catch fire, it was a constant activity for the men of the 603rd. Fulford had seen his friend George Houck at the 5 a.m. early-bird breakfast but didn't get a chance to talk to him,

Staff Sergeant Earl Fulford.

Photo printed with permission from the 1947 RAAF Yearbook.

and he didn't think too much about it when he saw Houck drive off in the low-boy. "I just thought that George was being sent to pick up a wreck somewhere," he said. "Nothing special."

Things would soon change, however. A number of the civilian mechanics who worked in the same hangar as Earl Fulford began peppering him with questions about what was going on as soon as he arrived for his shift that morning. It was, in fact, how Fulford first learned of the crash. "They kept asking me all day long, 'C'mon, tell us. What crashed? You must know. The word in town is that it was a spaceship with bodies of little spacemen.' I didn't know what to tell them other than I didn't know anything about it, but it sure got me to rethinking about George Houck and where he might have been going with the low-boy after breakfast."[9] S.Sgt. Harvie L. Davis, also of the 603rd AES, now 86 years old, remembered hearing the "scuttlebutt" at that time about the crash of a flying saucer. "Stories were going around, and I didn't—and still don't—doubt the people involved. I believe that it was a UFO."[10] John Bunch, now 77 years old, was also a member of the 603rd AES. "Everything was hush-hush. We all knew that something was going on, but we didn't know what. A lot of planes were coming in and going out, and the airstrip was shut down for a period. The base went into lockdown, and they checked us real close going in and out."[11] Eugene C. Helnes, now 78 years old, was a PFC in the 603rd AES in July of 1947. "It was definitely not a balloon," he told us. "I knew fellows who were out there at the site to clean it up. All the talk was of a crashed saucer—right up to the time that I left the base in mid-1949."[12] Reflecting today on his then growing awareness that something highly unusual had taken place, Earl Fulford told our investigation in 2006, "M.Sgt. Hardy [1st Sergeant Leonard J. Hardy of the 603rd AES] had a look on his face like he knew something that he wasn't telling us. It was clear that scuttlebutt was out in town almost immediately, especially about the bodies, but on base no one was telling us anything."

With the completion of his shift at 4 p.m. on this afternoon of July 8, Earl Fulford and a friend left the hangar with the intention of heading over to the NCO Club across the base for a couple of cool ones to help them deal with the rumors and contemplate their futures. As they approached Fulford's car, parked in the parking lot across the street from the hangar, he could see a large tractor-trailer rig coming down the street in his direction, apparently heading for Hangar P-3. "It had come through the main gate, past the parade ground, and made a left turn toward the hangars," he said. When the rig got close enough, Fulford could see that it was pulling a low-boy trailer and that the low-boy was carrying something under a tarp that was "about the size and shape of a Volkswagen Beetle." Fulford now also recognized the driver of the rig, none other than his friend, George Houck. According to Fulford, one of Houck's base duties was that of a "reclamation specialist," meaning that whenever there was wreckage somewhere to be hauled back to the base for disposal—be it an aircraft, a staff car or truck, and so on—the job was his. Seeing Houck behind the wheel of the rig, Fulford waived his arms for Houck to stop. With the engine idling, Houck leaned out of the driver's window slightly to hear what Fulford was about to say.

"Where you been, George?"

"Up north."

"What'cha got under the tarp?"

"I can't tell you that."

"Why not?"

"They told me not to say anything."

With that, Houck put the rig into gear and drove into Hangar P-3.[13] Recalling his run-in with the low-boy these many years later, Earl Fulford had no doubt that it occurred just the way he described to us, and that the driver was his old 603rd friend, George Houck. Fulford then related a little story to us involving Houck and himself that had taken place a few months before their July 1947 "close encounter." Another fellow 603rd airman by the name of Eldo Heath had apparently gone AWOL by "appropriating" a private airplane from the Roswell Municipal Airport, where he had been taking flying lessons, and flying it all the way to the state of Georgia. It was several months before Heath was located, and Fulford and Houck were summoned by their commanding officer (CO) to travel to Georgia by transcontinental train and return Heath to Roswell, which they did with a stopover at Sportsman's Park in St. Louis to take in a Cardinals game. The story had a happy ending—for Heath at least—in that the episode did not permanently stain his military record, as he would later go on to become a pilot in the new Air Force.

Our investigation located the still living, 86-year-old George Houck in 2005. He claimed not to remember his former 603rd buddy, Earl Fulford. But after reprising him with the saga of Eldo Heath, Houck said that he now remembered Earl Fulford. If you interview enough people, you can tell pretty early in the interview of how it's going to go. This one was one of those that wasn't going to go well, and Houck didn't disappoint. Perhaps sensing where we were heading with our questions, Houck became evasive. He claimed not to remember at all the incident involving Fulford and the tarp-covered object on the low-boy he was allegedly hauling to the big hangar in July 1947. "I don't remember that at all. It was a long time ago."[14] That was a far as we could get with George Houck, so we then asked Earl Fulford if he wouldn't mind giving Houck a call to relive old times and perhaps obtain some of the answers we were not able obtain. Fulford agreed. After his initial phone call to George Houck, Fulford gave us the results:

> Houck first claimed not to know me. Then, after a while, he finally relented, and we started to talk. Then I asked him if he remembered the incident in front of the hangar with the low-boy, and there was a long silence. Then Houck said, "What do you want of me?" I told him that I just wanted to know if he remembered it. After another long pause, Houck then shocked me a bit with, "Some things should not be discussed, Sergeant." Then he hung up.

Earl Fulford today.

Photo printed with permission from Earl Fulford.

Fulford did not give up, however, and would call George Houck another half-dozen or so times over the course of the next year. Houck, however, has retreated to the final fallback position of a defendant not wishing to incriminate oneself, but not wanting to "take the fifth" either, by simply telling Fulford, "I can't remember."[15]

That was not the end of Earl Fulford's brush with history in the Roswell story, however. It has been determined from interviewing surviving family members and friends of Mack Brazel, that he had been sequestered at the RAAF for about a week (July 8 to July 15), while the cleanup operation was taking place at his Corona ranch. The sea of strange debris from the crippled UFO that covered his sheep pasture had to be cleared, and as near as we can figure, this operation began on July 7 and was completed by July 15. It was the late Robert E. Smith who told our investigation in 1990 how this was accomplished. Smith, who was a sergeant in the First Air Transport Unit (the "Green Hornets"), said that several groups of 60 or more men were trucked out to the ranch, where they were told to "pick up everything not nailed down" in the pasture and place them in wheelbarrows for collection at a central point. The men went back and forth over the pasture until all of the larger pieces of debris were picked up. Then another group of 60 or so men would come in and go over the same ground picking up what the previous group had missed. That's how it was done. Smith also said that, "All of a sudden, there were a lot of people in dark blue suits on the base that I did not recognize." Crews for this purpose were brought in from Fort Bliss in El Paso, Texas, and possibly from White Sands near Alamogordo, N.M. Fulford was also enlisted.

The early morning of Wednesday, July 9 found Earl Fulford enjoying his 5 a.m. early-bird breakfast at the chow hall, as usual. Not so usual was the sudden appearance of M.Sgt. Earl Rosenberger, heading for Fulford's table. Rosenberger was a member of the 603rd AES, an old-time sergeant whose Date of Service went all the way back to World War I. Looking right at Fulford, Rosenberger snorted out, "I need a detail. Let's go!" It was too late for Fulford to look away and pretend that he didn't hear him (an old ploy that all potential "volunteers" in the military employ to lessen the chance of being chosen), plus Sgt. Rosenberger was looking right at him. Fulford reluctantly left his early-bird for the maw of the clipper and followed Rosenberger out the door where he joined 15–20 other enlisted men and noncommissioned officers waiting outside. A military bus then pulled up, and they were all told to get on. As Fulford told us:

> The bus ride took about two hours. The site was north-west of Roswell. We went north up Highway 285, then west on the Corona road, which was a gravel road back then, past a little school house and some other structures [this was in all likelihood the present-day ghost town of Lon, which is no longer on the map], and then turned south onto a dirt road. I remember seeing a little house [the Hines House], which was not far from where we were going. When the bus stopped, we were told to get out. A major

was in charge [this was Maj. Edwin Easley, the RAAF provost marshal], and armed MPs ringed the site, which was
situated at the base of gently sloping hills. Sgt. Rosenberger
then handed each of us a burlap bag and told us to "police-
up" the site and put anything that we found in the bags.

Fulford can only recall today that the site to be "policed" encom-
passed "hundreds of yards." Fulford and crew had arrived at the Brazel
debris field site on the J.B. Foster ranch. This was not the same site (known
as the "impact site") from which the egg-shaped vehicle or "pod" that was
transported through the center of Roswell on the low-boy was retrieved.
That site was much closer to Roswell. This site, simply known as the
"debris field," was nearer to Corona in Lincoln County, and was the location over which the outer surface of the unknown craft came apart for
reasons unknown, raining debris down on the desert floor below. What
remained stayed in the air a few more seconds, ultimately falling to Earth
at the impact site.

It was evident to Fulford and the rest of his crew that theirs was not
the first crew to police the site. They could see tire tracks from heavy
trucks all over the landscape, and the amount of recoverable material
appeared to be sparse. They were never once told what it was that they
were supposed to look for or what had happened there—just pick up
anything was not part of the landscape. "We knew from the day before
that something had crashed up there, so we figured that this must have
been the crash site." The men formed a single line abreast with a few feet
between each man and began traversing the pasture, picking up anything
that was "not natural" and placing it in the burlap bags. They performed
this procedure over and over again in every conceivable direction on the
site until 4 p.m., after which each man was told to empty his bag into a
wheelbarrow near the entrance to the pasture. When this was accomplished, the men boarded the bus and returned to Roswell, never to return to Brazel's pasture again.

Recalling the experience today, Earl Fulford remembers that during
the entire policing operation, he only picked up seven pieces of debris.
But they were enough to confirm his original suspicions regarding the
site. He told us:

I picked up small, silvery pieces of metallic debris, the larg-
est of which was triangular in shape, about 3 to 4 inches

wide by about 12 to 15 inches long. It looked like thin, light, aluminum foil that flexed slightly when I picked it up, but once in the palm of your hand, you could wad it up into a small ball. Then, when you let it go, it would immediately assume its original shape in a second or two—just like that! That was the only type of debris I saw that day. I thought to myself, "Hey, this is neat. I'm going to keep a piece for myself." But they searched us thoroughly when we got back to make damned sure that none of us had anything. Nobody picked up anything of size. We didn't see any other type of debris or pieces of debris with writing on them, and we didn't see any bodies. We also did not see any balloons or balloon material. They launched weather balloons from in between barracks where I lived back on the base every day. I was familiar with them, and the debris wasn't from one of those. When we got back to the base, everything that we picked up was taken to Hangar 3. We were then lined up and told one-by-one by our First Sergeant [M.Sgt. Leonard Hardy] in no uncertain terms that we didn't see anything, and we didn't say anything; and if we did from that point forward, we might be court-martialed. A few days later, I think it was on Saturday, our entire squadron was called together for a special meeting in Hangar 2 where we were addressed by our Squadron Commander, Maj. Harry Shilling. Also present was our second-in-command, Capt. Earl Casey, and a glowering First Sergeant Hardy who had been in my face a few days earlier. Capt. Casey gave a cautionary admonition to everyone present not to talk about anything they might have seen or heard in the past few days, but Maj. Shilling got right to the point, "You didn't see or hear anything. Nothing happened!"[16]

A few days earlier, PFC Harry Girard of the First Air Transport Unit (ATU) had found himself in a similar meeting in another hangar on the base about to be addressed by his commanding officer, Lt. Col. James R. Wiley. Girard had no idea why he was there or what the meeting was about. Col. Wiley addressed the group, "If you know something, you keep your mouth shut! If you don't, you may find yourself at Leavenworth [Prison], and you can read all about it there." Col. Wiley never told the group what that *something* was, or why talking about it could land them in Leavenworth. PFC Girard and perhaps more than a few others that day had no idea what their CO was talking about. Word probably had not yet reached them about the multiple flights made by aircraft of the First ATU that had flown UFO wreckage and "little bodies" recovered from the crash site out of Roswell in the preceding days. Interviewed in 2006, Harry Girard said that the meeting in the hangar "was unusual, because I had no idea what he was talking—actually threatening us—about. I do now, and maybe in another 50 years they will tell us what happened."[17]

Threats seemed to be the order of the day, the *modus operandi* for handling the problem. Lt. Steve Whalen was a 28-year-old navigator in one of the bomb squadrons of the 509th Bomb Group at the RAAF during that second week of July, 1947. Although nothing official had been said to base personnel, Whalen and his friends knew that something was going on at the big hangar, but they were afraid to inquire about it. "There were a lot of people who were real scared who were not talking," Whalen's son told us. "There were also a lot of planes taking off and landing in the middle of the night." A special meeting was then called by his bomb squadron's commanding officer—not to explain what was going on, but to issue a warning: "Stay away from the big hangar area no matter what, or you will run the risk of being shot on sight!" That was all. Until that meeting, Lt. Whalen had thought that the base commotion might have had something to do with "Goddard stuff" (Dr. Robert Goddard, the Father of American Rocketry, had conducted his rocket experiments just outside of Roswell). Whalen died in 1998, so he apparently followed his CO's orders to the letter.[18]

By Monday morning, July 14, 1947, things had pretty much calmed down at the Bank Bar in Roswell, as well as at Roswell Army Air Field. The press and the public had quickly lost interest in the Roswell crashed spaceship story a few days earlier when Gen. Roger Ramey issued his famous press release. In addition to the airmen on the base, the ranchers in the Corona area and key civilians in Roswell had been threatened into silence. The crash sites had been cleaned up, and most of the wreckage, including the bodies, had been shipped out. Life had returned to normal. Or had it?

At 2 a.m., the sleeping Sgt. Earl Fulford was suddenly awakened to the sight of a flashlight shining in his eyes and the unsmiling face of M.Sgt. Larry Sanchez staring down at him. Fulford's first thought was, "What's this? Did I miss early-bird?" Sgt. Sanchez barked, "Get dressed and follow me!" Still in that semi-shock state from being surprised in the middle of the night, Fulford dressed as quickly as he could and followed Sgt. Sanchez out of the barracks into the mist of the early morning night. Sanchez led Fulford to the front of Hangar P-3 where a large wooden crate was sitting all by itself. Also sitting in front of the hangar on the tarmac was an idling C-54 aircraft with its cargo door open. In a voice loud enough to be heard over the idling engines, Sanchez ordered Fulford, who had recently taken over the duties of a forklift operator from someone else who had been transferred, to load the wooden crate into the C-54. After locating and firing-up the forklift, Fulford carefully lifted the crate onto his machine, drove it over to the waiting aircraft, and deposited it inside the yawning cargo hold. With that, the cargo door slammed shut, and Fulford was told to leave as the plane taxied away toward the flight line. "I had no idea what was going on. No one told me a thing. I just followed orders. I do know one thing, however. Given the size of the crate, which was about 7 feet by 7 feet by 7 feet, whatever was in there had to weigh almost nothing. I could tell that right away when I first lifted it."[19] After returning and shutting down the forklift, Fulford left and walked back to his barracks. It was almost time for early-bird.

11

Loaned by Major Marcel
to Higher Headquarters
From Complicity to Cover-Up

Shortly after 1 p.m. on the afternoon of July 8, 1947, a silver Boeing B-29 "Superfortress" bomber nicknamed *Dave's Dream* taxied up to the flight operations building at Roswell Army Air Field. This was no ordinary flight, even by RAAF standards.

It had been personally ordered by none other than Col. William Blanchard, the base commander. Its command crew was not one of the regular ones chosen from three constituent bomb squadrons on the base: the 393rd, the 715th, or the 830th.

Instead of the usual cast of young lieutenants and captains, this flight was to be commanded by lieutenant colonels, including the Roswell deputy base commander himself (just below Blanchard in the RAAF command structure); two majors; and a captain—all from Blanchard's close staff. The enlistees on board were all experienced NCOs—tech sergeants and master sergeants—not the usual mixture of privates, corporals, staff sergeants, and others who were included as a matter of course in normal crews.

The flight was booked to go all the way to Wright Field near Dayton, Ohio (Wright Field would later that September combine with the adjoining Patterson Airport, home of the Foreign Technology Division, to form Wright-Patterson Air Force Base), after a "preliminary" stop in Texas at the Fort Worth Army Air Field, headquarters to the Eighth Air Force under the command of Brig. Gen. Roger Ramey, under whom Blanchard and the 509th directly served.

This flight was to have a special guest on board, Maj. Jesse Marcel, the head of intelligence for the 509th at Roswell. Marcel was carrying something special to higher headquarters on Blanchard's orders, and was told before departure that the flight was to go directly to Wright Field. Marcel had earlier that morning briefed all in attendance at a special staff meeting

The B-29 known as *Dave's Dream* was used to transport the wreckage (brought to the Roswell base by Maj. Marcel and Capt. Cavitt) to Fort Worth on July 8.

Photo printed with permission from the 1947 RAAF Yearbook.

after his return from a two-day fact-finding trip to the high desert of Lincoln County, where he had encountered a sheep pasture full of strange, shattered, foil-like, plastic-like debris. He brought as much of it back to Roswell with him as he could fit into his baby-blue, 1942 Buick Roadmaster convertible.

It would be soon after taking off from Roswell that Marcel was informed about a short layover at Fort Worth where, as we know, soon after the one-hour flight had touched down, Gen. Ramey announced to the world that a flying saucer had *not* been recovered by Marcel and the 509th command at Roswell, but merely the misidentified remains of a very common rubber weather balloon and kite-like, tinfoil radar target.

To seal the verdict, several pictures were taken of both Marcel and Ramey (by himself and with his chief of staff, Col. Thomas DuBose), each posing with these mundane items on the carpeted floor of the general's office.

To gild the lily, base weather officer Irving Newton was personally called and ordered by Ramey to report to his office and identify the remains as a weather balloon and a rawin-type radar target, and pose for a picture as well. A number of these photos went out over the wire services and were picked up by many newspapers across the country as a final solution to the previous day's excitement. The loud sucking sound then heard in and around Fort Worth was the air going out of a big news story as General Ramey "emptied" Roswell's saucer.

The July 8 flight was actually the second confirmed to transport debris out of Roswell since the crash. The first flight took place two days earlier on July 6. According to DuBose, it was ordered by Gen. Clements McMullen, deputy commander of Strategic Air Command (SAC) at the Pentagon, who ordered some of the original debris brought into Roswell by Mack Brazel that very day to be flown to Washington for immediate inspection. That flight passed through Fort Worth, where DuBose checked the container (a canvas pouch) holding debris samples prior to sending it on its way to its final destination. He did not look at the contents of the pouch.[1]

The second flight's destination was Wright Field, after a brief stop at Fort Worth. Piloting the plane was Roswell's deputy base commander, Lt. Col. Payne Jennings. The copilot was the base executive officer, Lt. Col. Robert I. Barrowclough. Rounding out the command crew were Maj. Herb Wunderlich of the First Air Transport Unit (the "Green Hornets") and Capt. William E. Anderson of the Air Base Squadron.[2]

All of the noncommissioned officers on the flight were from the 830th Bomb Squadron and included M.Sgt. Robert R. Porter who was the crew chief, T.Sgt. William A. Cross, T.Sgt. George M. Ades, and T.Sgt. Sterling P. Bone.[3] Also on this flight was Marcel, who had been ordered by Blanchard to accompany the material that he and CIC Capt. Sheridan Cavitt had brought back from the Foster ranch (supervised by Brazel) earlier that day.

The standard C-54 cargo plane at the base was not used to transport the wreckage. Instead, a B-29 bomber was readied for the unscheduled flight. Although it remains unclear why this choice was made, it reinforces the unusual circumstances of this flight.

It has been possible to piece together details about this particular flight from interviews conducted with firsthand witnesses who were either on the plane or on the ground at Roswell or Fort Worth. By comparing and combining their testimonies, one can reach certain conclusions regarding the nature of the debris that this second flight was ferrying, and how it might relate to Ramey's press conference and the photographs taken in his office that day.

Upon his arrival, as later related by Roswell PIO 1st Lt. Walter Haut, Marcel carried a box of genuine debris that he had held in his lap on the flight to Ramey's office. The box included the small I-beam that Marcel's son Jesse Jr. would describe years later as displaying undecipherable symbols along its inner surface. Marcel placed the box on Ramey's desk in the general's office. Ramey then directed Marcel into another room to indicate the crash location to him on a large wall map.[4]

When they returned to the main office, Marcel immediately observed that his box of real wreckage had been removed, and the remains of a weather balloon and a torn and mangled radar target were laid out on the floor. A reporter by the name of James Bond Johnson from the *Fort Worth Star-Telegram* was asked to step into the office and Marcel was then posed for two pictures with the substituted balloon remains, after which he was instructed by Ramey to not say anything to anyone, and that he would handle the entire situation. More pictures were taken of Ramey alone and with DuBose, and the remainder of the flight to Dayton, Ohio was *officially* cancelled.[5]

What was actually going on, however, was that Marcel had been abruptly removed from the flight to Wright Field and ordered to return to Roswell, while the real wreckage from the B-29 was transferred to another plane to complete the original mission. The resumption of this flight, contrary to Ramey's previous statement, was also confirmed by the local FBI office in Dallas in the now widely circulated telegram dated 6:17 p.m. CST on July 8. Marcel returned to Roswell the next day complaining to Haut about the "staged event" in Fort Worth in which he felt that he had, unfortunately and unwittingly, played a part.

Robert R. Porter, the flight engineer on the original flight, confirmed the extraordinary security measures that surrounded every aspect of the assignment. "Whatever was in the cargo hold was escorted by an armed guard who had been assigned to it from Roswell," he said. This would suggest that something extremely important or highly classified was on board.

Master Sergeant Robert Porter.

Photo printed with permission from the 1947 RAAF Yearbook.

Porter recalled that three or four shoebox-sized packages wrapped in brown paper, and one triangular-shaped package, also wrapped in brown paper and about 2 1/2 to 3 feet across at its base by 4 inches thick, were loaded onto the plane. These had been handed up to him through an open hatch on the B-29 while it was still going through preflight near the operations building. A staff car from Building 1034 had driven up to the plane and delivered the packages, which Porter personally received. All of them were extremely light and they were stored in the forward section of the plane. Although Porter definitely remembered Marcel on this flight, he did not recall any other debris. Unknown to him, actual material would be loaded just before the aircraft would begin its taxi to departure.[6]

1st Lt. Robert J. Shirkey was the former assistant operations officer for the 509th and the officer on duty when the July 8 flight to Wright Field taxied up to the flight operations building. He was responsible for drawing up its flight plan.

According to Shirkey, shortly after he had returned from lunch (about 1:15 p.m.), he was informed that a flight plan had to be drawn up for an unscheduled 2 p.m. flight to Wright Field. No sooner was he told this than the plane—a four-engine, B-29 bomber—taxied up to Flight Ops for checkout. Shirkey could see some of the crew inside the cockpit. He recognized Lt. Col. Payne Jennings in the pilot's seat but doesn't recall the others.[7]

Just then, he heard a loud voice behind him wanting to know if the flight was ready. Shirkey recognized Blanchard's voice. He replied that it was, and Blanchard stepped out into the hallway and waved to some people who were waiting outside

First Lieutenant Robert Shirkey.

Photo printed with permission from the 1947 RAAF Yearbook.

on the street side of the building to come on through. Blanchard backed up into the doorway to allow the men to pass, and in the process, blocked Shirkey's view of the procession down the hallway.

After asking Blanchard if he could step aside a bit so that he could see some of the action, he found himself standing "buckle to buckle" with the base commander as the men filed by them. There were at least half a dozen wearing dark blue suits ("FBI types"), none of whom he recognized, except for Marcel, who was carrying an open cardboard box filled with nonreflective, aluminum-looking "scrap metal." All but one of the other men were carrying similar open boxes of the same material.

One particular item in Marcel's box caught Shirkey's eye and still stands out in his mind today: "Sticking up in one corner of the box...was a small I-beam with hieroglyphic markings on the inner flange, in some kind of weird color, not black, not purple, but a close approximation of the two."

Following Marcel was one of the FBI types, carrying only a single piece of metal under his arm. It was about the size of a "poster drawing board" (about 2 feet by 3 feet). The men moved quickly through the building out to the waiting B-29, and he only managed a brief look. "Here it came, and there it went," he would later remark. The FBI types handed the boxes of material up through an open hatch on the plane, and all clambered aboard the flight.

Sometime shortly before or after the Marcel troupe made its hallway dash (Shirkey cannot remember which), he recalls an Army staff car driving up to the waiting aircraft, whereupon someone got out and handed a few plain packages up through an open hatchway to someone inside the plane. After the hatch closed, the engines revved up as the B-29 rolled down to the runway and made a speedy takeoff. Blanchard then turned and tossed a perfunctory "see you" in Shirkey's direction as he left the building. He never saw Blanchard again. Nine days later, Shirkey was transferred to the Philippines.[8]

Even though Porter had been advised by one of the officers on the flight (later identified as Anderson) that the material in the cargo hold of the plane was from a "flying saucer" and that he (Porter) was not to say any more about it, Porter still wasn't sure of its true nature, "...whether it was Brazel's material or something else."

According to Porter, when they landed in Fort Worth, the officers were permitted to disembark, but enlisted personnel were told to remain on board until the plane was secured, meaning that guards were posted around it. Afterward, they were allowed to go to the mess hall to eat, during which time the material was transferred to another plane, a B-25 that would fly it on to Wright Field. When they returned to the B-29 for the return trip to Roswell, they were informed that the material they had flown to Fort Worth under so much secrecy and security was simply a weather balloon.[9]

What about those suspicious packages that were loaded into the plane back in Roswell just before takeoff? Where might they fit into this story? As you will recall, three or four of the packages were of the shoebox variety, and the fourth was triangular in shape with the base edge being 2 1/2 to 3 feet across. All of the packages were wrapped in plain, brown paper and taped shut. Porter doesn't know what became of them after landing in Fort Worth. All he knows is that when the crew returned to the plane after eating a snack before the return trip to Roswell, the packages were missing. He assumed they had been transferred to another plane to be flown on to Wright Field. He was wrong, as it turned out, because there was no "on to Wright Field" intended.[10]

The answer leaps out when you look again at the Fort Worth photographs taken in Ramey's office. Scattered on a blanket of brown wrapping paper in the middle of the general's office, with all of its triangularity on display, is the torn-up tinfoil radar target. Folded, with a broken strut or two, it could easily fit the dimensions of the package received by Porter. Also on display in the pictures of Ramey and DuBose, and especially Newton, is one of the brown-paper-wrapped containers. It can be seen on the floor next to one of the chairs in the Newton photo, and behind the middle chair in the Ramey/DuBose photos.[11]

The July 8 flight from Roswell to Fort Worth was a special flight. Much secrecy and security, if not urgency, surrounded it. The high rank of the crew members indicates the kind of priority attention that would not be accorded a flight transporting merely rubber and tinfoil. The talk on board was that they were carrying pieces of an actual flying saucer, but the crew was warned to keep their mouths shut about it. If anyone on board knew the real mission of the flight, it would have been the highest-ranking officers, Jennings and Barrowclough, who were close to Blanchard. Marcel didn't know, and neither did Anderson, who also believed the cargo was not made on Earth. It was not until the start of the return flight that the crew was officially told that they had flown a weather balloon, and to forget about it. Similar before and after reactions are described in the July 9 flight to Fort Worth, which we contend transported a number of the bodies. The fix was in; everyone should just go home and act as though nothing happened.

So, if the balloon debris arrived from Roswell, did it originate there? Some have suggested that the White Sands Missile Range near Alamogordo was the source, and others say it was Wright Field or even Fort Worth itself. More likely, however, for the most obvious reason, which flies in the face of those who would maintain that Marcel and Blanchard himself would not have recognized a rawin target balloon, is that the balloon and target did indeed come from the base at Roswell. Why? Because the RAAF was launching such balloons from atop Roswell's tallest building on the average of twice a day in connection with the base's frequent test drops of unarmed atomic bombs.

But one other thing still remains certain. There are absolutely no witnesses to the recovery of a weather balloon or any other balloon device (or its reinvention by the Air Force in 1994, Project Mogul included) at the Foster ranch in June or July of 1947. The weather balloon, which was packaged up and shipped out on July 8, and which would serve as a prop for the official explanation of what actually crashed, came from the RAAF. It was not what Mack Brazel discovered and then brought into town. This scenario, as has been described by the actual witnesses, represents the best explanation available to us that supports the facts as we have come to know them.

12

The Secretary and the Spacemen

From all eyewitness accounts, something unusual was happening inside the RAAF hospital. Unfamiliar doctors and nurses rushed through the halls and into and out of rooms. Regular staff were sent back to their living quarters. No one was talking except for guarded whispers. MPs were posted around the outside perimeter as well as inside along the main emergency corridor. Ambulance trucks would pull up to the rear loading dock area that led directly to the OR. As 1st Lt. Rosemary A. McManus, a nurse with the base medical unit told us just weeks before passing away, "Something big had happened." She would acknowledge nothing more.[1]

The highly experienced hospital administrator, Lt. Colonel Harold M. Warne, had been exposed to the worst of human atrocities as a medic through WWII, and then at the first atomic base in the world. Even in 1947, planes would crash during training exercises, and bodies mangled and burned beyond repair had become all too common. But "something big" had happened here, and apparently it was not described in any medical journal. And even though Warne was in charge of the medical squadron, he was not directing this assignment. Therein may be the cause of his behavior as opportunities would later present themselves.[2]

All military hospital administrators had their own secretary. Warne was no different. His was a 27-year-old civilian woman by the name of Miriam "Andrea" Bush. Miriam was a graduate of New Mexico State College at Las Cruces, majoring in business administration. She would have graduated at the beginning of WWII, and because college campuses were principal recruiting grounds for the FBI at that time, all indications are that she also had a background in intelligence, which would explain why she would land a top security job at the RAAF after the end of the war in the South Pacific.[3]

Now, one item of crucial importance needs to be emphasized here. The RAAF hospital in 1947 did not have a morgue. That is why the base had a contract with a private mortuary, namely the Ballard Funeral Home. The city of Roswell did not have its own coroner at that time, so they received assistance from the state. All reports of the extra security and presence of outside personnel took place at the precise timing of a reported crash of a genuine flying saucer on that remote ranch north of town. Should civilian fatalities be involved they would have gone directly to one of Roswell's two funeral parlors. If they were military, they would have gone first to the base hospital and then to the private mortuary. Curious phone calls were made to the Ballard Funeral Home inquiring as to the availability of "children's caskets." A rather strange request on the face of it, but even more so from a facility without a morgue. Dry ice was called in from Clardy's Dairy during this same period of time. Also, there were follow-up calls to the mortician about recommended embalming techniques that would be the least detrimental to tissue and bodily fluids.[4] You get the picture. It sounds as though the RAAF hospital had some corpses beyond the realm of regular practice standards as regulated by the state coroner's office. And in any event, no morgue withstanding, the base hospital would have to do for the time being.[5]

It was dinnertime during one of the days highlighted by all of these strange circumstances. Miriam Bush would arrive at her parents' home from a rather memorable day at the base hospital. She would sit down with her mother and father, who was the first chiropractor to set up a practice in Roswell, and her brother George and sister Jean. Many years later both George and Jean recounted how upset Miriam became, and how she wouldn't touch her food. She then excused herself and started to sob uncontrollably as she raced into her bedroom. Both of them had great respect for her employment at the base. Did she lose her job? Did she lose a close friend? George sensed something worse. "Fear seemed to overcome her," he said. Dr. Bush responded immediately with similar concern for her well-being.[6]

The story she would confide was told between tears and near to shock. It sounded like a nightmare but her emotional response was too real. It was something she was not prepared for. None of them were. She was eventually able to describe how she had been performing all of her regular duties at the hospital earlier that day, but grew more and more curious as to all the additional personnel who acted totally indifferent to the normal staff. Whether it was out of frustration for being left out of all the commotion or just a desire to share all the excitement with someone, Warne would take her by the arm and quietly mention that she should accompany him to the examination room. Upon entering surroundings that normally would have been quite familiar, she immediately was surprised to observe a number of bodies on gurneys in the middle of the room. But something was wrong. Something became terribly wrong. At first she cried out, "My God! They're children!" But she soon realized that their body size was their only childlike quality. Their skin was grayish to brown in tone and white linens covered most of each body. But the heads, the heads were too large. And the eyes, those large eyes that wouldn't shut. "Those staring eyes," she said. Panic started to quicken her heart, and then it happened: "One of them moved!" All her father could do was listen with total disbelief and hold her as she wept. He was aware of all the talk of a crashed spaceship outside of town and the spacemen inside it. But now it had hit home. And there was nothing he could do about it. Eventually, she would cry herself to sleep, though one might debate if sleep would serve as any respite.[7]

Morning came all too soon, but Miriam wrestled with her professional training, and her fear grew more and more into anger at her boss, "Why did he have to show me something so terrible?" she thought. "Why did he have to involve me?" But the entire town of Roswell was abuzz with all the talk of the crash of a flying saucer on some ranch and "little men" that were found inside it...and some of them were possibly loose in town! Only the base south of town could provide the answers and only the hospital knew the truth. The morning newspaper carried headlines of it all just being about some old weather balloon. How silly, she thought.[8]

Much had taken place overnight while Miriam slept. A temporary morgue was set up, a large wooden crate was constructed and packed with dry ice, a tent was pitched, and a metal fence was erected around it on the far south end of the tarmac. In the meantime, most of the activity back at the hospital had returned to normal—as though nothing "big" had ever happened. The day was Wednesday, July 9, and the big shoe was about to drop on Miriam.

As did so many others merely performing their military duties at the RAAF, Miriam became immediately suspect. Any base personnel who saw anything out of the ordinary would have to be warned of the consequences of speaking out of turn, and the traumatized secretary was no exception.

Her brother George somberly described to us her demeanor that evening, as she said, "I am never to say another word about what I saw. None of you ever heard me say anything about it," she chided them. According to George and Jean, she displayed all the symptoms of being subjected to heavy-handed threats. She would become more and more paranoid over the entire ordeal. Yet she couldn't share even her worst fears with the very family who also knew the truth. There was nothing any of them could do and certainly nothing any of them could prove. The whole situation became rather hopeless. Best to do just as the military sternly advised—never to say another word.[9]

Miriam Bush and her brother George, during WWII.

Photo printed with permission from Patricia Bush.

No one ever questioned her truthfulness and she never did mention it again. But it had made such a lasting impression on her brother that years later when he would marry Patricia it was one of the very first private pieces of family history he confided to her. Sadly, no one was ever able to get through to Miriam again. Whatever she saw back in that examination room in 1947 haunted her relentlessly. She would marry within a year—someone she had just met—move to California, and try to forget the unforgettable.

After nearly 40 years of a loveless, "arranged" marriage, she would finally file for divorce in 1987. A tremendous weight was lifted off her shoulders; she was not distraught or depressed about the failed relationship. Such was the distinct impression from her sister-in-law Pat who would speak to her over the phone on a regular basis. Within months of the separation, Pat sensed a subtle change becoming the focus of each new conversation. Miriam was becoming increasingly paranoid. She was deeply concerned about being watched and followed, which to Miriam's sister Jean all seemed to be connected in some way to 1947 and the very purpose of Miriam's 39-year marriage to a homosexual.[10]

Patricia Bush would receive one last call from Miriam in December of 1989. She had become obsessed with the fear that someone was spying on her day-to-day activities. Nothing Pat could tell her would eleviate her dread. Still, no one in the family suspected that time was about to run out for Miriam.[11]

The very next day, Miriam would check into a motel just outside of Los Angeles in the town of Fremont, strangely using her sister's name. She was unaccompanied, and would not be found until the next morning. The coroner's report concluded that she had committed suicide by wrapping a plastic bag around her head—a rather prolonged and gruesome way to take one's own life. According to the Bush family, scratches and bruises also covered her arms. Other suspicious details suggest that Miriam's fears may not have been totally unfounded. The truth she possessed about Roswell had died with her—death being the great silencer.[12]

Major Jack Comstock.

Photo printed with permission from the 1947 RAAF Yearbook.

When our fellow Roswell investigator, Victor Golubic, found Dr. Jack Comstock, the base's chief surgeon back in 1947 just a few years later and asked to comment on the unearthly visitors at the old RAAF hospital, he denied having any such knowledge. And Miriam Bush? "I have no memory of such a person," he said, denial being the second greatest silencer.[13]

13

"Get These [Bodies] Over to the Base Hospital!"

They didn't look like they were from Texas. —Frank Kaufmann, CBS *48 Hours*, 1994

The first book ever published about the Roswell Incident dealt mainly with events surrounding the Corona sheep rancher Mack Brazel, who initiated the Roswell chain of events when he discovered one of his sheep pastures almost totally blanketed with strange wreckage following a severe lightning storm.[1] There was no suggestion that Brazel had found anything other than wreckage—there were no bodies, and the wreckage found on his ranch consisted mostly of very small, very thin pieces of debris suggesting a midair explosion and the notion that perhaps the main part of the stricken craft, whatever it was, had crashed elsewhere, at a second site.

This second crash site was provided by a story told to close friends and family members by a deceased soil conservation engineer who lived in Socorro, N.M. by the name of Grady L. "Barney" Barnett. Before being chased away by the military, Barnett claimed to have seen a downed flying saucer along with its dead crew up close while working on the Plains of San Agustin just to the southwest of the town of Magdalena, 150 miles west of Brazel's sheep pasture. The suggestion was that the UFO, after possibly being struck by lightning near Corona, exploded in the air, raining debris down on the Foster ranch. What was left of the craft then careened out of control to the west, finally falling to Earth on the Plains of San Agustin. Although the retellers of Barnett's story could not provide a year when Barney's chance encounter was supposed to have occurred, Berlitz and Moore assumed that it must have been 1947, and simply stapled Barnett's account to the Brazel story to close the circle for *The Roswell*

It was thought by the original Roswell investigators that the Roswell UFO crashed west of Socorro, N.M. on the Plains of San Agustin, near the town of Magdalena, not far from the Very Large Array (VLA) of radio telescopes (featured in the movie *Contact*).

Photo courtesy of Tom Carey, 2003.

Incident. Barnett was known by everyone to have been a "straight shooter," but there were major problems with his account, not least of which was a complete lack of corroborating witnesses, the lack of a date for his encounter, and the distance of the alleged "Plains of San Agustin" crash site from Roswell, which was much too far for the RAAF to have become involved in any recovery operation there.

By 1991, new first- and secondhand witnesses to alien bodies had been added to the expanding Roswell story, but the location of the supposed second site came into question. In their book, the investigative team of Kevin Randle and Don Schmitt, who had reopened the investigation of the Roswell case three years earlier, kept the Barney Barnett story in their Roswell crash scenario, but moved Barnett's close encounter from the Plains of San Agustin 152 miles east, to a low bluff about 2 miles east/southeast of Brazel's pasture.[2] The move was based upon information of heavy military activity at that location and timeframe that the team had gathered from local Corona ranchers. They then speculated that Barnett must have been in Lincoln County and not Catron County on the day of his discovery. There was no evidence of that, but it was the only way to include Barnett's alleged discovery that there were indeed bodies recovered from the UFO crash, but that they were recovered near the Brazel debris field. With three new witness accounts of alien bodies—Sgt. Melvin E. Brown, the RAAF cook from K Company who accompanied the bodies from the crash site to the Roswell base in the back of a truck;[3] Capt. Oliver W. "Pappy" Henderson, the First ATU pilot who flew wreckage and bodies from Roswell to Wright Field in Dayton, Ohio;[4] and the Roswell mortician, Glenn Dennis, who claimed to have inadvertently arrived at the Roswell base hospital during an attempted "alien autopsy"[5]—all signs pointed away from the Plains of San Agustin. In 1994, Randle and Schmitt dropped the Barney Barnett story altogether from their Roswell UFO crash scenario, and again moved the final crash site—now termed the "impact site"—to a site much closer to Roswell.[6] This site—known as the Corn Ranch Site or the Kaufmann Site—later turned out to be bogus, as its location was based upon the testimony of a single, alleged eyewitness who himself was later discovered to have been be a purveyor of false information.[7]

On the morning Mack Brazel was making history in his Corona sheep pasture, he was accompanied by a 7-year-old neighbor boy, Dee Proctor, who often visited Brazel from an adjoining ranch owned by his parents, Floyd and Loretta Proctor. In the ensuing 59 years up to his death in 2006, Dee Proctor never allowed himself to be formally interviewed by anyone about what he witnessed with Brazel that day so long ago. In 1995, however, he took his dying mother to the second site.[8] This site turned out to be the exact same site identified by Randle and Schmitt as the "impact site" in 1991. Today, we believe that the "Dee Proctor Body Site" is a legitimate site, the second in the straight-line trajectory of *three sites* involved in the Roswell UFO crash, where Mack Brazel found two or three alien bodies a few days after they were blown out or ejected from the stricken craft when it exploded over the debris field on the evening of July 3, 1947. The rest of the ship or an escape vehicle, along with the remainder of the doomed crew, remained airborne and continued in an east/southeast direction for another 30 miles before crashing in a flat area with low, rolling hills 40 miles north/northwest of Roswell. Based on new evidence, we located the third and final crash site—the true impact site—in

2005. It was at this last site, about which Mack Brazel knew nothing, that an additional two or three dead aliens and one live one were discovered by civilian archaeologists. The following witness accounts presented in this chapter all pertain to recovery activities that took place on the Foster ranch at or near the Dee Proctor Site during the July 7–8, 1947 time frame.

In July of 1947, Ed Sain was a private first class in the 390th Air Service Squadron attached to the 509th Bomb Group at the RAAF. As did most others in the 390th ASS, PFC Sain possessed the Top Secret security clearance that was required for security personnel whose main duty was to

Corporal Raymond Van Why.

Photo printed with permission from the 1947 RAAF Yearbook.

guard the Silverplates. Sain was just about to turn in for the evening (July 7) when the chief of security, Maj. Richard Darden, burst into the barracks: "C'mon Boys! We've had a crash." Sain and a 390th ASS buddy of his, Cpl. Raymond Van Why, were told to report to the ambulance pool outside of the base hospital ASAP. After the short walk to the hospital, the two airmen were directed to a waiting "box-type," military ambulance, which they quickly entered. They drove north of town for half an hour or so, then headed west "into the boondocks" of Lincoln County. Because it was dark outside, they could not see where they were going or where they had been. The ambulance finally came to a stop in the lee of a small bluff, around which there had been a beehive of activity just a few hours before. Except for a few tents that had been erected at the base of the bluff and a number of floodlights that had been set up, there wasn't much to see but desert. "Maj. Darden and Maj. Easley [head of the 1395th MP Company] were both there, which was unusual," Sain told us. Sain and Van Why were each given a handheld searchlight and told to guard the entrance to the site from a tent set up for that purpose. Their orders were to "Shoot anyone that tries to get in!" According to Sain, "We had plenty of food to last us the night, and thank God that no one showed up. So we didn't have to shoot anyone. We were relieved before first light and back on the base at daybreak."[9] Due to a combination of Ed Sain's age and his accent, it was difficult to understand him over the phone at times. We also felt that he was not giving us the whole story regarding that night in the desert. A call to Sain's son Steven (with whom we had talked prior to speaking with his father) confirmed our suspicions. It had taken Steven Sain and his brother almost 30 years to get anything out of their father regarding Roswell. "He was extremely reluctant to talk about it," Steven said. "He said that he was under a security oath and feared for his life if he said anything. He wouldn't talk about it for a long time, and he still won't watch any TV shows or read any books about Roswell. It's only been recently, however, that he has started talking to us."

According to Steven Sain, his father told him that he had been an MP at the RAAF at the time of the Roswell Incident. His job had been to "guard the bodies at the crash site" by guarding the entrance to the site with another fellow. "He referred to the bodies as 'little green men,'" Steven said, "when he told me, and said that they were kept in one of the other tents until being transported to the base. My father said that everything was strange that night, and he must have seen the ship at some point, because he told me that it was the strangest thing he had ever seen in his life."[10]

Raymond Van Why passed away in 2001 at the age of 76. According to his widow, Leola, her husband was usually pretty closed-mouthed about the nine and a half years he spent in the military. "He was a security guard who guarded the *Enola Gay*, and when he got out of the Air Force, he shredded his service records." According to Mrs. Van Why, her husband first talked about Roswell after he got out of the service in 1954 when, upon reading an account in the newspaper or a magazine of an alleged spaceship crash, he shouted out, "I saw that!" He then told her that, when he was stationed at Roswell a few years earlier, he had been a guard at a crash site "out in the desert" where a spaceship had crashed. "My husband told me that it *was* a UFO that had crashed, that it was a round disc." We then pressed her on that point, "How did he know that?" "Because he was out there and saw it!"[11]

Van Why wasn't the only one. Sgt. LeRoy Wallace, a 6-foot 9-inch Cherokee Indian from Arkansas, was assigned to the 390th ASS as an MP three months prior to the Roswell Incident. According to his widow, he was called away one evening to go to a crash site outside of Corona "to help load the bodies." When her husband returned home early the next morning, the first thing she noticed, besides his disheveled appearance, was the smell. "The stench on his clothes was the worst smell you'd ever want to smell. It was worse than any combination of smells you could imagine. I had him strip off his clothes. We ultimately burned them and buried the ashes." She said that her husband bathed frequently with lye soap and an old Army scrub brush after that, and would wash his hands up to 10 times a day to the point of becoming raw. "He walked around for two days after he returned home and did not sleep, and for the next two weeks, when he ate, he wore gloves because the smell was still on his body." Wallace was transferred out of Roswell three months later.[12]

The witnesses keep coming. After World War II, 26-year-old Sgt. Frederick Benthal was serving in the Army Air Forces as a photographic specialist at the Anacostia Naval Air Station in Washington, D.C. In 1946, he had helped set up the photographic equipment for Operation Crossroads in the Pacific, involving special cameras for filming the two atomic bomb tests conducted there. According to Benthal, after reporting to work one morning in early July of 1947 with a friend, Cpl. Al Kirkpatrick, they were told to pack their bags for a flight to Roswell, New Mexico. They flew in a B-25 "Mitchell" medium bomber, leaving around 10 a.m., and made one stop along the way, during which they were told not to leave the plane. On the flight, the two men studied the dossiers of persons who might be expected to be at their destination. These individuals included J. Robert Oppenheimer of Los Alamos ("Father of the Atomic Bomb") and Gen. Curtis "Bomber" LeMay of WWII fame and the future head of the Strategic Air Command. The plane landed in Roswell around 5 p.m., and the men checked into the base transit barracks for the evening. The following morning, Benthal and Kirkpatrick were picked up by a covered military truck and headed north of town. During the trip, both men changed into rubberized suits that were very hot, but apparently offered some kind of protection—protection against what, they did not know.

When they arrived at the site, Benthal saw several tents that had been set up near a small bluff, and what appeared to be a refrigerator truck. He also witnessed covered trucks leaving the site that were obviously carrying wreckage of some sort. He could see thin strips of wreckage sticking out the backs of the trucks as they departed. Other empty trucks continued to arrive at the site. Benthal witnessed a lot of enlisted men going back and forth in various directions, as well as two majors whose names he did not know. He and Kirkpatrick were then split up, as Kirkpatrick was ordered into one of the empty trucks that headed out to another location (the Brazel debris field site), while Benthal was taken to a nearby tent and told to stand by. An officer then came out of the tent and told Benthal, "Get your camera ready!" Then the officer looked into the tent and made a loud comment that someone was coming in, whereupon a number of officers then exited the rear of the tent. Once inside, the officer told Benthal to stand back, and then pulled back a tarp that was on the floor of the tent, revealing several little bodies lying on a rubber sheet. Benthal and the officer slowly but purposefully moved around in a circle with Benthal taking pictures of the bodies lying in death beneath them. "They [the bodies] were all just about identical, with dark complexions, thin and with large heads," Benthal said. "There was a strange smell inside the tent that smelled something like formaldehyde."

Benthal was shooting his pictures with a standard-issue Speed Graphic camera that had a holder, each with two shots. Although it was daylight outside, it was dark inside the closed, rubber-lined tent. Because it was so dark inside the tent, the flash bulbs gave off a blinding light when a picture was snapped. After taking each set of two pictures, Benthal would give the holder to the officer. This procedure was repeated many times as the two men circled the bodies. The entire session lasted about two hours, after which Benthal was told to leave. About that time, Kirkpatrick returned from the other site in a truck that Benthal could see was loaded down with wreckage. Benthal and Kirkpatrick were dismissed from the site and returned to the base in Roswell. They were debriefed on the ride back to the base and told not to talk to anyone. "My camera case, cameras, and all of the film had been confiscated before we left the site. We were given bunks in the barracks overnight, in a small room upstairs, rather than in the larger room [downstairs] that had many more bunks."

The men were awakened around 4 a.m. the next morning and taken to the mess hall where they ate the early-bird breakfast. After breakfast, they boarded the B-25 and headed back to Washington. When they got back to Anacostia, they were again debriefed, this time by a Marine officer—a lieutenant colonel—by the name of Bibbey, who asked them if they knew what they had photographed. Benthal and Kirkpatrick both responded, "Yes, Sir." To which Lt. Col. Bibbey instructed them that they did *not* know what they had photographed! Then Lt. Col. Bibbey asked the question again.

Recalling the episode in 1993, Benthal observed, "Not long after that, I was assigned to Antarctica to take pictures of pieces of equipment to study the effects of cold [on them]."[13]

One of the MPs Frederick Benthal might have seen guarding the crash site was Cpl. William Warnke of the 390th ASS. Warnke, now 78 years old, was normally assigned to guard the Silverplates on the flight line at the base, but he recalled being sent "out in the boondocks" in July of 1947 to stand guard.[14] Another might have been Cpl. Leo Ellingsworth, who in July 1947 was a member of the 830th Bomb Squadron at the RAAF. In 1950, as Ellingsworth was about to be shipped out of the country, he told his brother Ross a story that Ross did not know whether to believe or not. Leo Ellingsworth passed away years ago, and Ross Ellingsworth is now in an assisted-care facility in Texas. Fortunately, Leo Ellingsworth also told the story to his niece, Monte Dalton, before he died. According to her, Ellingsworth had been assigned to a detail one night with a lot of other men who were ordered to a location "out in the boondocks" to pick up "bits and pieces of material." According to him, the men "walked shoulder-to-shoulder all night long," back and forth across the site, picking up whatever they could find and placing it in a container that each man had been given. When they were finished, each man emptied the contents of his container into a wheelbarrow as he departed the site. "My uncle also told me that he saw 'three little men,'" she said.[15]

It was Glenn Dennis who first introduced "smelly" alien bodies at the RAAF base hospital into the Roswell story. Dennis began talking publicly about it in the late 1980s and early 1990s, and has repeated his story in numerous documentaries about Roswell since then. Often referred to as the "Roswell mortician" for viewing audiences, Dennis was a 22-year-old embalmer employed at the Ballard Funeral Home in downtown Roswell.

On the morning of July 8, 1947, Dennis claimed to have received a series of telephone calls from the mortuary officer at the base, first inquiring about the availability of child-size caskets, then later about various embalming techniques for bodies that had been "out in the desert" for an extended period of time. Thinking that there might have been a plane crash—not unknown to Roswellians with the air base so close to town—Dennis offered his assistance. It was declined on the premise that the calls to Dennis were simply for

Roswell mortician Glenn Dennis.
Photo courtesy of Tom Carey, 2003.

"future reference just in case." Later that afternoon, Dennis received a call instructing him to pick up and transport to the base hospital a local airman who had just been injured in a motorcycle accident in town (besides providing mortuary services to the base, Ballard's Funeral Home also had the base contract for providing ambulance services when requested). Upon arriving at the emergency wing of the base hospital, Dennis got out of his vehicle and proceeded to walk with the injured airman up the ramp and into the rear of the building. Along the way, Dennis passed several box-type military ambulances that were parked close to the hospital. One of them had its back door swung open, and Dennis could see that it contained what appeared to be the front end of a canoe-like structure with strange writing or symbols along its side. It appeared to be made of metal, and its metallic surface had a bluish hue to it, as if it had been subjected to intense heat.

Once inside the hospital, Dennis then claimed to have bumped into a nurse he knew who was coming out of a side room holding a towel over her nose and mouth. Seeing Dennis, she exhorted to him, "What are you doing here? Get out! Get out of here as quickly as you can, or you will be in a lot of trouble!" On his way out of the building, Dennis was allegedly accosted by a black sergeant and a red-haired captain who called Dennis an "SOB," told him that there had been no crash, that he had seen nothing, and that if Dennis didn't get out of there right away and keep his mouth shut, he might require the services of an embalmer himself. It was a shaken and angry Glenn Dennis who drove back to Ballard's, followed all the way by an armed military escort, just to make sure. A day or two later, Dennis met up with his nurse friend at the Officers' Club on the base to try to find out what had happened at the hospital. Dennis could tell right away that she was nervous and not feeling well. They ordered lunch and Cokes, but neither touched their food, as the nurse tried to describe the scene at the hospital. She told Dennis that she had gone into a side room to get some supplies when a military doctor whom she had never seen before turned around from what he was doing and told her to stop what she was doing and come over, that she was needed at once to take notes. It was then that she noticed the overwhelmingly foul smell in the room and three dead "foreign bodies" lying on gurneys. Two of them were in bad shape and appeared mutilated, while the third one seemed to be intact. It was over the intact one that several doctors were hovering. She described the creatures as being 3 1/2 to 4 feet tall, with long arms and frail bodies. They had oversized heads, and the bones of the head were similar to those of a newborn baby, meaning that they were pliable and could be moved slightly. Each hand had only four fingers—no thumbs—with suction-cups on the tips of each finger. The eyes were sunken and oddly spaced. The ears and nose were simply holes in the side of the head and on the face, and the mouth was only a small slit. She did not notice what, if anything, they were wearing, as she was overcome by the horrible smell and became sick. She asked to be excused and left the room, and that was when she had run into Dennis in the hallway. She said that the doctors also became sick from the smell and had to abort the attempted autopsy. The nurse then took out a prescription pad and drew on it a picture of what she could remember that the "foreign bodies" looked like. She gave the drawing to Dennis and excused herself because she was still feeling sick. Dennis never saw the nurse again. According to Dennis, she was transferred to England a week or two later, and a letter that he sent to her a few months after that came back simply marked DECEASED. Dennis told Roswell investigators that he later learned that the nurse had been killed in plane crash during a training exercise. He also said her name was Naomi Selff.

After several years of searching without success for any record of a military nurse by the name of Naomi Selff, or any record of a plane crash in England involving American nurses during the pertinent time frame, Glenn Dennis was confronted by Roswell investigators with this information in the mid-1990s. His surprising and disappointing response was, "That wasn't her real name. I gave you a phony name, because I promised her that I would never reveal it to anyone."[16] In any court of law, when someone is caught in a lie, that person is said to have been "impeached" as a witness, meaning that his or her testimony, as evidence, cannot be relied upon. Even though we know of witnesses who have told us that Dennis had told them about the phone calls from the base for child-size caskets way back when they happened, and of witnesses who have told us that Dennis had told them about his run-in at the base hospital long before Roswell became a household word—still, Dennis was found to have knowingly provided false information to investigators, and must technically stand impeached as a Roswell witness. There is no way to get around that fact without believable, clarifying information from Dennis himself. To date, such information has not been forthcoming.

We continue, however, to investigate the alleged activities that took place at the RAAF base hospital during the time of the Roswell Incident. We have identified a number of first- and secondhand witnesses, including a nurse, who have attested to bodies coming into the base hospital at that time, as well as to activities suggesting that something highly unusual indeed was taking place there. One such person was Cpl. Arthur Fluery. In July of 1947, Fluery and a buddy of his, Paul Camerato, had just transferred over from the motor pool to the base medical unit (Squadron M) a month or two earlier to become ambulance drivers. At the time of the incident, Fluery was assigned to provide special transportation between the airstrip and the base hospital for an expected increase in the number of people flying in and out of the base. This Fluery did. "There were doctors, both military and civilian," he said, "flying in from all over the world it seemed, at least from all over the country, whom I picked up and drove over to the base hospital. I never saw so many planes coming in and going out in such a short span of time. I didn't know what was going on, but I had heard the rumors. My job was simply to drive the ones coming in to the hospital, and drive the ones going out to the airstrip."[17]

Another man who *did* see the bodies was Elias "Eli" Benjamin. His wife had told us as much, but it would be several years before he would tell us himself. As a retired career Air Force man, Benjamin feared for his pension—and still does—if he ever talked about Roswell. Benjamin and his wife had come into the International UFO Museum & Research Center in Roswell in 2002 to see the exhibits, as did the one million or so other visitors who had preceded them since the museum opened its doors in 1991. Against her husband's wishes, Mrs. Benjamin stopped into the museum director's office to tell someone about her husband. After hearing Mrs. Benjamin's story, especially the part about bodies and the hospital, Julie Shuster, the museum director, felt that a private interview with Mr. Benjamin was warranted. It was soon apparent, however, that there was a major problem—Mr. Benjamin was nowhere to be found. He had left the building when he saw his wife and Julie Shuster looking around for him—a reluctant witness, to put it mildly. Since that day, we managed to track down the former member of the 390th ASS and meet with him half a dozen times to try to gain his confidence. In the process, we learned that Benjamin's main fear, similar to so many others who were and are reluctant Roswell witnesses, was his belief that he, as a retired Air Force veteran, might lose his pension if he said anything about those long-ago events. We assured Benjamin that we knew of no instances whatsoever of someone losing his pension for talking about Roswell. Besides, the secretary of the Air Force issued a proclamation in 1994 that absolved anyone with knowledge about

Eli Benjamin at the site of the old base hospital.

Photo courtesy of Tom Carey, 2005.

the Roswell Incident who believed that they were still subject to security or secrecy oaths regarding the matter. The other thing that we noticed was that Benjamin was still deeply moved, if not troubled, by what he witnessed back in 1947, and he broke down in tears on several occasions when talking to us about it. His wife also revealed that her husband still has trouble sleeping comfortably and would for years wake up suddenly in the middle of the night, shaking. In 2005, the 80-year-old Eli Benjamin finally agreed to tell his story. He subsequently appeared as a featured Roswell witness on the *Sci Fi Investigates—Roswell* TV show that first aired on November 8, 2006.

In July of 1947, Eli Benjamin was a private first class with the 390th ASS at the RAAF. Possessing a Top Secret clearance, PFC Benjamin was authorized to provide security support for the most highly classified operations of the 509th Bomb Group. In addition to his primary job of guarding the Silverplates, one of his secondary duties was that of a recovery specialist, which involved the grim activities associated with the aftermath of plane crashes.

The morning of Monday, July 7, 1947 found PFC Benjamin walking back to his barracks after a night of guard duty on the flight line followed by breakfast at the chow hall. Just minutes away, sleep was awaiting him. "Something's going on..." he thought to himself, as he stood at attention and saluted the playing of the national anthem and the morning flag-raising ritual at base headquarters on the south end of the esplanade. He knew that the base commander, Col. William Blanchard, normally held his weekly staff meetings on Tuesday mornings, but on this day Benjamin thought there were way too many staff cars and other vehicles parked in the headquarters parking lot for a regular staff meeting. When Benjamin finally arrived back at his barracks, "Word was given to my squadron to be on the alert for special duty," he said. Such was life in the 509th and the Strategic Air Command, and sleep would have to remain a secondary consideration. The word finally found PFC Benjamin: "Benjamin! Get your gun and report to Hangar P-3 for guard duty." Benjamin gave us the following account:

> I got myself ready, got my gun, and reported to the big hangar, as ordered. As near as I can recall, it was late afternoon or early evening at the time. While looking for my OIC [officer in charge] to get instructions for duties at the hangar, I came upon a commotion taking place at the main

entrance to the hangar. Some MPs were trying to subdue an out-of-control officer who, among other things, appeared to be drunk as a skunk. I found out later that the officer in question was from my squadron and was the very officer to whom I was to report for a special detail. This officer—whose name I cannot now recall—was to have overseen the transfer of several "Top Secret items" from the big hangar to the base hospital, and I was there to help escort the transfer. I was later told that he had been to the crash site and had seen the ship. When this officer reported to the hangar and saw the small bodies, it was apparently too much for him to handle, and he just lost it. At this point, having just arrived myself, a Major or Lt. Colonel came out of the hangar, looked over the situation, and pointed at me. "You! Come over here," he said. "You're now in charge of this detail. Get these over to the base hospital!" He then pointed to three or four gurneys inside the hangar, each of which had something on it that was covered by a sheet. On one of the gurneys, whatever was under the sheet appeared to me to be moving. I saluted my acceptance and understanding of his order, and instructed the rest of the men in the detail to load the gurneys with their payload into the back of a truck that had just arrived for the purpose. Up to this point, I had no idea what we were transporting to the hospital. I would know soon enough, however. As the men were loading the truck, one of the gurneys slipped during the handoff, and the sheet covering it fell away, revealing the grayish face and swollen, hairless head of a species that I realized was not human. My orders were to deliver these to the base hospital's emergency room [Building 317] and remain there until relieved.

Almost 60 years after the event, the fog of time prevents Eli Benjamin from recalling the names or faces of the other men assigned to "escort duty" that day. They may well have been from other squadrons on the base or even from other bases brought in from the outside (known as "augmentation troops") to prevent the comparing of notes later on. Benjamin continued:

Upon arriving at the emergency room ramp, we proceeded to unload. I went in with the first gurney and stood aside near the doorway as the medical people took control of the gurney. A half-dozen or so medical and nonmedical officers quickly removed the covering sheet. I couldn't see too well from where I was standing because of the number of officers gathered around the gurney, but I could see well enough to make out that a very small person with an egg-shaped head that was oversized for its body was lying on the gurney. The only facial features that stick out in my mind now are that it had slanted eyes, two holes where its nose should have been, and a small slit where its mouth should have been. I think it was alive. The medical people were mostly just staring at it, but I'm not sure. After the rest of the gurneys were brought into the room, I was dismissed and told to return to my squadron, which I did. There, I was debriefed and made to sign a nondisclosure statement regarding what had just taken place. I was told that if I ever spoke about it, something bad would happen, not only to me, but also to my family. I heard later that the one species that was still alive was apparently taken to Alamogordo, then shipped to Texas or Ohio.

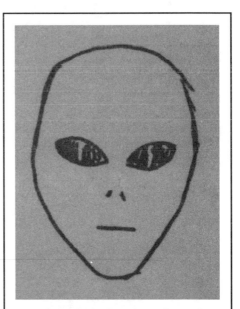

For her part, Mrs. Benjamin confirms her husband's account of his involvement in the Roswell events of July 1947. She further states that they have been married since 1949, when he first confided the story to her, and that his memories of that night—seeing the swollen faces and slanted eyes of the "species"—remain with and haunt her husband to this day.[18]

Don Schmitt's drawing of an alien Eli Benjamin witnessed, based on Benjamin's description.

Photo courtesy of Don Schmitt, 2005.

After telling his story before the cameras of *Sci Fi Investigates* in the big hangar on the old Roswell base where it all happened back in 1947, all the emotional Eli Benjamin could say after the cameras stopped filming was, "Do you think I will lose my pension?"

14

Who's Flying, Anyway?

The late Len Stringfield, who was the first researcher to take UFO crash retrievals seriously, met with a doctor he described as his "prime medical contact" for information regarding the alien bodies from Roswell. From that source he heard detailed descriptions of the unique body structure of the recovered crash victims.

Later, Stringfield was able to talk with a doctor who had participated in an autopsy of another such specimen. This new witness, according to Stringfield, provided a great deal of additional data: "From him, in time, I was able to envision the body entire," Stringfield wrote. "I learned of its internal chemistry and some of its organs—or, by human equation, the lack of them."[1] Stringfield, working with such information from his medical sources, was able to draw a number of conclusions: The being was humanoid, 3 1/2 to 4 feet tall, and weighed about 40 pounds.

The being's head was proportionally larger than a human head. The being had two large,

The late ufologist Leonard Stringfield.

Photo printed with permission from Dell Stringfield.

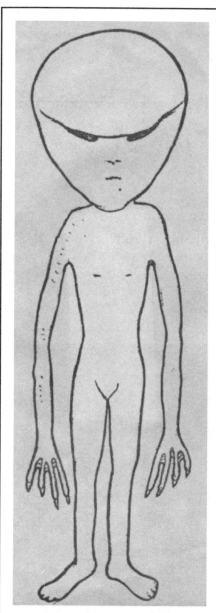

A 1978 composite drawing by Leonard Stringfield of a Roswell alien.

Photo printed with permission from Dell Stringfield.

round eyes, though one source did suggest the eyes were "Oriental or Mongoloid, deep-set and wide apart." Its nose was vague, with only a slight protuberance. Its mouth was a small slit and opened only into a slight cavity. The mouth apparently did not "function as a means of communication or as an orifice for food ingestion," and there were no teeth. There were no earlobes or "protrusive flesh extending beyond apertures on each side of the head."[2]

The being's body had no hair on its head, though according to Stringfield, one of his medical sources said that it was covered with a slight fuzz. The neck was thin, as was the torso. The arms were long and thin and the hands reached close to the knee. "A slight webbing effect between fingers was also noted by three observers," he wrote.[3]

"Skin description is not green," Stringfield continued. "Some claim it was beige, tan, brown or...pinkish gray, and one said it looked almost 'bluish gray' under deep-freeze lights....The texture was described as 'scaly' or 'reptilian' and as 'stretchable, elastic, or mobile over smooth muscle.'" He noted that "under magnification, I was told, the tissue structure appears mesh-like....This information suggests the texture of the granular-skinned lizards, such as the iguana and chameleon."[4]

Melvin E. Brown, a sergeant with the 509th Atomic Bomb Squadron at Roswell AAF in 1947, described bodies recovered at the crash scene when he was given the task of guarding a number of them after they were placed in the rear of a military ambulance truck. According to Brown, they were smaller than humans, and their skin was yellowish-orange in color, and had a texture similar to that of a lizard—leathery and beaded, but not scaly. Given the circumstances of his opportunity to observe the bodies, the discrepancy between his and Stringfield's accounts of the skin color and texture could have been the result of decomposition or simply a difference in lighting conditions. Regardless, it is intriguing that Brown spoke of lizard-like skin, as Stringfield's sources did.[5]

Stringfield was able to also learn something about the internal organs and their structure. There was no apparent reproductive system and no genitalia. There was a colorless fluid prevalent throughout the body, and, according to Stringfield's sources, "without red cells"—there were no lymphocytes. Not a carrier of oxygen. No food or water intake is known. No digestive system or GI tract. No intestinal or alimentary canal or rectal area described."[6]

Further confirmation of autopsies has come from another source. Dr. Lejeune Foster, a renowned expert and authority on human spinal-cord structure, who had a clinic in San Diego in 1947, was called on to perform a special assignment for the military. She was not sent to Wright Field as one might assume, but rather to Washington, D.C., where she stayed for approximately one month.

Possibly, because Dr. Foster had worked undercover for the FBI during the Second World War, and as a result had a top security clearance, she was flown to Washington to examine the spinal structures of the bodies retrieved near Roswell. She reported that her information from a high-ranking source was that one had been found alive but critically injured. According to the doctor, it had been rushed to Washington, where it soon died of its injuries.

Dr. Foster saw one or two of the bodies. Her task was to check their bone structure, spinal cords, and vertebrae, and to make comparisons between their and human anatomy. Because of her medical specialty, there was tremendous curiosity regarding the cervical spine, and the thoracic spine below and behind the chest that anchors the ribs. Dr. Foster was asked to examine the spinal canal that protects the spinal cord itself. Of special interest were the spinal nerves that carry impulses to move muscles or carry information to the brain from the sense organs in the skin, muscles, ligaments, and internal organs. Dr. Foster observed differences in the number of vertebra, not so much with bone structure, but the absence of specific internal organs. She did not elaborate further.[7]

As did the other doctors who saw the bodies, Dr. Foster portrayed the beings as short, with proportionately larger heads than those of humans. She said they had "strange eyes."

According to family members, Dr. Foster was very upset upon her return from Washington. Her housekeeper, who also was a dear personal friend, sadly saw a change that only got worse. She became distant and seldom talked to anyone but her medical patients. As she had been debriefed, she had been told that if she talked about what she had seen she would lose her license to practice medicine and that she risked being killed! "Someone in the government is trying to keep me quiet," she often said.[8]

15

Who Goes There?

The 509th Bomb Group at Roswell Army Air Field in 1947, as the Air Force's first operational SAC unit, was perhaps *the* elite military unit in our country's entire Armed Forces. The RAAF was chosen to house the 509th Bomb Group because of its central location on the North American landmass, and it offered the added security feature of being situated on the ground "in the middle of nowhere." All of its officers and enlisted personnel were handpicked for its mission, and had to pass extensive security background checks for the jobs they were intending to perform. Located just 7 miles south of the city of Roswell itself, the RAAF was in a perpetual state of high security and readiness. Military Police patrolled the fence perimeter that enclosed the base, as well as most of the sensitive areas within the base: the flight line with its compliment of Silverplates at the ready, the hangars and repair facilities, and the long, windowless, concrete building where the famed Norden bombsight was kept. The use of terminal force was authorized (one witness we interviewed told of an airman who was shot and killed by an MP near the flight line as he was running toward his aircraft; he was apparently late for takeoff and attempted a shortcut across an area where the use of lethal force was authorized, and failed to stop when challenged). At the main gate located at the north end of the base facing the city, armed MPs controlled the main entrance from an enclosed security booth. In addition to an intelligence office, the base also had a counterintelligence office, whose civilian-clad officers checked out possible security risks and breaches, trying to combat the very real threat of espionage. Airmen stationed at the base in those days have all told us of the tight security that was always in place, 24 hours a day, every day. The need for security was "drummed into us" from the moment of their first arrival, as one witness told us. "Need-to-know" has always been a way of life in the military, but it was carried to an extreme at Roswell, as 509th personnel were told not to discuss with anyone, not even their wives and family—at the risk of federal imprisonment—anything that took place on the base or in the course of carrying out their duties. As a reminder just in case anyone might have thought that the "loose lips sink ships" mentality of WWII was a thing of the past, large signs were placed at strategic locations on the base that warned:

WHAT YOU HEAR HERE

WHAT YOU SEE HERE

WHEN YOU LEAVE HERE

LET IT STAY HERE!!

So it is that we have spoken to many widows of former 509th airmen who were at Roswell in 1947 who have told us, when asked about their husbands' knowledge of the Roswell Incident, "He never said anything about it." Although we find it difficult to understand today how someone could remain silent for the rest of his life, not even telling his wife, that he was witness to the events that are the subject of this book, we respect that possibility whenever we encounter it. We admit that we couldn't do it, but there is no doubt that more than a few 509th personnel from America's "greatest generation"—whether out of a sense of patriotism or fear of retaliation—did just that. On the other hand, what easier way is there for an elderly widow to terminate a conversation with a complete stranger on a subject that she may not want to discuss—for whatever reason—than to say that she knows nothing because her husband told her nothing? End of conversation. Fade to black.

Fortunately for us and for history, our witness list of those who *have* talked to us about the 1947 Roswell events now totals more than 600 and counting.[1] This chapter will demonstrate to the reader how we fill in detail and flesh out the timeline in our story. It pertains to the preparations for the alleged July 9, 1947 "body flight" to Fort Worth, Texas.

This was the unscheduled, special flight of a single B-29 from the 393rd Bomb Squadron, known as the *Straight Flush*, that flew from Roswell Army Air Field to Fort Worth Army Air Field at the suspiciously low altitude of only 8,000 feet (B-29s normally flew at an altitude of about 25,000 feet). In place of its normal payload that day was a cargo consisting of a single 4-foot by 5-foot by 15-foot wooden crate in the bomb bay. Surrounding the crate in the bomb bay was a contingent of half a dozen or so armed security guards. Because the bomb bay of a B-29 was not pressurized, the

Straight Flush had to fly low enough so that the security guards in it would not succumb to oxygen starvation. The low altitude also suggests that there might have been something biological in the crate. Upon landing in Fort Worth, the bombardier on the flight was overheard to remark that he recognized an old friend—a mortician—from his college days among the officers waiting in the greeting party on the tarmac. He was immediately ordered to "Shut up!" by the aircraft commander. The enlisted crewmembers on the flight were by this time starting to put two and two together. They had heard the talk back in Roswell about a "spaceship" crash north of town a few days earlier. The day before, they read in the *Roswell Daily Record* and heard on the radio that a downed flying saucer had been recovered by the 509th and was being shipped to "higher headquarters"—that meant Fort Worth. There had also been talk of strange little bodies. And when the wooden crate was loaded into the bomb bay of their B-29 under armed guard, all of the enlisted crewmembers were ordered to stand at the far wingtip and face away from the aircraft, so they could not see what was going on. This order, of course, only served to embolden some of the crewmembers to take a glance. On the flight to Fort Worth, therefore, it did not require much of a stretch to think that the large crate in the bomb bay possibly had something to do with the "spaceship crash" that everybody was talking about back home (the officers on the flight already knew, as they had been briefed separately prior to takeoff). Now, after hearing about a mortician waiting for their flight, and then hearing one of the officers on their flight boast, upon taking off for the flight back to Roswell, that they "just made history," the crew started entertaining the thought that the wooden crate might have had something to do with the "little bodies." One of the crewmembers was especially convinced of this. Unknown to the others at the time, Private Lloyd Thompson, a gunner on the *Straight Flush* that day, recognized a flight physician from the Roswell base hospital who had treated him a week earlier for a sore shoulder, and who was now on the flight to Fort Worth with the security detail attending to the wooden crate. On the hour-long return flight to Roswell, after the wooden crate had been unloaded in Fort Worth, the *Straight Flush* flew at its normal altitude of 25,000 ft.

The information we have been able to gather about the flight of the *Straight Flush* is the result of interviews conducted by us with three of its crewmembers on that July 9, 1947 flight: Pvt. Lloyd J. Thompson, a waist-gunner and assistant flight engineer who passed away in 2003; S.Sgt. Arthur J. Osepchook, another gunner; and S.Sgt. Robert A. Slusher, the radioman. All other crewmembers that we have identified as being on that flight have either passed away, were killed, or refused to talk to us when we came calling. Besides Osepchook and Slusher, there is only one other member of the crew known to possibly still be alive, Lt. James W. Eubanks, the flight's navigator.

Lloyd Thompson was the first former crewmember to come forward in the late 1980s when he wrote a letter to a UFO group, *Just Cause*, who then passed along his letter to UFO crash/retrieval researcher, the late Leonard Stringfield (1920–1994). Beginning in the late 1970s, Stringfield had published a series of unsourced monographs about alleged UFO crashes, a subject that was a taboo for UFO researchers up to that time because of its sensationalist nature (Thompson's account, authored by Stringfield, appeared in the *MUFON UFO Journal* in 1989). However, Thompson would not allow Stringfield to identify him by name, thereby forcing Stringfield to refer to him only as "Tim" in the article. It wasn't until 2000 that Thompson "came out of the closet" when he gave a public presentation about the *Straight Flush*'s flight to a local UFO group in the town where his son lived. Schmitt (as well as Stringfield) had interviewed Thompson several times over the years, but it was during a 2005 interview that Carey had with Thompson's son Lowell, after his father had passed away, that we were able to learn additional details about the flight and its aftermath that his father never revealed publicly.

Robert Slusher has always been open and up-front with us regarding what he knows and what he doesn't know about the flight, without embellishing. In 2002, he appeared on-site at the old Roswell base to tell his story for our 2-hour Sci Fi Channel special, *The Roswell Crash: Startling New Evidence*. We interviewed Arthur Osepchook in 2004. He was very cautious about the flight and could offer no additional details of his own on the subject beyond noting the unusual nature of the flight and affirming the accounts of his crewmates, Thompson and Slusher. He was expansive, however, in recalling the excitement and talk on the Roswell base at the time about a "spaceship crash" and the "little bodies" supposedly found among the wreckage.

Our investigation located James Eubanks in 2003, but after learning the subject of our telephone call, he quickly terminated the conversation with, "I can't remember," and hung up. He soon changed his phone number to unlisted and is now unavailable to us.

Several years ago, a woman who operated a local museum in another state visited the International UFO Museum & Research Center in Roswell. She claimed to know a Native American "back home" who had been stationed at Roswell in 1947 and had "guarded the bodies."[2] She said that he was still alive, and she left his name with the museum director. She warned, however, not to try to contact him directly, as he would not talk to anyone who had not been introduced through her. After several years of trying without success to arrange a telephone or an in-person interview with the gentleman by going through the woman, we decided to take matters into our own hands by calling him directly. We felt that we had nothing to lose at that point, in 2005, as the years were rapidly slipping away. Edward Harrison answered the telephone himself, and contrary to the woman's warning, agreed to talk, however cautiously, about his participation in the 1947 events at Roswell.

Corporal Edward Harrison, now 81 years of age, was the sergeant of the guard in charge of a small detachment of Native Americans at the RAAF ordered to report to the far southwest corner of the base for a special duty assignment. He could remember the name of only one of the airmen in his charge that day, "a full-blooded Omaha" by the name of PFC James J. Lyons (now deceased). He did not remember the exact date, only that it occurred in July of 1947, "during the time of all the talk on the base about the crash of a spaceship" (we believe the date was July 8). When Cpl. Harrison and his men reported to the designated location at the far end of the base as ordered, they were somewhat surprised to be met by their commanding officer, Lt. Col. John S. Loomis of the 1027th Air Material Squadron, who was sitting in a Jeep in front of the locked gate of an 8-foot-high chain-link fence enclosing a large tent. Harrison had never known a tent to be in that location on the base before—near the trash incinerator—and, judging by the fresh earth piled up at the base of the fence posts, he surmised that the fence and tent had only recently been erected. He estimated the perimeter dimensions of the fence to be approximately 20 feet by 20 feet. The tent inside was about 15 feet by 15 feet by 10 feet at its central peak. It was one of those old olive drab Army tents used in WWII to sleep 4 to 6 soldiers (uncomfortably) in the field. After exchanging salutes with Col. Loomis, Harrison was ordered to post armed guards around the outside of the fence with orders to "Shoot anything that isn't a rabbit." According to Harrison, this was an unusual but not unheard-of order, considering the nature of the assignments his detachment had been given in the past. What *was* unusual to Harrison, however, was the sudden appearance of a tent and fence in the remotest part of the base, which he was being asked to secure with terminal force, if necessary. "Something not normal is going on here," Harrison thought to himself, as he saluted his understanding and acceptance of the order to Col. Loomis, who then quickly departed. After instructing his men, Harrison departed by Jeep as well. He had also arranged for several changes of the guard covering the next 24 hours. Early the following morning (July 9) Harrison drove his men to the tent to relieve the guards on duty only to discover that the guards, the fence, the tent, and whatever was in it, were gone! Scratching his head in bewilderment at this latest surprise, Harrison noticed a freshly graded dirt road and a set of large tire tracks in the soft morning earth that came from the general vicinity of the flight line up to where the tent had been, and then continued off in the direction of Bomb Pit #1—another highly secure location on the base, where the atomic bombs were loaded into the B-29s. When asked by our investigation almost 60 years later if there was a foul smell coming from the tent, Harrison replied, "Maybe, but it was hard to tell because of the ever-present smell of aviation fuel from the aircraft engines that permeated the air in that part of the base." Not having further orders or a need to know what was going on, Harrison and his men departed the site and never returned.[3]

Other men were able to get considerably closer to Bomb Pit #1. Corporal William L. Quigley had already finished working his day shift in the armaments shop of the 393rd Bomb Squadron[4] at the RAAF, and the evening found him in his room in the enlisted men's barracks getting ready to turn in, when the sergeant of the guard unexpectedly appeared at his door, saying, "Corporal Quigley, I have a job for you. Follow me!" Not particularly pleased at this turn of events, as it was getting late and he had already worked his 8-hour shift that day, Quigley unhappily complied. Both men then went outside and got into a waiting Jeep that quickly whisked

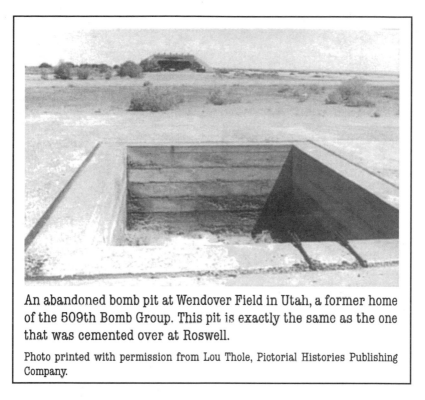

An abandoned bomb pit at Wendover Field in Utah, a former home of the 509th Bomb Group. This pit is exactly the same as the one that was cemented over at Roswell.

Photo printed with permission from Lou Thole, Pictorial Histories Publishing Company.

them across the flight line to Bomb Pit #1. Quigley knew that this was one of the most sensitive locations on the base, but he didn't know what this had to do with him. He was ordered to get out of the Jeep and to stand by.

"The Pit," as it was known, was a large, cement-covered, rectangular hole in the ground containing a hydraulic lift big enough to raise an A-bomb 10 feet up and into the bomb bay of a waiting B-29. When the bomb-loading procedure was in progress, armed MPs normally secured the area, and a 7 1/2-foot-high canvas screen-type barrier was placed around the perimeter of the bomb pit directly underneath the B-29 so that no one on the outside could see what was going on inside.

Quigley was handed an M-1 carbine rifle and joined three others, two officers and one enlisted man, who were also holding carbines and who were also obviously standing by with that "what am I doing here?" look on their faces. It was only now that he became aware of a B-29 not far from where they were standing, partially obscured by canvas screens. (In addition to the canvas screen barriers in place around The Pit proper, this time there was a second set erected in parallel around the inner ring of

A B-29 with screens erected to block onlookers' views of the loading process from a bomb pit.

Photo printed with permission from the U.S. Air Force.

screens which, according to Quigley, formed an alley between where the guards were to walk their security details.) The four were then led over to the B-29 and taken inside the outer ring of canvas screens and were given their orders. "I felt like I was walking in a tunnel," Quigley would say in 2006. "I couldn't see in, and I couldn't see out."

Each of the four guards walked a quarter of the perimeter in this circular tunnel, as assigned. Quigley's station was to walk back and forth from the tail of the aircraft to the right wingtip (he remembers seeing the tail number of the B-29 he was guarding that night—#291). His orders were to challenge anyone and anything that moved, and the use of terminal force was authorized. A few hours into his shift, around 3 a.m., Quigley thought he heard something outside the perimeter. "Who goes there?" he challenged. Nothing. "Stop and identify yourself!" Still nothing. Knowing that his orders were not to leave the "tunnel" under any circumstances, Quigley continued walking his detail. A little later, he noticed some movement against one of the outer screens. This time instead of challenging, "I just took my rifle-butt and rammed it against the screen as hard as I could where the movement was and called for the sergeant of the guard, but no one came. I don't know what I hit, but it was something solid. I heard later that I had butt-ended a 'CIA-type' [using today's terminology] who was checking security around The Pit that night." At the end of Quigley's shift, instead of heading back to his barracks for some much-needed sleep, he and the other three guards were driven over to squadron headquarters, where all were told to sign a piece of paper that stated, as Quigley tells it today, "It didn't happen" (meaning that Quigley did not guard The Pit that night/morning). Quigley thought this to be highly unusual at the time, but because he was more concerned about getting some sleep, he quickly signed the statement and left. It would be the only time he was ever asked—actually, ordered—to sign such a statement.

Recalling the episode today, Quigley, now 78 years old, prefaced what he was about to say with, "I have never talked to anyone about this before. There have been phone calls, but I always told them that I didn't know anything. I understand, however, that the ban on talking about this has been lifted, and I can now talk. You will be the first to hear this." He continued, "I didn't know what to make out of it at the time, but it was a highly unusual situation. The double row of canvas barriers was not normal and way, way out of the ordinary." This suggests that the second row of canvas screens was erected in this instance to prevent the *guards on duty* from seeing anything that was going on around them. Quigley went on:

> I had never pulled guard duty in my life, either before or after that night. Normally, the MPs provided the security for an operation like that, but I heard a little later that something "bigger than the A-bomb" was going on, and that the MPs didn't have a high enough security clearance for it. That would explain why I was chosen for this special duty, because I possessed the highest security clearance that an enlisted man could obtain—higher, at least, than anyone else I knew. I guess they could find only one other enlisted man in my squadron with the required clearance and therefore had to substitute two officers to fill the other two guard spots. This took place during the time of all the buzz on the base about UFOs. All the time I was walking my detail that night, I never heard any sound whatsoever coming from The Pit area behind the inner ring of canvas screens. I believed at the time that I was guarding a B-29 with an A-bomb aboard in its bomb bay. A few days later, after all the excitement had died down, I heard that I had guarded the alien bodies that everyone was talking

about that were stored in The Pit that night in preparation for flying them to Texas the next day.

We already knew from our investigation that the *Straight Flush* was the B-29 that allegedly flew several alien bodies to Fort Worth, Texas on July 9, 1947 (several other bodies, we believe, had been flown out a day earlier, directly from Roswell to Wright Field in Dayton, Ohio, on a C-54 piloted by Capt. Oliver "Pappy" Henderson). Because we have not committed to memory the tail-numbers of every B-29 in the 509th Bomb Group's inventory, a quick check was made by Carey for the tail number of the *Straight Flush*. Fully expecting that it would turn out to be #291, it was a shock and a disappointment to discover that it was in fact #301. This would seem to suggest that William Quigley's interesting story had nothing to do with the Roswell Incident—that it was just another situation involving high security on a base full of high security situations. Out of curiosity, however, and to put a period on this story, we wanted to know which B-29 bore the tail number #291. Further research showed that #291 belonged to a B-29 known as the *Necessary Evil*.[5] That name rang a bell with Carey, who recalled he had a copy of a picture of a B-29 with that name that had been sent to him by Robert Slusher. Sure enough, Carey located it, and there was Robert Slusher standing right by the *Necessary Evil* in clear view with the rest of its crew! Thoroughly confused now, because Slusher was known to have been a crewmember on the July 9 flight of the *Straight Flush*, Carey decided to call Slusher for an explanation of this apparent contradiction.

The articulate Bob Slusher, now 81, was up to the challenge. "The *Necessary Evil* was our regular aircraft," Slusher told Carey, "and we were surprised when we were told to report to another aircraft, the *Straight Flush*, for a special flight to Fort Worth that day [July 9, 1947]. We found out later that the cargo we were carrying that day—a large wooden crate— would not fit properly in the forward bomb bay of the *Necessary Evil*. So at the last minute, the *Straight Flush* was substituted in its place."

We can now meld these separate witness accounts into a scenario that suggests the impromptu security measures that were employed to keep the secret during the 24-hour period preceding the "body flight" from

Roswell to Fort Worth of July 9, 1947. This flight involved a *second* set of bodies to be brought to the base. Unlike the previous set of alien bodies—found closer to Roswell in Chaves County and brought in two days before—these had been found closer to Corona in Lincoln County, and all were dead. They also smelled. After an aborted attempt at conducting an autopsy at the base hospital (terminated due to the smell), it was decided to fly the bodies out as soon as possible to a facility that was better equipped to handle such a procedure. In the meantime, the bodies were placed in body bags, packed in dry ice within a large wooden crate, and removed to the remotest part of the base in the hope that the smell, if it could not be contained, would at least not reach the rest of the base. To block its view from curious eyes, the crate was placed in a tent, and to prevent whoever was guarding the tent from taking a peek inside, a tall fence was erected around it. Enter Cpl. Harrison's high-security detail at the tent with "shoot-to-kill" orders, but with no idea what it was they were guarding. When it came time to move the crate over to Bomb Pit #1, it was done under cover of darkness in order to minimize the chance of being observed (sometime after midnight on the morning of July 9), and the twin military doctrines of "compartmentalization" and "need-to-know" were employed to keep Harrison and his men from learning too much about what might be going on. Therefore, instead of accompanying the crate over to the bomb pit, they were dismissed just prior to its transfer.

After the crate was lowered into The Pit, the *Necessary Evil* taxied over from the flight line and assumed "loading position" over the bomb pit for the night (the actual loading of the crate into its bomb bay was scheduled for the following morning—in daylight). Who, then, should and could guard the crate? They couldn't use any of Harrison's men, because word would surely get back regarding the new location of the crate, and they might then be able to connect the dots. They also did not want to chance a security breach by expanding this responsibility to any other unit on the base, such as the 1395th MP Company (most MPs also did not possess high enough security clearances for this situation). It was decided that the best way to prevent leakage was to keep everything compartmentalized within the 393rd Bomb Squadron. A quick roster-check of the men of the 393rd Bomb Squadron revealed only two available enlistees, one of whom was Cpl. William L. Quigley, with security clearances high enough to permit them to stand guard for something that was, "bigger than the A-bomb."

The testimony of Edward Harrison and William Quigley, neither of which has ever before been published, serves to put an exclamation point on the testimony of the crewmembers who were aboard the strange flight of the *Straight Flush* on July 9, 1947 that something highly classified and unusual had taken place. Taken in isolation, each participant's testimony could be dismissed as nothing more than just another day in the life of someone stationed at a SAC base in the late 1940s. But our job is to connect the dots, to put the pieces of the puzzle together. And we have sufficient dots and pieces of the puzzle in the form of related and credible testimony to do that. When we plug in Harrison's and Quigley's accounts of the strange and secret goings-on at the fenced-in tent and Bomb Pit #1 to what we know about the unusual and highly classified flight of the *Straight Flush* the following day, a more complete and fortified picture of the Roswell time line comes into focus, as well as some of the steps employed by the military to contain knowledge of the unfolding events.

16

Boys, We Just Made History!

The entry in the *Straight Flush's* flight log for July 9, 1947 read, "DEH, Ship #7301. B-29. Cross-country. Forth Worth and Return. Flight time: 1 hr. 55 mins." It was the day after Brig. Gen. Roger Ramey had put an end to all the excitement and public clamor for more information about the flying saucer reported to have been recovered by the 509th Bomb Group at Roswell Army Air Field.

It was shortly after lunch when a flight crew went to the skeet range to test their shooting skills. They had spent the morning attending "ground-training classes" in Russian history, Russian language, and hand-to-hand combat, and their official duties for the day were completed. The aircraft commander, Capt. Frederick Ewing, had shattered 48 of 50 targets. Pvt. Lloyd Thompson, who was on base skeet team, did nearly as well with 47 out of 50, while S.Sgt. Robert Slusher, a radioman, left to join baseball practice for the base team, the RAAF "Bombers." Still, the buzz about the flying disc and the "little bodies" preoccupied the shooters, and the NCO in charge of the skeet range talked about nothing else. It was about 3 p.m. when the officer of the day (a rotating guard position) came by the skeet range in a Jeep and told the men to stay together and stand by. "This could be serious," said Capt. Ewing. Slusher was pulled from the baseball field and rejoined the rest. Something was up. A bus then picked them up and transported them to the flight operations building near the flight line.

All the other flight crews had been released for the day. The operations officer, Maj. Edgar R. Skelley, instructed the crew to stand by, because he had an unscheduled flight for them. Not knowing what to expect, the crew thought that it might be a last-minute test flight to prep a plane for a mission the next day. This thought did not change when the enlisted crewmembers were ordered to preflight a B-29, nicknamed the *Straight Flush* (#301) that was waiting on the concrete tarmac just behind the flight operations building. This was because the *Straight Flush* was not this crew's regular aircraft. Theirs was a B-29 nicknamed the *Necessary Evil* (#291). The preflight of a B-29 was an involved, lengthy affair because it had four separate engines, each with individual systems, that had to be checked out. The entire process took about an hour to complete. During this time, the officers of the crew had remained inside the flight ops building, where they were cleared and briefed for the impending flight. With the preflight completed, the commanding officer of the 393rd Bomb Squadron, Lt. Col. Virgil Cloyd, appeared and told the crew, "This is a routine mission. Do exactly as you are told, and don't discuss it." Maj. Skelley then instructed the crew to board the *Straight Flush* and taxi it over to Bomb Pit #1.

The nose of the B-29 *Straight Flush*, #301.
Photo printed with permission from the U.S. Air Force.

Bomb Pit #1, known to flight crews simply as The Pit, was housed in a cul-de-sac located to the southwest just off the main tarmac of the flight line. Signs were posted around the bomb pit area that read:

LETHAL FORCE WILL BE

USED ON ANYONE

TRESPASSING WITHIN

200 FEET OF THIS AREA.

The only areas of the base that had unobstructed views of the bomb pit were the air traffic control tower near the flight ops building, and portions of the flight line. While the huge airplane positioned its open, forward bomb bay directly over the pit for loading, it was then that the crew noticed that The Pit was covered by a large, canvas tarp. But there was no atomic bomb in the bomb pit that afternoon. "Did you see what I saw?" Cpl. Thaddeus Love, a tail gunner who was on the flight, was overheard asking another crewmember. "No talking!" was Capt. Ewing's quick retort.

The enlisted crewmembers and NCOs were ordered to deplane and stand at the far wingtip of the aircraft facing away from the bomb pit. As this was unusual, even for A-bomb loading, they still did not know what was going on. They also did not know that their own aircraft, the *Necessary Evil*, had spent the night and part of that day parked over The Pit while a ground crew tried in vain to ready it for this flight. When it still was not ready by midafternoon, it was decided to substitute another aircraft, the *Straight Flush*, in its place. The canvas cover over the bomb pit was pulled away, exposing a large rectangular wooden crate. All indications suggested it had been hastily constructed, as it was unpainted and unmarked. Its size—approximately 4 feet high, 5 feet wide, and 15 feet long—made for a snug fit as it was hoisted into the forward bomb bay of the waiting B-29. Four special security guards dressed in full MP Class-A uniforms positioned themselves at each corner of the sealed box. One of them was a major, one was a captain, one was a lieutenant, and one was an NCO. Three additional MPs positioned themselves inside the aircraft in the fore and aft crew compartments. After the bomb bay doors closed, the enlisted men and NCOs had to wait before reboarding the aircraft, while Lt. Martucci, the bombardier on the flight, conducted a security check of the cargo in the bomb bay. It wasn't until the *Straight Flush* was airborne that the rest of the crew were told of their official destination: Fort Worth Army Air Field, home and headquarters of the "Mighty Eighth" Air Force to which Roswell's 509th Bomb Group was attached. This was definitely no quickie test flight.

The normal flight time from Roswell to Forth Worth was about one hour, but with the aid of slight tail wind, the flight this day took only 55 minutes. Upon landing at the base, they taxied the *Straight Flush* across the tarmac over to a waiting contingent of officers, a development that only added to the mystery of the unidentified cargo in the bomb bay. Lt. Martucci was overheard to remark excitedly to no one in particular that he recognized one of the officers in the greeting party as an old friend from his college days, "Hey! I know that guy. I went to school with him. He's a mortician." This implied that whatever was in the crate might be related to his friend's profession. Lt. Martucci's reminiscence was cut short with a stern admonition from Capt. Ewing to "Shut up!" that came through the crew's earphones loud and clear.

Once the aircraft came to stop, the crate was unloaded. One of the crew wasn't sure, but he thought he remembered seeing a gurney being wheeled out toward the crate. The enlistees and NCOs in the crew were ordered to remain on board, while all of the officers disembarked the aircraft to talk to the officers in the receiving line. Lt. Martucci deboarded the aircraft with the MPs in the bomb bay and immediately went over to chat up his old friend. The entire party plus the crate and the gurney then departed for one of the gray buildings lining the flight line, after which the remaining crewmen, who had been waiting in silence for 15 minutes, were permitted to leave the aircraft to stretch their legs. They had been ordered, however, not to talk to anyone on the ground. Sandwiches and soda were brought out to them for a snack, which, considering the time of day, turned out to be their dinner. When they were just about finished eating, the flight officers, as well as one or two of the MPs, returned to the aircraft. Capt. Ewing and Lt. Martucci, however, were not with them. Just then, Ewing and Martucci could be seen exiting the flight operations building with another officer. All three walked quickly across the tarmac and boarded the *Straight Flush*. Maj. Jesse A. Marcel, the intelligence officer of the 509th Bomb Group in Roswell, who had been flown to Fort Worth the day before with a plane-load of wreckage that he had collected from the crash site (and who had been unwittingly used as a prop by Gen. Ramey at the press conference the day before), was a "guest passenger" on the flight back to Roswell. One of the crewmembers observed that Marcel, "appeared to be down and very sad that day." After everyone had boarded the aircraft and had settled in for the return flight, the aircraft commander, Capt. Ewing, who had ordered Lt. Martucci to keep quiet moments before, now issued another curious but stern lecture aimed at the entire crew. They were told in no uncertain terms that this had been a "routine flight," and that they were never to say another word about it—even to their wives! "Forget everything that you saw today!" One crewman would later remark, "For weeks, rumors were plentiful, and we were hard-pressed to maintain the silence we had been ordered to keep." After the *Straight Flush* lifted off the runway at Fort Worth for the return flight to Roswell, according to surviving crew members, the irrepressible Lt. Martucci apparently could not contain himself any longer and was heard to exclaim to everyone within earshot, "Boys, we just made history!"

This account of the flight of the *Straight Flush* suggests that something more important than Gen. Ramey's laundry was being flown to Fort Worth that day. The secrecy of an unscheduled flight, the security surrounding an unmarked wooden crate, a low-altitude, cross-county flight, the curious behavior of certain officers on the flight, a flight surgeon dressed as security officer, a mortician waiting for the flight, the gurney, the stern admonitions to keep quiet, and the remark about making the history books was all out of the ordinary—even if A-bombs were known to be aboard. When interviewed many years later with the benefit of hindsight and reflection, the surviving crewmembers to a man stated that they definitely suspected on the return flight, and believe now, that several alien cadavers were inside the wooden crate they had flown from Roswell to Fort Worth that day. In answer to the question regarding the possibility of a foul smell emanating from the crate, all stated that they were unaware of such a smell, but they were not permitted anywhere near the crate.

The flight crew that day, from the 393rd Bomb Squadron at the RAAF, was led by Capt. Frederick Ewing, the aircraft's commander and pilot. Ewing was killed in an unfortunate air accident five years later while piloting his B-47 "Stratojet" medium bomber in an attempt to help another B-47 that was having difficulty with its landing gear. Ewing's copilot on the *Straight Flush*, Lt. Edgar Izard, retired from the Air Force and was last seen selling insurance in Roswell in the 1950s. To our knowledge, he was never interviewed and is now presumed dead. Lt. Elmer Landry was a fill-in on the July 9 flight for Sgt. David Tyner as the flight engineer. He too has never been interviewed and is presumed dead. Lt. James W. Eubanks, the flight's navigator, was located a few years ago living in Forth Worth. In a

2003 telephone interview with Carey, when informed of the nature of the call, Eubanks simply said, "I can't remember," and hung up. Follow-up telephone calls by Carey in the ensuing months went unanswered. Eubanks then changed his phone number to an unlisted number. It is not known, therefore, if he is still alive or not. Lt. Felix Martucci, the talkative bombardier and security officer on the flight who made the "Boys, we made history!" statement, was located in 1990 living in a military retirement community in San Antonio, Texas. Because of his suggestive statement on the flight, our investigation especially wanted to interview him to find out what he had meant by it. We also wanted to learn more about his mortician friend, and why he was waiting for his flight that day. Schmitt had briefly spoken to an unresponsive Martucci on the telephone, and when Len Stringfield, from whom we had initially learned about Martucci, followed up with a call to Martucci on his own, a woman answered and shouted a loud "No!" into Stringfield's ear before slamming down the phone. A hoped-for, in-person, "ambush" interview with Martucci at his residence in San Antonio unfortunately fell through when Martucci failed to appear. Martucci subsequently obtained an unlisted telephone number to thwart efforts to contact him, thereby avoiding having to answer the questions. We do not know for sure, but he has in all likelihood passed away by this time—without ever revealing to anyone the true details of his self-proclaimed history-making flight.

Of the enlisted men and NCOs on the flight, Cpl. Love died six months before we located his widow in the early 1990s with the help of Barbara Dugger and Christine Tulk, the granddaughters of the late Chaves County Sheriff, George Wilcox, who was heavily involved in the Roswell Incident. Both were also schoolteachers, one of whom (Tulk) by coincidence worked at the same school as Love's widow. After informally learning of their mutual connection to Roswell at school, Tulk told Dugger, who also spoke to the woman. Love's widow did not deny anything that Tulk and Dugger were saying and suggesting, but she did not say much on her own either. Dugger then called Schmitt, whom she already knew from an earlier interview, and it was quickly decided that an in-person interview was in order. Schmitt, Dugger, and Tulk then drove from Roswell to El Paso. Schmitt got out of the car and went to front door of the widow's house, while Dugger and Tulk remained in the car. Schmitt knocked on the door. The door opened just a crack so that Schmitt could barely see the woman's face. After introducing himself, Love's widow responded to Schmitt, "Yes, I know who you are. But, before my husband died, he asked me never to say another word about this, and I have no intention of breaking that promise. I wish I could help you. I'm very sorry." With that, she closed the door, and that was that. What is the explanation here? Never say anything about a *weather balloon*?

Robert Slusher, now 81 years old, introduced himself to our investigation in 1990 after a talk by Schmitt and fellow Roswell investigator Kevin Randle, at the Alamogordo Civic Center. He was able to corroborate much of what Lloyd Thompson had told Stringfield and Schmitt previously about the July 9 flight. He was sincere, did not embellish, and what he did not know, he simply stated that he did not know. He kept his testimony to what he personally knew, and his story has not changed over the years in follow-up interviews by us. Slusher was among those Roswell witnesses who were presciently brought to Washington, D.C. in 1991 by the Fund of UFO Research for the purpose of videotaping their individual testimonies for posterity in *Recollections of Roswell*. Slusher also appeared on location at the site of The Pit on the extinct base in Roswell to tell his story for our 2002 Sci Fi Channel production, *The Roswell Crash: Startling New Evidence*. Slusher is still living and spends much of his time traveling the country with his wife.

Arthur Osepchook was interviewed by Carey in 2003 and 2006. Although he could not recall many of the details, he remembered "the crate flight" and the feeling at the time that, "Something big was going on." Carey went through the list of crewmembers on the July 9 flight, all of whom Osepchook was able to confirm as being on that flight. He confirmed the trip to the skeet range and especially the air of excitement on the base about the rumored crash of a "spaceship" with "little bodies" inside. Even more than his colleagues, Osepchook was emphatic that he knew there was *something*—"something special"—in the crate. He did not elaborate on how he knew this or what he thought might have specifically been in the crate, but his recollection of post-flight reaction no doubt contributed to his notion that something highly unusual was afoot, even before the *Straight Flush* touched down in Roswell. "We were told that 'nothing was going on' in order to kill such speculation on our part," he said.

Staff Sergeant Arthur Osepchook.

Photo printed with permission from the 1947 RAAF Yearbook.

"Then, after we landed, a big meeting was called of the entire squadron in one of the hangars to tell us that there were no such things as *flying saucers* and that it [a crash of one] didn't happen." Osepchook told Carey that he had "papers" from his military days that were stored away somewhere, and he promised to look for them. Arthur Osepchook is now 83 years old and lives in Alabama.

Lloyd Thompson began corresponding with the late Cincinnati UFO researcher Leonard Stringfield in 1989. A responsible, "by the book" member of America's "greatest generation," Thompson felt compelled to get the truth out about the Roswell Incident, but wished to remain anonymous in doing so. It was for this reason that Stringfield would refer to Thompson only as "Tim" in his sixth published monograph about alleged UFO crash/retrievals as well as in an article published in the November 1989 *MUFON UFO Journal* ("Roswell & the X-15: UFO Basics"). Still a cautious and circumspect man, Thompson was invited to but chose not to attend the 1991 *Recollections of Roswell* assemblage of Roswell Incident witnesses in Washington, D.C. In 2000, however, Lloyd Thompson finally went public when he gave a presentation about his participation in the Roswell Incident to a local UFO group in the town where his son lived. It is from Thompson's account in the aforementioned MUFON publication regarding the July 9, 1947 flight, from his 2000 presentation, as well as from Schmitt's own telephone interviews with him, that we have drawn to construct the basic history of that flight. Thompson passed away on April 13, 2004.

In conducting an investigation such as this, we have found that surviving family members will sometimes talk when the departed eyewitness would not. Not always, but sometimes. Further, family members can also supply additional details to information already supplied by a deceased witness. Such was the case with Lloyd Thompson. Carey called Thompson's son Lowell in 2005 after he learned of Lloyd's death from his widow. Lowell Thompson was able to provide additional background information about his father that was of a personal nature, as well as new details concerning his father's involvement in the Roswell Incident. According to Lowell, his father never said a word about Roswell until 1984, after reading the first book about Roswell. After dinner one evening, he asked his family to return to the dinner table. Lowell told us:

> He was in a somber mood. I thought that he was going to tell us that he was divorcing my mother! He held up a copy of *The Roswell Incident* and said, "I didn't think that I would ever be able to tell you this. I thought it would be secret until my death. But, I checked this book out from the library last week. I've gone through it, and they pretty much have everything in here." He went through the basic story and then showed us an old logbook of his with an entry for a flight which, I believe, was dated July 9, 1947. So, that's how it all got started. Later, he got in touch with Stringfield.

This postprandial revelation also explained for Lowell why his father had always encouraged him to take out UFO books when they went to the library. "Ever since I was 8 years old, wherever we lived, he told me to do this, but never explained why. My father read a lot of UFO books. He also had me clip from the newspaper any articles or news stories about UFOs and put them in a scrapbook. Now I know why."

Besides fitting neatly into the Roswell time line, from the moment the wreckage from an unknown aerial device and the remains of its crew started arriving at the RAAF, until arrival at their final destination at Wright AAF in Dayton, this chapter illustrates the classic, historical, military reaction to a UFO event. Secrecy, "compartmentalization," "suspension of disbelief," intimidation, and so on, were all part of the extraordinary security measures employed. Hasty and momentous decisions, however seemingly myopic to us now, were made, perhaps out of panic, perhaps out of ignorance, all for the primary purpose of keeping the secret—not only from the Russians, but also from the American people.

17

If You Say Anything, You Will Be Killed

Today, we would refer to the threats made by some members of the military as civil rights violations or even war crimes if committed in time of war, and their perpetrators would be brought to a swift justice and punished severely. Especially when such acts involve excesses by the military establishment upon the helpless, whether military or civilian—the resulting outrage by the media can reach fire-storm proportions. Military reprisals against civilians, even in times of war and against enemy civilians, is repugnant to our value system, and something that will not be tolerated by the United States citizenry.

Occurring as it did sometime during the first week of July 1947, the Roswell Incident happened at the time of the first wave of flying saucer sightings around the country that summer. The latest "sighting of the day" commanded front-page attention in most newspapers, as was the case with events in Roswell. As an anxious and excited nation—and world—awaited more news of the discovery, things were about to change. Moving quickly to kill the story, our government used a combination of appeals to patriotism, claims of "national security," bribery, threats of long prison sentences, and outright thuggery in the form of death threats to contain the story. As a result, the Roswell Incident turned into a two-day story and was quickly out of the public consciousness.

Those in the military who were involved in the retrieval of the wreckage, the bodies, and what was left of the crashed UFO itself, were the easiest to deal with. Roswell Army Air Field was a SAC base, so everyone who worked there, military and civilian, was already familiar with the base policy of not talking about things that went on at the base, even to family members—ever. To drive home this point, the enlisted men involved in the cleanup at the various sites were detained in groups and "debriefed" (sworn to secrecy under the guise of national security). Long prison terms were promised in case anyone was thinking of talking, and we have also heard that bribes of $10,000 or more were used to assure the silence of those who saw the bodies. The *officers* involved, especially career officers, were less of a problem. In order to advance a career in the military, one does not defy orders or breach security. One key officer who was heavily involved in the recovery operations even promised President Truman (via Truman's aide) that he would keep the secret forever. He did until he was on his deathbed many years later.

Controlling civilians, however, was a different matter.

Except in time of war or under conditions when Martial Law has been declared, under the Constitution, the U.S. military has no direct authority over U.S. civilians. The military could keep its own house (the men of 509th Bomb Group stationed in Roswell and up the chain of command) quiet, but how to keep the civilians from exercising their God-given, Bill of Rights-guaranteed freedom of speech? And there were a lot of civilians involved in the Roswell Incident all along the way: from the initial discovery of pieces of wreckage by civilians near Corona, to the discovery of the craft itself closer to Roswell, to the recovery operations at the Roswell base itself, and finally to the shipment of the wreckage and bodies to Wright Field in Dayton, Ohio.

Aside from the Corona ranchers whose homes were indiscriminately ransacked[1] in our military's mad search for "souvenirs" from the crash, and the rancher Mack Brazel who started it all and who was dealt with directly by the military, other civilians involved in the 1947 Roswell events were dealt with through civilian authority figures. The highest-ranking of these was Dennis Chavez, a U.S. senator from New Mexico. He was "enlisted" by the Army Air Forces to intimidate Roswell radio station KGFL, whose ownership had secured an exclusive, recorded interview of Mack Brazel, during which Brazel told of finding strange wreckage and the bodies of "little people." Walt Whitmore, Sr., the station's majority owner, was threatened by Sen. Chaves with the loss of the station's broadcasting license if it went ahead with its plans to air the Brazel interview (KGFL had planned to "scoop" the other Roswell media outlets with the interview). KGFL minority owner Jud Roberts was also similarly threatened, and for good measure, a high-ranking member of the FCC in Washington, D.C also threatened Whitmore and Roberts with the same message. It worked better than was hoped for, as Whitmore caved in completely by not only turning over the taped Brazel interview, but also by becoming a willing accomplice in the military's campaign to silence civilians. One of his broadcasters, Frank Joyce, had also been called by "a military person in Washington," and had been "read the riot act" to shut up about the crash. Joyce had been the first media person to interview Brazel and knew Brazel's original story, including the part about Brazel finding little bodies. Incensed about being told what to do by someone in the military, Joyce let him know where to go. The angry voice in Washington shot back, "I'll show what I can do!" and hung up. A day or two later, Joyce's boss, Walt Whitmore, Sr., told Joyce to get into his car, and that they should go for a ride. Joyce did so, and then noticed a strange-looking man in a strange-looking uniform sit-

Walter Whitmore, Sr.
Photo printed with permission from Mrs. Walter Whitmore, Jr.

ting in the back seat. The man did not speak. Whitmore drove north out of Roswell for more than an hour to a remote shack off Corona Road. He was told by Whitmore to get out of the car and go into the shack. This Joyce did, still not knowing what was going on. Joyce stood alone in the shack for a few minutes, wondering what was taking place, when in walks none other than Mack Brazel himself. "You're not going to say anything about what I told you the other day, are you?" Brazel asked Joyce. "Not if you don't want me to," responded Joyce. "Good. You know our lives will never be the same." With that, Brazel walked out, and Joyce never laid eyes on him again. Joyce then returned to Whitmore's car for the ride back to Roswell, and the stranger in the back seat was gone. Apparently the military was not sufficiently convinced of Joyce's pledge not to say anything, and he was shortly thereafter gathered up and physically removed to a Texas hospital for a year or so under circumstances that are still not clear to him. A Roswell native, Joyce did not return to Roswell upon his release.[2]

The Roswell base guest house, where Mack Brazel was sequestered for a week, still stands where it stood in 1947.

Photo courtesy of Tom Carey, 2006.

We know of at least one instance when the military authorities took matters into their own hands by employing thuggish tactics directly to a civilian eyewitness to scare her into silence. Perhaps they thought they could get away with it because the witness was a mere child. Perhaps they hadn't gotten their game plan together yet. Frankie Dwyer was a 12-year-old schoolgirl in July of 1947, and her encounter with the bullying and threatening military officer haunts her to this day. Frankie's father was a crew chief with the Roswell Fire Department. At the time of the incident, Frankie had just been to the dentist and had stopped at the fire station to wait for her father to take her home. While she was waiting, a highway patrol officer by the name of Robert Scroggins came into the station with a mischievous look on his face. "Hey, guys! Want to see something?" Scroggins reached into his pocket and took out something that he wadded up in his hand. "Watch this," he said. He then held his hand out about a foot over a nearby table and opened it. Something silvery fell from his hand to the surface of the table without a sound. Then, as if by magic, it spread out like quicksilver into a small, thin, irregular sheet of *something* in one or two seconds. Everyone who was there that day, including Frankie Dwyer, had a chance at it. It could not be cut with scissors, scratched, burned, or permanently creased. No one there could figure out what it was. Scroggins said that he had gotten the piece from "someone in Corona."[3] A day or two later, Frankie Dwyer was at home with her mother tending to chores when there was a hard knock on the door. Opening the door revealed a tall man with wide shoulders and a dark complexion dressed in an MP uniform. He was looking for Frankie Dwyer. After Mrs. Dwyer introduced her daughter to the ominous MP, two other MPs escorted Mrs. Dwyer into another room. With a thick New York accent, the first MP started to question Frankie about the incident at the fire station and wanted to know what she had actually seen. Satisfied that the 12-year-old had seen plenty, he took out his billy-club and started pounding it into his open palm as he tried to pound home his reason for the visit. "You did not see anything. You got that? If you say anything, not only will you be killed, but the rest of your family will be killed too. There's a big desert out there. No one will ever find you."[4] With that, a shaken Mrs. Dwyer was returned to her terrified daughter, and the men left.

Frankie Dwyer Rowe.
Photo courtesy of Tom Carey.

In researching Frankie Dwyer Rowe's story over the years, we followed the evidence trail to conclude that the MP who most likely confronted Frankie that day was a former Brooklyn, N.Y. policeman by the name of Arthur Philbin, who was a security officer with the 390th Air

Service Squadron that was part of the 509th Bomb Group in 1947. Lt. Philbin, in addition to being tall and dark with wide shoulders, ran the guard house on the base and had a reputation of being an all-around tough-guy. He also was the base liaison with the Roswell Police Department and Sheriff's Office on matters that affected both the base and the town. Philbin died many years ago, so it was impossible to turn the tables and interrogate him about his Roswell days. Therefore, we never published anything about Philbin or anything that mentioned his name. We also never mentioned his name to Frankie Dwyer Rowe. In 2005, we got an idea. Why not try a line-up similar to what the police do when they parade a number of people in a group that includes the suspect before the witness? The hope is that the witness will be able to pick out the suspect from the rest of the group. Sometimes the witness can, and sometimes not. No harm in trying. We knew that Lt. Philbin's picture was in the 1947 RAAF yearbook. He is shown on a page along with the pictures of 16 other officers—enough for a line-up by any standard. We then made a photocopy of the pertinent page from the yearbook and mailed it to Frankie Dwyer Rowe with the simple question, "Do you recognize anyone on the enclosed page as the person who came to your house and threatened you back in 1947?" A few weeks later, we received an envelope in the mail bearing Frankie Rowe's return address. Inside the envelope was the folded, photocopied page that we had sent to her. There was no accompanying letter, just the page with the pictures of 17 officers of the 390th ASS on it. There was simply a single circle drawn around one of the pictures—the picture of Lt. Arthur Philbin.

Chaves County Sheriff George Wilcox was the authority figure utilized by the Army on the ground in Roswell to help contain the story. A picture of him on the telephone and looking like a deer caught in the headlights was prominently featured on the front page of the July 9, 1947 edition of the *Roswell Daily Record*. But Wilcox was doing more than just answering telephone calls. He refused to give out any details to inquiries regarding what was going on, because he was, "helping out the fellows from the base."[5] He also completely rolled over in the face of the military full court press by allowing himself to be used as the enforcer to intimidate local Roswellians into keeping their mouths shut about what they witnessed. It was his task to deliver the threat of the ultimate sanction to those who saw or knew about the bodies recovered from the crash. Glenn Dennis, the Roswell mortician, allegedly knew about the bodies from a nurse friend who was involved in the autopsy of one of them at the base. Dennis had been threatened at the base hospital by an officer, and like Frank Joyce, Dennis became incensed at his treatment by the officer and told him where he might go. The next day, Dennis's father received a visit from Sheriff Wilcox and a deputy to tell him that his son "was in trouble at the base."[6] No doubt the veiled death threat of the previous day was part of the message delivered by Wilcox.

Ruben and Pete Anaya in 1947 were Montoyistas, supporters of then lieutenant governor and future New Mexico senator, Joseph Montoya. After the incident that shook him up so badly, the two Anaya brothers and their families were paid a visit at their homes by Sheriff Wilcox. According to Pete Anaya and his wife Mary, who were interviewed again in September 2002 about this incident, Wilcox delivered the ultimate sanction to them if they talked about what they knew: "If you say anything, you will be killed. And your entire family will be killed as well."[7] It is not known to how many others Sheriff Wilcox delivered the message on behalf of the Army, but what is known is that he never ran for sheriff again. According to family and friends, the Roswell events "destroyed him." Now, we know why. When asked about all this just a few years ago, a former deputy of Wilcox's responded, "I don't want to get shot." After the story had been contained, and things had died down a bit, the Army paid a visit to Sheriff Wilcox and his wife, Inez. To praise or reward him for a nasty job well done, you may ask? Think again. The message delivered to the startled couple was that unless they kept quiet about everything, not only would they be killed, but their children would also be killed. Sheriff Wilcox died in 1961. Asked by her granddaughter years later whether she believed the threats or not, Inez Wilcox looked at her with a straight face and clear eyes, and said, "What do you think?"[8]

18

It Looks Like Something Landed Here!

One of the most prized possessions a prosecuting attorney can have in his arsenal to impress a jury is a witness from the camp of the defendant who can provide pertinent and persuasive "inside" information and insights as to the true nature of the defendant's actions and motives regarding the case at hand. Such witnesses are said to have "flipped," "turned state's evidence," or have otherwise become "cooperating witnesses" for the prosecution. This practice is usually done in exchange for not prosecuting a case against the cooperating witness or for a lighter sentence.

In "prosecuting" the Roswell Incident as a case of extraterrestrial visitation, we have found from experience that the witnesses who will or will not talk to us fall into fairly predictable categories of "most likely" to "least likely" to talk (assuming that they know something, everything else being equal). Those in the "most likely" category include the civilian witnesses not on government pensions, followed by former noncareer enlistees and noncommissioned officers who are not on government pensions. In the "least-likely" category are retired career military officers (and the higher the rank, the less the chance there will be of their saying anything) followed by retired, career enlistees (usually NCOs), retired civilians on government pensions, and civilian professional people (doctors and lawyers). There are exceptions to these rules, to be sure. For example, retired Air Force General Arthur Exon talked to investigators directly about his remembrances relating to the Roswell events at Wright-Patterson AFB when he was stationed there in 1947, and about seeing two distinct crash sites between Corona and Roswell as he flew over the region a year or two later.[1] But Gen. Exon is definitely the exception here. Most deny any knowledge of the Roswell Incident or use the "I can't remember" dodge, and a few even deny being at Roswell at the time when we know they were.[2]

This wall of silence even carries over to the surviving family members after the witness has passed away. For instance, General Roger Ramey, the architect of the Roswell cover-up, passed away in 1963, but his wife is still alive. All sorts of rumors have flown around over the years that the general told his wife that the Roswell events really involved a crashed UFO. All attempts to interview Mrs. Ramey have been frustrated by her son who has been performing an Academy Award-worthy reenactment of Horatio at the Bridge.[3]

Most investigators agree that there would be no case to pursue were it not for the testimony of a handful of key witnesses, some of whom, it can be said, flipped. Certainly, without the sheep rancher Mack Brazel, who reported finding strange wreckage to the sheriff in Roswell, there would be no public record of the event. Against Air Force orders, he later told family members some—but not all—of what happened. Without Maj. Jesse Marcel's direct testimony to investigators that he believed the wreckage he saw back in 1947 was "not from this Earth," the case would have remained moribund in perpetuity. Chaves County Sheriff George Wilcox, a civilian who flipped, cooperated with "the boys over at the base" at the threat of death to him and his family if he talked. And Wilcox's chief deputy, to this very day, tells investigators, "I don't know anything." Even though, by his own admission, he—not Wilcox—ran the daily operations at the sheriff's office.[4] The provost marshal at the RAAF in July of 1947, Maj. Edwin Easley, never told investigators anything other than that, as a retired military officer, he was sworn to secrecy and couldn't talk. But in his final days, he confessed to family members about seeing alien bodies from the crashed UFO.[5] Unlike him, former Roswell counterintelligence Captain Sheridan Cavitt took his secrets with him to his grave.[6] And on and on.

Certainly, one of the most important military witnesses to flip was the retired Army Counter Intelligence Corps Master Sergeant Lewis S. "Bill" Rickett. Rickett died in his Florida home in 1992, but not before he became a cooperating witness to Roswell investigators by telling them what he knew about the 1947 Roswell events—which was plenty. Because of Rickett, we have another firsthand witness to the strange wreckage and the suggestion of a second (or third?) UFO crash site other than the Corona site, closer to Roswell. Because of Rickett, we know that the Air Force hired University of New Mexico meteor expert, Dr. Lincoln La Paz, in September of 1947 to try to determine the speed and trajectory at the time of impact of the crashed UFO. According to Rickett, he drove La Paz all over New Mexico for the better part of a month on this project, taking measurements and soil samples and interviewing local ranchers. La Paz's conclusion was that the crashed craft was an extraterrestrial device. Because of Rickett, we know that there were at least two formal reports written about the Roswell UFO crash, one by the aforementioned Dr. La Paz and one by his boss, counterintelligence Captain Sheridan Cavitt. Because of Rickett, we know that Cavitt, contrary to his statements to investigators right up to his death in 1999 that he was not involved at all in the Roswell events of July 1947, was *heavily* involved. Rickett confirmed that it was Cavitt who had accompanied Marcel and Brazel back to Brazel's ranch on that fateful Sunday, July 6, 1947 (Cavitt had denied ever meeting Brazel). Cavitt was also involved at the UFO impact site—not a balloon site as he told Air Force investigators in 1994.

Master Sergeant Lewis "Bill" Rickett.

Photo printed with permission from Mrs. Lewis Rickett.

According to Rickett, Cavitt asked him to go with him to a place "in the boondocks." "I don't believe what I've seen, and I just thought it would be advisable for someone else to see it," he told Rickett. They drove in a staff car to a remote site about 45 minutes out of Roswell. According to Rickett, the site itself was of generally flat terrain with low, rolling bluffs. He recognized the provost marshall from the RAAF as well as a contingent of MPs ringing the area with weapons drawn. Also evident were about 60 or so pieces of what appeared to be very thin aluminum scattered about. As Rickett walked the site under the approving eye of Cavitt, he was both amazed and bewildered at what he was seeing: "It looks to me like something landed here," he said. "But if it landed here, I don't see any tracks. I don't know how anything could have landed here and not leave tracks." (At the Foster ranch debris field site, witnesses reported seeing a long gouge and several skid-marks, so this was clearly another site, thus confirming Gen. Exon's observation.) As for the strange wreckage, it was very similar to that found on the Foster ranch—thin, light, and strong. Rickett picked up a piece of it, about 4 inches by 10 inches, placed it over his knee, and tried to bend it. He couldn't. Cavitt and Easley laughed at him because they had tried and failed at it too. Rickett had never seen a piece of metal that thin that could not be bent. "The more I looked at it, I couldn't imagine what it was," he said.[7]

Two months later, in September of 1947, Rickett was given another field assignment. He was ordered to assist Manhattan Project scientist Dr. Lincoln La Paz, from the University of New Mexico at Albuquerque. La Paz was a famous meteor expert, as well as a nuclear scientist, and had just arrived at the base in Roswell after being briefed in Washington, D.C. Their special assignment: to determine the speed and trajectory of the unknown object that had crashed northwest of town.

Rickett described to our investigation that he and La Paz discovered a possible touchdown point about 5 miles northwest of the debris field on the old Foster ranch. Not only did they recover a small number of pieces identical to the material Rickett had handled before, they were startled to find that the sand in the high-desert terrain had crystallized, apparently as a result of exposure to tremendous heat. There was also one last item discovered that didn't match any of the debris described heretofore: a seamless black box. Rickett told us that it was a little bigger than a shoebox, like shiny plastic, and didn't weigh anything. Try as they may, "there was no getting inside of it, that's if there even was an inside," laughed Rickett.[8]

They spent a total of three weeks interviewing witnesses and making calculations, which were contained in La Paz's official report. Rickett never had a chance to see the document, because it, along with the new physical evidence, was delivered directly to the Pentagon. The professor did confide to the plain-clothes intelligence specialist that, based on all the new data and hardware they'd collected and tested, the original object was an "unmanned interplanetary probe."[9] Sgt. Rickett continued to search for answers. Unfortunately, his supervising officer, Capt. Cavitt, refused to discuss the matter with him.

One year later, Rickett met once again with Dr. La Paz, this time in Albuquerque. La Paz remained convinced that the object that exploded near Corona was from another planet. In all his confidential meetings with various government agencies, he said he had learned nothing that contradicted that position.[10]

The very next month, while on assignment in Washington, D.C., Rickett met with fellow counterintelligence agent Joe Wirth. Rickett asked about the status of the materials recovered at Roswell the previous year. According to Wirth, the government's top researchers had yet to identify its metallurgic makeup and still "hadn't been able to cut it."[11]

One can well imagine Bill Rickett's surprise when, after more than 40 years of silence, he received a very unexpected evening phone call in 1991 from his former commanding officer. "Happy Birthday, Bill," exclaimed the voice on the other end of the phone, "Its Cav, your old boss." After exchanging pleasantries, Cavitt queried, "Have you been talking to anyone about what happened back in 1947?" Rickett identified one of the coauthors, whom Cavitt had met as well, and Cavitt pressed the issue, "What have you been telling him?" Pressing further, Cavitt added, "We both know what really happened out there, don't we, Bill?" To which Rickett responded, "We sure do." After a short pause Cavitt responded, "Well, maybe someday....Goodbye, Bill."

Lewis "Bill" Rickett, who passed away in October 1993, never heard from the officer who introduced him to the Roswell Incident again.[12]

Bill Rickett.

Photo printed with permission from Mrs. Lewis Rickett.

19

You and I Never Saw This

Throughout the many years we have been conducting our investigation into the events that have come to be known collectively as the Roswell Incident, we have come to know (and know of) many of the eyewitness participants. We have been fortunate enough to have interviewed several hundred of these, although others had passed away either before we could locate them or before investigators even knew about Roswell. Still others have refused our requests for interviews, or when granting interviews, have been less than truthful with us.

We have dubbed our investigation's resistive or untruthful witnesses as Roswell's "reluctant witnesses." Many, perhaps most of these, have already passed away, taking what they knew with them to their graves. Former Roswell radio station KSWS reporter Johnny McBoyle, who had somehow made his way to the crash site before it was fully secured by the military and tried to report his observations to Lydia Sleppy for the AP wire, not only refused to talk to investigators, but also refused to tell his wife and family about it, even upon being urged to do so by them on his deathbed.[1] He died in 1991, just a few weeks before his wife. A few, to be sure, did relent at the end and gave deathbed confessions to their families. Countless widows, however, have slammed down telephones in our ears and doors in our faces with a parting shout, "He never said anything!"

There is a dwindling number of reluctant Roswell witnesses still out there who, if they talked, would go a long way toward putting all of us out of our misery regarding Roswell. One of these was Dee Proctor, who managed to avoid every attempt at being interviewed by Roswell investigators over the years. Perhaps the youngest participant in the Roswell events, he was 66 years old when he passed away suddenly in 2006. Another is Tommy Thompson, the former deputy sheriff of Roswell in 1947 whom we have interviewed several times in his home. Although we know that the Chaves County Sheriff's Office was heavily involved in the 1947 events, and although he has told us that he basically ran the day-to-day operations of the sheriff's office, he tells us that he has no recollection whatsoever of the Roswell Incident, because he was "out of the office that day" and never bothered to ask his boss, Sheriff George Wilcox, about it. Thompson is now in his 80s and in declining health.[2]

Perhaps the best known of Roswell's reluctant witnesses was first made known to Roswell investigators in a 1979 interview of the former Roswell base intelligence officer, Maj. Jesse Marcel, who could only identify him as "Cav."[3] Marcel recalled that "Cav" was a captain who headed up the Counter Intelligence Corps (CIC) unit at the Roswell base back in '47, that he was from West Texas, and that it was Cav who had accompanied him and the sheep rancher, Mack Brazel, back to the Foster ranch to investigate the rancher's find. A check of records and documents quickly identified "Cav" as retired Lt. Col. Sheridan W. Cavitt, who was indeed the officer who headed up the CIC unit at Roswell AAF from June of 1947 until the Air Force became a separate branch of the armed forces in September of 1947. With so many potential spies lurking in and about Roswell at the dawn of the Cold War, the CIC was tasked with locating them, keeping track of them, and neutralizing them, as well as dealing with other potential breaches of security.

Sheridan Cavitt in the 1990s.

Photo printed with permission from Kevin Randle.

When located in retirement by Roswell researchers in the early 1990s, Sheridan Cavitt at first denied that he had ever been stationed at Roswell. Upon being confronted with documented evidence to the contrary, he admitted that, yes, he had been stationed there in the late 1940s, but it was after the time of the Roswell Incident. Confronted again with documentary evidence that he had arrived in Roswell prior to the famous incident, Cavitt then fell back on the "I can't remember" defense used by so many others of his generation who do not want to say anything, but do not want to tell outright lies either. Questioned further, he said that he had never met the rancher, Brazel, and had not gone out to the Foster ranch to inspect the strange wreckage with Marcel. In short, there was no "Roswell Incident" that he could recall, and if there was one, he was not involved. While Cavitt was still telling this tale to civilian Roswell investigators, he was telling a different story to Air Force investigators who were conducting their own investigation of Roswell in conjunction with the one being conducted by the United States Congress' investigative arm, the Government Accounting Office (GAO) in 1993 to look into the Roswell case.[4] Now he remembered it, but it was only a solitary, mundane weather balloon that he and Rickett, and perhaps Marcel, found (Cavitt wasn't sure about Marcel's participation). That was it. There was no sheep rancher and no strange wreckage to stupefy Maj. Marcel, Col. Blanchard, and the world. End of story. Oh, really?

Thanks to the persistence of civilian Roswell investigators, including our investigation, we have been able to piece together some of Sheridan Cavitt's involvement in the 1947 Roswell events, primarily from key interviews conducted with his immediate subordinate at Roswell in 1947, M.Sgt. Bill Rickett,[5] and from several interviews with Cavitt and his wife, Mary.[6] In fact, it was Cavitt's wife who supplied us with some of the most interesting, filling-in-the-blanks comments about her husband, starting with, "He won't tell you anything. They've told him not to, and he won't. That's why they chose him for many of the assignments he's had—because he knows how to keep quiet. And I couldn't help you either, because he doesn't tell me anything."

Mary Cavitt, 1990s.
Photo printed with permission from Kevin Randle.

We now know for sure that Maj. Marcel's "Cav," Captain Sheridan Cavitt, accompanied Marcel to the Foster ranch to inspect the strange wreckage found and reported by Mack Brazel. This was confirmed by Bill Rickett and secondarily by a secretary in the CIC office. After the jeep carry-all that he drove out to the site was filled with wreckage and he was shown *something else* by the rancher, he drove back to the base and reported his findings to the Roswell base commander, Col. Blanchard, as well as to his superiors in a separate command in Washington, D.C. This was on Monday, July 7, 1947, which was the day before Marcel would arrive back from the ranch. Although Cavitt told the Air Force investigator that he only made the one trip, we know from Bill Rickett that he made at least two more trips—one to the "impact site" close to Roswell, and another to bring Rickett out to see it and offer an opinion. As we saw in a previous chapter, Cavitt, according to Rickett, wanted another set of eyes from someone he trusted to see the wreckage. Cavitt told Rickett, "I just thought it would be advisable for someone else to see it."

M.Sgt. Bill Rickett, 1945.

Photo printed with permission from Mrs. Lewis Rickett.

Cavitt told Rickett where he should walk amongst the pieces of wreckage while soliciting Rickett's opinions as to what he was seeing. Looking at the thin pieces of metallic-looking wreckage strewn about the site, Rickett asked Cavitt, "Is it hot? [radioactive] Can you touch it?"

To which Cavitt replied, "Yeah. Be my guest. That's what I wanted you to ask me."

Rickett continued to walk the site. He picked up a 4-by-10-inch piece of very thin, feather-light, slightly curved wreckage he thought was aluminum, and tried to bend it over his knee. Try as he might, he could not bend it. By now, Maj. Edwin Easley, the provost marshal from the base, had joined Cavitt in watching Rickett struggle with trying to bend the unbendable. Cavitt turned to Easley and laughingly commented, "Smart guy. Trying to do what we couldn't." Completely dumbfounded and frustrated by this turn of events, Rickett exclaimed to Cavitt and Easley, "For God's sake! What in the hell is this stuff made out of? It can't be plastic. Don't feel like plastic. But it just flat feels like metal."

Summing up his observations of what he saw at the crash site to investigators, Rickett could only scratch his head after the passage of so many years and say, "I never saw a piece of metal that thin that you can't bend. The more I looked at it, I couldn't imagine what it was."

Indicative of the extreme secrecy that attended the recovery operation is a brief conversation that Rickett had with one of Easley's MPs who was guarding the site, someone whom Rickett knew. Out of earshot of others, the MP confided to Rickett, "I don't know what we're doing, but I do know this. I never talked to you in my life—not out here." Picking up on this theme, Rickett chimed in, "Right. What you see out here, you never saw."

This sentiment was reemphasized to Rickett shortly thereafter as he and Cavitt were about to depart the site. In the presence of Maj. Easley, Cavitt, in a purely perfunctory manner, as if he were lecturing a child, said to his subordinate, "You and I never saw this. You and I have never been out here. We don't see any military people out here. We don't see any vehicles out here." To which Rickett could only respond, "Right. We never left the office."

Sheridan Cavitt passed away in December of 1999. Playing the part of the good soldier to the end, he never told his wife or family some of the things you have read in this chapter, and he never acted upon a request he received in a letter from his old CIC/AFOSI boss at Kirtland AFB in Albuquerque, Doyle Rees, shortly before his death: "When you call the press conference to tell the world, let me know, because I want to be there."[7]

20

It Wasn't Ours!

When Corona sheep rancher Mack Brazel heard a strange, muffled explosion among the thunderclaps during a severe lightning storm ("The lightning seemed to be attracted to a single location on the ranch," he would later tell his son Bill) late one evening in early July 1947, he had no idea what it could be. Some of Brazel's neighbors also told of hearing the explosion. The following day, as he gazed upon one of his pastures now covered by pieces of silvery wreckage, he still had no idea what it was. Without electricity or a radio and with only monthly newspapers, he had not heard about the flying saucers that had made their historical appearance only two weeks previously. It wasn't until Brazel had paid a visit to

A U.S. Air Force flying disc. The attempted development of such disc-shaped craft was still 10 years in the future in 1947.

Photo printed with permission from the NASA Ames Research Center.

his close neighbors the following day, and to a Corona bar a few evenings later, that he heard about them—as well as a possible reward for finding one. Early the following morning, he would find something else on his ranch, something that convinced him to drive to Roswell to report his finds, thus securing his place in history and initiating one of the greatest mysteries of the 20th century.

Leaving the *something else* for another day, what was it exactly that was deposited in small pieces concentrated so densely in a fan-shaped area of up to 1 1/2 million square feet in Brazel's pasture that summer of 1947? From various sources, both military and civilian, who actually saw and handled pieces of the wreckage, the most interesting consisted of the following:

1. A large amount of small to palm-sized pieces of smooth, very thin, very light but extremely strong "metal" the color of aluminum, which could not be cut, scratched, bent, or burned. Some of the larger pieces displayed a slight curvature to the surface.

2. An apparently large quantity of palm-sized and larger pieces of a very thin and very light "metal" or "cloth" with "fluid" properties. This type of wreckage also could not be cut, scratched, or burned, but it could be temporarily deformed. As startled witnesses tell us, "I wadded up a piece of it in my hand, and it felt as though there was nothing there. Then, I placed it on a smooth surface, and it unfurled itself and flowed over the flat surface like liquid mercury back to its original shape without so much as a crease." (It is this so-called "memory metal" that we refer to today as the "Holy Grail" of our Roswell investigation, because locating a piece of it would provide irrefutable proof, we believe, of the extraterrestrial nature of the Roswell Incident.)

3. A quantity of thread-like, monofilament "wires" that could not be cut, scratched, burned, or permanently deformed. These could be coiled, and when a light from a flashlight was shown in one end, it could be seen coming out the other end. These, it has been suggested, adumbrate today's fiber optics technology.

4. A small, black, seamless box that could not be opened.

5. A light, seamless, dull-aluminum flange or strut that could not be cut, scratched, or burned.

6. A number of thin "I-beams" about 18 to 30 inches long by 1/4-inch wide by 3/8-inch thick containing "writing" in the form of unintelligible symbols along their lengths; these "beams" were as light as balsa wood, but they could not be cut, scratched, or burned; they could be flexed slightly but not broken.

7. A number of thin strips of thin, aluminum-like "metal" about 3–4 feet long by 3–4 inches wide containing a hieroglyphic-like "writing" on them.

It should be noted that debris similar to what has just been described was also found at the impact site in proximity to where the remainder of the intact craft allegedly crashed—but not in the large quantities found in Brazel's sheep pasture on the Foster ranch. So, what can we make out of such items as those just described? Were they truly as exotic in nature and origin as they appear, or just misidentified everyday items (tinfoil, sticks, and rubber), as the U.S. Air Force would have us believe? To answer this question, let's let the people who actually handled the materials tell it like it was.

We know that Mack Brazel told the *Roswell Daily Record* on July 8, 1947 that what he found was certainly "...no weather observation balloon." Later, he confided to a few family members that it was "the strangest stuff he had ever seen" and, according to his son Bill, the Army admitted to his father that they had definitely established that "...it wasn't anything made by us."

The RAAF base intelligence officer, Maj. Marcel, thought from the very first, until he died in 1986, that the wreckage was from an extraterrestrial spacecraft. His son, Jesse, Jr., has confirmed to us that his father was already talking about the wreckage in terms of it being from a flying saucer during his early morning visit home with some samples prior to reporting back to the base from his trip to the Foster ranch. What about Marcel's boss, Col. William H. "Butch" Blanchard? What did he have to say about it? We know from several firsthand sources that at first he thought it might be a Russian device, but then realized it wasn't. However, when pressed by his family at the dinner table for an answer on a number of occasions, he would stare off into space as if in a trance and repeat over and over again, "The Russians have things you wouldn't believe."[1]

The former mayor of Roswell, William Brainerd, tells the story of when Col. Blanchard returned to Roswell a few years after the event, and he found himself in Blanchard's presence at an official function. Later the same day, he was sitting across from Blanchard at dinner. During the course of the meal, he asked Blanchard about the 1947 incident. "[It was] the damnedest thing I ever saw," was Blanchard's only comment.

As for Blanchard's boss, Gen. Roger Ramey, commanding officer of the Eighth Air Force in Fort Worth, we know from public records that Ramey was the architect of the weather balloon cover story that chilled press interest in the story for three decades. But what about in less public settings? What did he say about it then?

We located a firsthand witness several years ago who had been stationed at Fort Worth AAF back in 1948. An enlisted crewman on a B-29, he was waiting on the tarmac to board his aircraft along with the rest of the crew. Also waiting with the crew on this day was Gen. Ramey himself. One of the officers in the crew was overheard to ask Ramey about the 1947 Roswell events: "What about it, General? What was that stuff?" To which Ramey responded, "It was the biggest lie I ever had to tell....[It was] out of this world, son, out of this world."[2]

We also have two living, secondhand witnesses with whom we are still in contact who say that, before Gen. Ramey died in 1963, he told his wife that the 1947 Roswell crash involved a "spaceship," and not a weather balloon as he had previously stated publicly.

Retired Gen. Arthur E. Exon was a lower-ranked officer in 1947 when he was stationed at Wright Field in Dayton. As a member of the Air Material Command where the Roswell artifacts were sent after the recovery, and as the later base commander at Wright-Patterson Air Force Base (in 1964), Exon was in a position to know things, even if he did not have firsthand access to the Roswell artifacts. He knew people who did. According to Exon, after conducting a series of metallurgical tests upon the Roswell wreckage, the overall consensus among the scientists involved in the testing was that, "...the pieces [of wreckage] were from space."

M.Sgt. Bill Rickett is one of the key eyewitnesses in the Roswell chain of events. It is Rickett who, before he passed away in the early 1990s, filled in a number of blanks and connected several dots in the Roswell timeline for us. In September of 1947, he was assigned to drive the University of New Mexico's meteorite expert, Dr. Lincoln La Paz, around New Mexico to help La Paz try to ascertain the speed and trajectory of the object that crashed two months previous. In doing so, La Paz interviewed many local ranchers and ranch hands for any bits of information

Retired Air Force General Arthur Exon.
Photo courtesy of Tom Carey, 2002.

they might possess. Both Rickett and La Paz submitted separate reports of their findings up their respective chains of command. Some months later, La Paz requested that Rickett meet him at the Four Corners Restaurant (now known as Clines Corners) at the intersection of Rt. 40 and Rt. 285 east of Albuquerque and north of Roswell. During lunch at the restaurant, La Paz reiterated to Rickett his belief that the Roswell crash represented "an unmanned, interplanetary probe."[3]

Rickett also related some firsthand accounts of several interesting and revealing conversations that he had over the years with fellow counterintelligence colleagues he knew along the way concerning the 1947 Roswell events. One, a former CIC operative named Claire Miller, actually disbursed the funds for the cleanup of the Roswell crash sites. Rickett ran into Miller years later in Washington, D.C. After trading pleasantries, mostly about the luck of finding one another still alive after so many years, Miller, perhaps anticipating the question, all of a sudden blurted out to a startled Rickett, "The answer's still the same. Don't ask me!"[4] End of conversation and reunion.

Another former CIC operative that Rickett knew was a fellow named Joe Wirth, who is presumed dead by now, and no one ever interviewed him. Rickett recalled, however, a conversation he had with Wirth in the early 1960s in Washington, D.C., when Wirth was then working as a civilian for the Park Police there. Years before, Wirth had rebuked Rickett when Rickett dared to ask him about a box of wreckage Wirth had received from CIC Capt. Sheridan Cavitt and had flown with it out of Roswell in a C-54, presumably to Washington, D.C., where Wirth worked. This time around, Wirth confided to Rickett. However, still wary 15 years after the fact, Wirth suggested that the two of them go outside into the parking lot to avoid the chance of being overheard. Continuing the conversation, Wirth revealed to an astonished Rickett, "Honest to God, they still haven't figured out what that stuff is!"[5]

For his part, having been to one of the Roswell crash sites and having handled some of the wreckage himself, Bill Rickett had seen and heard enough to reach some conclusions of his own. Although admitting to not knowing the entire Roswell story, he felt that he did know enough to conclude, "The Air Force's explanation that it was a balloon is totally untrue. It was not a balloon. I never did know for sure exactly what its purpose was, but...it wasn't ours!"[6]

We have had a conversation with a gentleman who lives in Dayton. His daughter had come home from college for the summer and had taken a job as a lifeguard at a local swim club. According to his daughter, she had made the acquaintance of another female lifeguard. In discussing their respective families, the friend of his daughter confided to her that her father was an officer who worked at Wright-Patterson AFB in a scientific capacity, and that he had just received a promotion to work on a project that was analyzing *pieces of metal from a UFO that had crashed in New Mexico back in the 1940s!*

21

The Pieces Were From Space

From the moment that a craft of unknown origin descended tragically from the summer skies and crashed in the high desert of New Mexico in 1947, high-level officials outside of Roswell clamored to get the materials into their hands for analysis.

At that time, and certainly as a consequence of World War II, there were a large number of national laboratories that specialized in a wide variety of military technologies. But there was only one facility that was dedicated to the science of reverse engineering: the FTD.

The Foreign Technology Division (FTD) at Wright Field in Dayton, Ohio, was a key intelligence organization responsible for the breakdown and analysis of all weapons and equipment captured during the war. When the military got their hands on something of foreign design—or of an even higher level—the captured technology would go to FTD for dissection.[1] As we have detailed throughout this book, Wright Field was Maj. Jesse Marcel's original destination when he made his first trip escorting wreckage from Roswell Army Air Field.

Instead, that flight was diverted after takeoff to Fort Worth, Texas, where Gen. Roger Ramey announced to the press that what Maj. Marcel had recovered was, in fact, the remains of a weather balloon. Officially, the flight scheduled to carry Marcel to Wright Field was cancelled, and he was ordered, after a one-night layover, to return to Roswell AAF. But an official FBI teletype message from its Dallas office to Director J. Edgar Hoover disputed that version of events, alleging that a clandestine flight carried the recovered Roswell material to Wright Field as originally planned, and that the FTD had made preparations for its arrival while the Army was still in the midst of spinning its weather balloon story to the media.[2]

Brig. Gen. Arthur E. Exon described to us what happened after the flight reached the FTD. Exon, then a lieutenant colonel, was an administration student in technology at the FTD. "We heard the material was coming to Wright Field," he said. Analysis of the debris was performed in the FTD's various labs: "Everything from chemical analysis, stress tests, compression tests, flexing. It was brought into our material-evaluation lab. I don't know how it arrived, but the boys who tested it said it was very unusual." Exon also described the material: "[Some of it] could be easily ripped or changed," he said, but did not elaborate. "There were other parts of it that were very thin but awfully strong and couldn't be dented with heavy hammers....It was flexible to a degree." According to Exon, "Some of it was flimsy and was tougher than hell, and the [rest] was almost like foil but strong, It had them [the FTD analysts] pretty puzzled."[3]

The lab chiefs at Wright Field set up a "special project" for the testing of the material. "They knew they had something new in their hands," continued Exon, "the metal and material was unknown to anyone I talked to. Whatever they found, I never heard what the results were. A couple of guys thought it might be Russian, but the overall consensus was that the pieces were from space. Everyone from the White House on down knew that what we had found was not of this world within 24 hours of our finding it." When asked what he thought about the components' physical makeup, he said, "...I don't know, at that time, if it was titanium or some other metal...or if it was something *they* knew about and the processing was something different."[4]

Gen. Exon's experience with the recovered Roswell remnants wasn't limited to the work at Wright Field. A number of months later, he told us, he flew over central New Mexico and checked out the crash site he had heard about while stationed back east, "[It was] probably part of the same accident," he said, "but [there were] two distinct sites. [At] the northwest [site], pieces found on the [Foster] ranch, those pieces were mostly metal." The general also confirmed having seen the gouge that others had reported. Exon said, "I remember auto tracks leading to the pivotal sites and obvious gouges in the terrain."[5]

When asked about the bodies, he said, "I know people that were involved in photographing some of the residue from the New Mexico affair near Roswell. There was another location where...apparently the main body of the spacecraft was...where they did say there were bodies." Asked if the bodies had been sent to Wright Field, Exon said simply, "That's my information...people I have known were involved with that."[6]

Gen. Exon also commented about specific information originating in Roswell: "Blanchard's leave was a screen. It was his duty to go to the site and make a determination. Blanchard couldn't have cared less about a weather balloon."[7] This bit of inside information was also mentioned by Lt. Col. Joseph Briley, who was assigned as the operations officer at headquarters at Roswell in 1947.

Arthur Exon and wife.
Photo courtesy of Tom Carey, 2002.

"Blanchard's leave was a blind," mused Briley. "He was actually setting up a base of operation at the crash site north of town."[8] We have also been told by airmen and NCOs who were there that Blanchard clandestinely moved his office to the basement of one of the enlisted men's barracks on the base to get away from the press. He may also have checked in at the base guard house (a.k.a. "the brig") for a time.

Exon elaborated, "I know that at the time the sightings happened, it was [up] to Gen. Ramey...and he, along with the people at Roswell, decided to change the story while they got their act together and got the information into the Pentagon and into the president."[9]

Because of how publicly outspoken Exon, a high-ranking officer, was about the incident, we anticipated the reaction in Washington. During the GAO investigation of Roswell in 1994–95, Exon was interviewed by a number of high-level congressional staff members. One of the discussions took place at his home on December 2, 1994. Exon was extremely guarded in these talks, and one of the staff members entered into his report, "Gen. Exon is afraid. He was afraid he was being monitored at that point. He was probably afraid his whole house was bugged."[10]

It is ironic to point out that two of the principle characters in the entire Roswell saga went on to play intricate parts in the U.S. government's 22-year official investigation of the UFO phenomenon—namely, Gen. Roger Ramey and the FTD. Ramey, for all of his stoic efforts to discredit all of the flying disc reports at that time, would become a consultant to the Air Force Project Blue Book. And in 1952 he was called their "saucer man" and one of their top "UFO experts." Ramey played an important role debunking the subject and conducting damage control for the Air Force throughout the mid-1950s. We contend that they could always use a good weather balloon to pull out whenever a case got too hot.[11]

And most curious of all, the FTD supported Project Blue Book with its resources and was responsible for conducting analysis work on what the Air Force investigators gathered. In fact, AFR 80-17, an Air Force regulation issued by the U.S. Department of the Air Force in Washington, D.C., was the official form used by Project Blue Book! The document also states that, "If the final report is deemed significant, the FTD will send the report of its findings to AF Systems Command, Andrews AFB, Washington, D.C., which will send a report to Headquarters USAF."[12]

The obvious implication is that both Ramey and the FTD were completely aware of the true nature of the Roswell material. Until they could amass all the intelligence necessary to provide the complete picture from a national security standpoint, the situation would remain fluid and the search for answers would continue. Meanwhile, total secrecy was the only means by which they retained complete control over the predicament. Startling as it would seem, after 60 years, the scenario hasn't changed much—four official explanations for Roswell notwithstanding. As were all the others who had been in Roswell at the time of the recovery, at Fort Worth when Marcel brought the material to the office of Gen. Ramey, or at Wright Field to marvel and shudder at the possibilities, Arthur Exon was convinced that the wreckage had come from something not manufactured on this Earth.

22

Deathbed Confessions
"Ohh...the Creatures!"

In courts of law, so-called deathbed confessions are accorded special weight and consideration because of the belief that when a person knows that death is pending, that person will want, in the end, to have his or her conscience cleared and leave truth as a lasting legacy. Perhaps the most significant deathbed testimony has been that of former provost marshal at the Roswell Base in 1947, Maj. Edwin Easley. When first interviewed by Roswell investigator Kevin Randle, all Easley would say was that he couldn't discuss the Roswell Incident, that he was still sworn to secrecy. Over and over, Easley would repeat that same phrase to each question that Randle asked.[1] Sometime thereafter, he in fact confirmed to his two daughters and granddaughter his participation. When he lay dying at Parkland Hospital in Dallas, Texas in June of 1992, his granddaughter brought him a gift while her mother and aunt kept vigil at their father's bedside. She held it up to her grandfather's eyes in the hopes that he would appreciate her thoughtfulness. With a look of total astonishment, he turned from the outreached arms of the young girl and sighed the words "Ohh,

Major Edwin Easley.

Photo printed with permission from the 1947 RAAF Yearbook.

the creatures!"[2] What was the gift, you ask, that brought such an intense reaction from an intrepid man who maintained his silence for 45 years? It was simply a copy of the first Randle and Schmitt book, *UFO Crash at Roswell*.[3]

Easley wasn't the only one. Just before he passed away in November of 1995, former Roswell base adjutant in 1947 Maj. Patrick Saunders wrote on numerous copies of the paperback edition of the Randle and Schmitt book *The Truth About the UFO Crash at Roswell*, which he sent to family and close friends, this cathartic statement: "This is the truth, and I still haven't told anyone!" (See Appendix III.) Months before he died he confided to other close friends that they were faced with a technology greater than ours, and that "we had no idea what *their* intentions might be."[4]

As participants in the Roswell events of 1947 expire at an ever increasing rate, it should be expected that we encounter more confessions of the "deathbed" variety as time passes, and such is indeed the case. Sarah Mounce, whose husband, Pvt. Francis "Frank" Cassidy, was an MP in the 1395th Military Police Company at Roswell in 1947, relayed to us the information that her husband, during his final days in 1976, confessed to guarding Hangar P-3 and seeing the bodies inside;[5] and another woman, Wanda Lida, told us that her husband, Cpl. Robert J. Lida, during the last remaining months of his life in 1995 finally told her of his involvement in the Roswell events of 1947. After seeing a program on TV that featured the Roswell Incident, she at last asked him, "Well, Dear, is it true?" He answered, "Well, I suppose its time I should tell you. I've been meaning to for a long time. It's true."

Cpl. Lida had been an MP with the 1395th at Roswell in 1947, and confirmed to Wanda that he was simply "grabbed" one day and told to report to Hangar #3. He was given a gun and told to stand guard at the hangar with other similarly marshaled base personnel. While on guard duty there, he waited for an opportunity to look inside the building. Lida swore to his wife that he observed wreckage scattered about inside and a number of "small bodies" being prepared for shipment elsewhere. Asked if she believed her husband when he told her this, Wanda replied without hesitation or reservation, "Absolutely! He was telling me the truth when he knew he didn't have much longer."[6]

Sgt. Homer G. Rowlette, Jr., was a member of the 603rd Air Engineering Squadron at the RAAF in 1947. He was career military and retired as an NCO after 26 years of dedicated service to his country. Before passing away in March of 1988, he finally conveyed to his son Larry the following startling information about his involvement with the "crash of the flying saucer." His father was part of a cleanup detail sent to the impact site north of Roswell. Larry was told that his father had seen everything. He had handled the "memory material," which, according to Homer, was "thin foil that kept its shape." If that wasn't enough, he described the actual ship, which was "somewhat circular." But what followed caught his son completely by surprise: "I saw three little people. They had large heads and at least one was alive!" His father ended by adding that there were *three* sites—the one just north of Roswell, and two others near Corona.[7]

Sergeant Homer Rowlette.

Photo printed with permission from the 1947 RAAF Yearbook.

According to Larry's sister Carlene Green, "My father was a very honest, honorable, and trustworthy man. He never lied to me." Her father had never mentioned his tenure at Roswell to her until just two weeks before he died. Homer was only given days to live. Carlene, who at the time knew nothing about the story her dad had secretly passed on to her brother, was nervously waiting with her father as he lay on a gurney in the hospital about to be wheeled into the operating room. Still totally lucid, he painfully motioned for her to come close so he could speak, in case he didn't have another chance, which was clearly the impression his daughter had at the time. She had no idea he would confess the following: "I was at Roswell when they recovered the spaceship in 1947. I was involved.

I saw it. It's all true." Homer told Carlene that he was sorry for never saying anything before, but he was told to "keep quiet, or else!"[8]

One of the earliest examples of a deathbed confession came from the late Sgt. Melvin E. Brown, who was with K Squadron back at the time of the incident. Brown would take the historic first manned landing on the moon in July of 1969 as an impetus to tell his family the truth about Roswell. Unfortunately for Brown, they were reluctant to believe him. Still, his wife and two daughters remembered his stern warning not to tell anyone else because, "Daddy will get into trouble."

In 1986, as Brown was on his deathbed just outside London, England, his daughter, Beverly Bean, said that her father talked about Roswell exclusively. He reiterated over and over that "it was not a damn weather balloon." Brown's wife and oldest daughter still refuse to discuss the matter. Beverly Bean, however, wanted everyone to know what her father had told her with his own dying words:

> It was approaching dusk when one other soldier and I were stationed in one of the ambulance trucks at the recovery site. Everything was being loaded onto trucks, and I couldn't understand why some of the trucks had ice or something in them. I did not understand what they wanted to keep cold. Our orders were not to look under the canvas tarp in the back. The moment we had a chance, I pulled back the covering. There were bodies...small bodies...and they had big heads and slanted eyes.

His family still fears government reprisal should they say too much.[9]

But Brown was not the only one to report bodies at the crash site. Capt. Darwin E. Rasmussen, the 718th Bomb Group operations officer (part of the 509th), told family members just before dying that the Roswell Incident was true, and that four bodies had been recovered. Elaine Vegh, Rasmussen's cousin, told us that she had personally heard the officer tell her father that he had no doubt that flying saucers were real because he'd helped to retrieve the bodies from the one that crashed at Roswell.[10]

After the *Unsolved Mysteries* broadcast of September 1989, a former cancer ward nurse from the St. Petersburg Hospital in Florida came forward to describe the final testimony she personally heard from one of her elderly patients. The nurse was Mary Ann Gardner, who worked at the hospital from 1976 to 1977. The patient, a woman (Gardner couldn't remember her name), had been alone in the hospital. Feeling concern for her because she had no visitors, Gardner spent as much time as she could listening to the woman's stories—especially the one about the crashed ship and the "little men" she had seen.

According to Gardner, "Basically...they had stumbled upon a space-ship of some kind and...there were bodies on the ground...little people with large heads and large eyes. Then the army showed up...and chased them away...the army people were everywhere and...told them that if they ever told anything about it, that the government could always find them."

The dying woman explained that she had been with a team of archaeologists and was not supposed to be there. The team had been "hunting rocks and looking for fossils...she had gone along with a friend." Gardner said the women was still frightened about official retaliation and soon had nothing more to say about the incident. "The woman kept looking around as if she was frightened about something and said to me, 'They said that they could always find us, so I'd better not say anymore.'" Gardner then asked her, "Who? Who can find you?" The woman then answered in a low, wary voice, "the government." Within days, she expired.[11]

From all eyewitness accounts, the Roswell incident left a devastating impact on the Chaves County Sheriff, George Wilcox. Just before his widow Inez passed away, she related a story to her granddaughter Barbara, who told us, "She said that the event shocked him. He never wanted to be sheriff again after that. My grandmother said, 'Don't tell anybody. When the incident happened, the military police came to the jailhouse and told George and I that if we ever told anything about the incident, not only would we be killed, but our entire family would be killed!'" Barbara added:

> They called my grandfather, and someone came and told
> him about this incident. He went out there to the site;
> there was a big burned area and he saw debris. It was in

the evening. There were four 'space beings.' Their heads were large. They wore suits like silk. One of the 'little men' was alive. If she said it happened, it happened! My grandmother was a very loyal citizen of the United States, and she thought it was in the best interest of the country not to talk about it.

Inez Wilcox expired shortly thereafter at the age of 93.[12]

William Kramer is a retired, former Air Force brigadier general and FBI agent who lives in Las Cruces, N.M. In two separate telephone interviews conducted 10 years apart, in 1996 and 2006, Kramer told us about a deathbed confession given to him in the early 1990s by a family friend by the name of Joseph Shoals. Kramer would not reveal Shoals' name during the first interview in 1996 because this was a deathbed confession, and he didn't want to jeopardize Shoals' pension for his surviving wife. By 2006, Shoals' wife had also passed away, and Kramer was free to talk. According to him, Shoals had been in the Army at Fort Bliss in El Paso, Texas. In July 1947, Shoals was in the TDY Barracks with a number of other soldiers who were awaiting orders to be shipped out for permanent assignment to another base. Soldiers in such circumstances were normally given menial tasks, such as "policing up the area," to keep them busy until their orders came through. According to Shoals, an NCO came into the barracks one day and simply said, "You, you, you, and you! Come with me!" Shoals was among those in the group of about 20 soldiers who were chosen that day. The group was marched to two waiting troop trucks, which they boarded and then headed out. According to Kramer, Shoals told him that they were driven north into the desert near Corona, and told to "pick up chaff" that crews who had been there before them might have missed. "Bill, we literally walked arm-in-arm, in lock-step, across the pasture picking up anything that looked foreign. We spent two hot and nasty days out there, and when we were done, there wasn't enough stuff found to put in a wheelbarrow. I didn't find anything. When we got back to Fort Bliss, we were told that if anyone ever asked, we were never there." According to Kramer, Shoals later went on to a distinguished military career that included helping to develop the Patriot missile.

Meyers Wahnee was a full-blooded, Comanche Indian who had pi-loted B-24 "Liberator" bombers during WWII. Fondly known as "Chief" by his crewmates, Wahnee was a top-tier security officer by 1947. In July of that year, Capt. Wahnee was ordered from Fort Simmons in Colorado to Roswell Field in New Mexico to oversee the transport of a "Top Secret item" from Roswell to Fort Worth via a special B-29 flight. The item in question was a single, large, wooden crate that Wahnee was to accom-pany in the bomb bay for the duration of the flight to Forth Worth. Appar-ently motivated by a featured segment about the Roswell Incident in 1980 on the popular TV show *In Search Of*, Wahnee finally broke his silence on the matter with his family during the final year of his life. According to his daughter Blanche, in a 2005 telephone interview with our investigation, her father told them:

1. The Roswell Incident was true.
2. He had flown with the alien bodies from Roswell, N.M. to Fort Worth, Texas (see Chapter 16).
3. There were three sites.

On his deathbed, according to Blanche Wahnee, her father gave his family one final caveat: "Whatever you do, don't believe the government. It really happened."[13]

In 2001, Dr. Roger Lier, the noted "alien implant" physician, informed us of a Roswell witness that he and "Alien Hunter" Derrel Simms had been researching. They had been talking to the witness's surviving sons, but the case was requiring much more time to research—time they did not have. Dr. Lier provided us with their investigative file to continue the investiga-tion. We quickly proceeded to interview four of Marion "Black Mac" Magruder's five sons: Mark, Merritt, Mike, and Marion, Jr., who told us about their father's unexpected brush with the Roswell Incident. Honor-ing his security oath, he had kept it from them until he felt it was safe to tell—when he felt that it was no longer a secret—"after he saw all of the books and TV shows about Roswell in the 1980s and 1990s."

The summer of 1947 found Lt. Col. Marion M. Magruder in class at the Air War College at Maxwell Field in Montgomery, Ala. The class was filled with officers whose ranks ranged from general all the way down to lieutenant colonel, which was the lowest rank permitted. The officers cho-sen for the class were deemed to represent the "best and brightest" in their respective branches of the military, as well as future leaders heading into the post-war era. Magruder's class at the Air War College was scheduled to last approximately one year, from July 1947 to June 1948, when the officers would receive advanced training in military history, decision-making, and geo-political strategy.

The Air War College class had just commenced in mid-to-late July 1947 when they were all flown up to Wright Field in Dayton, Ohio. Their "opinion" was desired on a matter of utmost urgency and importance. Not knowing what to expect, the curious officers were led into a room where they were told about the recovery to Wright Field of an extraterrestrial spaceship that had crashed just two weeks previously near the town of Roswell, N.M. Most of the officers had not been aware of the crash and were startled when some of the wreckage was brought out for them to examine. The real shocker, however, was yet to come. After

The Air War College class of 1947–1948; Black Mac Magruder stands in the exact center of the front row.

Photo printed with permission from Mark Magruder.

everyone had a chance to examine and handle the wreckage, they were taken into another room. There, they were shown something that would haunt Marion Magruder for the rest of his life.

While lying on his deathbed 50 years later, Black Mac recalled again his brief encounter with the live alien he witnessed only that once at Wright

Field with his Air War College class. The class had been told that it was a survivor from the Roswell crash. Magruder's son, Mike, had heard the story before, but this telling was meant for his granddaughter, who was there with her father. He told her that the "creature" was under 5 feet tall, "human-like" but with longer arms, larger eyes, and an oversized, hairless head for its small frame. Its other features, as described by Magruder, were similar to the descriptions of others over the years who have claimed to have seen the Roswell aliens: a slit for a mouth, no nose—just two small orifices—and no ears; again, just two small orifices. In his mind, Magruder emphasized the human-like qualities of the small, child-like creature, but he told his granddaughter that there was no question that it "came from another planet." Unknown to Magruder, even on his death-bed where he passed away on his 86th birthday in 1997, were the general terms used to describe the Roswell aliens by two military officers who had seen them two weeks before Magruder: Capt. Oliver "Pappy" Henderson, the pilot who had flown the first set of Roswell aliens—including the one that was alive—to Wright Field on July 8, described their appearance as reminding him of the cartoon character "Casper the Ghost"; Maj. Jesse Marcel, the Roswell base intelligence officer who was dispatched to the

Black Mac Magruder, in the cockpit of his Grumman F6F Hellcat during WWII.

Photo printed with permission from Mark Magruder.

crash site on July 6, told a subordinate that they had the appearance of, "white, rubbery figures." Magruder used the term "squiggly" to describe the living specimen he saw at Wright Field. It would not be too much of a stretch to suggest that all three men were using their own terms to describe the same thing. According to Mike Magruder, his father later learned that the military had been conducting experiments on the alien he saw, but it later died. "It was alive, but we killed it," he said. Magruder had no way of knowing that Roswell photographer Jack Rodden, Sr., told his son the very same thing.

CIC officer Sheridan Cavitt played a major role in the entire Roswell affair. As the head of counterintelligence at Roswell he would have been privy to most every aspect of the historic event—not that he ever admitted much to investigators. Still, his lasting legacy will be that he became the lone, star witness for the Air Force Project Mogul Report. Ironically, his testimony to us and to the Air Force is a huge contradiction; from not being at Roswell at the time of the incident, to being there but saying that nothing out of the ordinary took place, to going out to the ranch—not with Maj. Marcel, but rather with M.Sgt. Rickett?—and finding absolutely nothing, to finally going out with Marcel and recovering—you guessed it—a Mogul balloon.[14] On one occasion, his wife apologized to us when he wasn't in the room: "You have to understand," she said, "my husband is sworn to secrecy and can't tell you anything."[15] But that didn't stop us from trying. In fact, when Cavitt was terminally ill and given a very short time to live, we discussed a plan with his son Joe, an attorney, to get his father to write out a sealed statement, which could be released posthumously. Frustrated, Joe informed us each time he broached the topic with his father, and the answer was always that "he was not ready."

Unfortunately, the intelligence officer was *never* ready and quietly passed away with no awards or special proclamations from the president, the CIA, the NSA, or the DOD for preserving one of America's greatest secrets. Sheridan Cavitt remains a testimony to the fact that when you know too much, you forfeit your very freedom. As his son Joe said, "It was like having a father who lived in a bubble. You literally had only half a father."[16] Apparently, the government had the nonnegotiable half. This couldn't have been more evident than what was described to us by his attending physician just days before he died. "He sat next to his bed [in the hospital] with a room full of immediate family who were reminiscing and exchanging personal stories. But not Mr. Cavitt. He just sat there not saying a word. It was though he was afraid that he would say something."[17]

Such is the control, fear, and intimidation held over these individuals, in some cases for up to 60 years. What would seriously compel them to withhold a story of this magnitude from even their immediate families? And then at the most poignant moment just prior to their death, finally break the silence and reveal what obviously weighed on them relentlessly for so many years? It is perplexing for those of us in these modern, cynical times, when the government is often held in contempt. But not for those in the "greatest generation"—no, their actions regarding Roswell over the past six decades only solidifies that title. They knew how to keep their secrets. Call it devotion to duty, post-WWII patriotism, or just being a good soldier who respected the military code of honor.

Are we then to believe that any of the aforementioned examples were the results of mere weather balloons and wooden crash dummies? It is with a great sense of bewilderment that we ask, why do all of these witnesses— to the supposed mundane—clearly have an obsession with "small bodies?" Should we be shocked that nary a one has ever suggested they were made of wood, as the military would want us to believe? Are we to conclude that they are all lying—deceiving their loved ones at the end of their lives? To the surviving families, it remains a feeble, futile exercise at best. And for those few whose true love of family would inevitably outweigh love of country—though it may have taken a lifetime of denial—we strongly maintain that their dying words meet all the criteria for reasonable doubt.

23

A Voice From the Grave
The Sealed Statement of
First Lieutenant Walter G. Haut

It is debatable whether a deathbed confession carries more weight than a signed testament. Legally, the latter is much more binding, in that it is a lawfully signed and witnessed document intended as a final statement. The individual is ensuring the transfer of personal possessions, or in the case of controversial or secret information, the creation of a sacred trust with particular beneficiaries to place in their custody private material to ensure that their final wishes are carried out. In most situations, immediate families serve as custodians, until after the testament author's death, the property held in confidence to facilitate his or her last desires. In this chapter, we will reveal 1st Lt. Walter G. Haut's signed testament about his experience in Roswell in 1947.

During WWII, Haut was a B-29 bombardier on 20 bombing raids over Japan.

First Lieutenant Walter G. Haut.

Photo printed with permission from the U.S. Air Force.

Haut received numerous medals, including the Purple Heart, and in the summer of 1946, he was assigned with dropping the measuring instruments during Operation Crossroads' atomic tests at Bikini Atoll in the South Pacific. It is therefore fascinating that what Haut is most famous for was that as the public relations officer for the 509th Bomb Group at the RAAF, he released to the media one of the most famous press releases of all time. And for the next 55 years that's about *all* he would admit about his involvement. Finally, in November of 2002 Walter Haut declared his intentions regarding specific information he possessed about the Roswell Incident of 1947.

To say that the revelations were illuminating to his surviving family would be an understatement. Truly, they were shocked. In an atmosphere of ridicule and rejection of Roswell testimony from other witnesses, Walter Haut had chosen instead to eternally preserve his story as a solemn vow. But it was a vow that involved someone outside his immediate family.

We had the pleasure of meeting Walter Haut the very last day of our initial visit to Roswell in February, 1989. This was our anticipated one trip to New Mexico, where we fully expected to solve the entire mystery in a single investigative jaunt. We confidently set out to confirm the weather balloon explanation—or something just as earthly. But after having met with Mack Brazel's son Bill and his wife Shirley, then with Walter Haut and his wife "Pete," we seriously started to consider that we may have been wrong. Little did we realize at the time just how wrong.

Haut's story was at that time, as it remained for the next 15 years, that he received orders from his boss, Col. Blanchard, to put out a press release. He typed it up and distributed the announcement to the local media. End of his involvement. However, what shined through all of our remaining

Walter Haut.

Photo courtesy of Tom Carey, 2004.

questions about the RAAF's supposed blunder over making such an out-landish claim, was the deep and loyal friendship Haut had with the colo-nel up until his death. In fact, Haut fondly spoke of him as though he were a "close uncle." A look of admiration and respect would come over his face whenever he referred to Col. Blanchard—as he affectionately called him, "the old man."

Certainly, it was not at all uncommon for a high-ranking military man such as Blanchard to take a young officer under his wing and lead him up the ladder. But who was "Butch" Blanchard to Walter Haut? What place does he have in American history? And was he as incompetent as Roswell skeptics would want us to believe? As one of the Air Force debunkers said, attempting to denigrate Blanchard's character and reputation, "Blanchard was a loose cannon!"[1]

Blanchard graduated from West Point in 1938. From that moment on he was placed on a fast track for promotion, and by the end of WWII was perceived as a role model for the future of the Army Air Forces. As the deputy commander of the 58th Bomb Wing, he flew the very first B-29 into China to establish strategic bombing operations in the Japanese is-lands in 1944. As preparations for a full-scale invasion of Japan commenced, Blanchard was next assigned as commander of the 40th Bomb Group, B-29 squadron, and subsequently as the operations officer of the 21st Bomber Command. This is where he and Gen. Curtis Lemay prepared and super-vised plans for the first atomic bomb to be dropped on Hiroshima. With orders for a second bomb, Blanchard was originally assigned to pilot the flight over Nagasaki. Col. Charles Sweeny would command the B-29 "Bock's Car" in his place. With the surrender of Japan, he was Gen. Roger Ramey's right-hand man in 1946 as the CO of the 509th Atomic Bomb Group in Operation Crossroads. One of the officers he oversaw was Walter Haut, with whom he quickly became good friends.

After his tenure at Roswell, Blanchard was assigned to the Strategic Air Command, Eighth Air Force Headquarters as director of operations in 1948. From there he was in charge of the atomic training of B-36 crews, our first intercontinental bombers. After commanding B-50 and B-36 bomber units of SAC, he was made deputy director of operations for that unit in 1953. Next, he would become inspector general for the Air Force, then deputy chief of staff for programs and requirements at AF headquar-ters in Washington, which led him to AF planning and operations. He would also become a senior AF member of the Military Staff Committee of the United Nations. And lastly, he was vice chief of staff of the USAF and certain for the Joint Chiefs. By that time he had reached four stars, but sadly died at his desk at the Pentagon in 1966 from a heart attack. Gen. William Blanchard, who couldn't identify a common weather balloon at Roswell in 1947 achieved all of this and more by the age of 50!

Is it any wonder that Haut had the utmost esteem for and confidence in his military boss as the ultimate role model? In fact, there is little doubt that Haut could have followed him all the way to the rank of general. Such was the personal bond between these two men. When "the old man" needed someone to drive his wife and kids back home to Chicago, Haut was his man. When the base commander was touring some Washington dignitary around the base, Haut was always at his side (while Ramey followed from behind). And when Blanchard suddenly died, Haut didn't read about it in the paper, and he didn't get a phone call from some military underling. A special emissary arrived in Roswell from Washington and went to Haut's home with the somber news. This was normally a courtesy afforded only immediate family. And to Blanchard, that is exactly what Haut was.

We have explained the close association of these two men in order to address this continuing argument: Walter Haut basically kept silent for more than 50 years; why profess any hidden truths for posthumous disclosure? Why withhold any details about such an important story? Why not write a book? Why not at least profit your family? After all, isn't it human nature for one to have milked this account for all it was worth? The more simple answer as to why he never spoke to a fuller extent about Roswell was because *he promised Butch that he would not.* To Haut, it was a matter of his word to the most trusted friend and commander he had in his life. It was his lifelong testimonial as well as an indication of just how highly he regarded his former commanding officer. True, national security, protection of loved ones, and secrecy oaths may have played into his decision. But more importantly, Blanchard had asked him not to.

There were always subtle hints in Haut's life that he was withholding secret information or protecting someone in particular. For example, he would receive many Christmas cards from the former head of CIC at Fort Worth, Milton Knight. We were puzzled by his longtime acquaintance with an individual completely out of his regular circle of military associates. But one card especially caught our eyes: It included a note that read, "I still say that there were no bodies at Fort Worth." The inference was quite obvious. Unfortunately, Walter couldn't elaborate any further as to what had set off the debate. From our first meeting it was clear that all of his experience in dealing with the press made him quite proficient at playing dodge ball.

Instead, Mr. Haut preferred to play it safe by remaining on the periphery. He was always happy to pass on limited information to us about others who were involved, maybe to temporarily avoid renewed focus on himself. Our position has always remained simple: Col. Blanchard, who was the base commander and who would have been privy to every aspect of the case + Walter Haut, his most trusted ally and friend = Walter Haut must possess a great deal more information than he's admitting to us.[2] But he had made a promise. Albeit reluctantly, we couldn't help but admire the man's loyalty.

Ironically, it was inevitable that Walter Haut would become the greatest champion of all the believers in Roswell. His testimony was always consistent as to the limited capacity of his participation. But at the end of each public appearance or media interview he would always hit it out of the park with his closing remarks: "It wasn't any type of weather balloon," he would say. "I believe it was a UFO! Just don't ask me why."[3] But being the intrepid investigators we are, we persisted. After all, Haut had given us the final solution to the longstanding mystery—he told us that he believed it *was* a UFO. How did he come to accept that? What did he really know?

The IUFOM&RC in downtown Roswell.

Photo courtesy of Tom Carey, 1998.

Of our close to 100 research trips to New Mexico before he died, Haut was almost always included in our rushed schedule. But beyond our fading hope that he would someday take us into his confidence, mainly, he was our friend, and he was Roswell's greatest ambassador. Not that he ever claimed the Roswell Incident really happened. In many regards he was standing up for all his military comrades long passed and forever silent. He also remained one of our last connections to one of the most important events in history. We just had to come up with a respectable device that would enable him to preserve the truth—without breaking his word to his departed friend.

After Haut founded the world-famous International UFO Museum & Research Center in his chosen home of Roswell, we believe that somehow, deep down, he was doing what the old man would have wanted him to do. He was still keeping his word; he was not breaking any promise. He provided a public repository for information related to the event. But more importantly, he established a facility for the preservation of the Roswell Incident as a historic event. Such may have been the reasoning for others such as Maj. Patrick Saunders just before he passed away—let others discover the facts, and when the time is appropriate you write in their book, "Here's the truth and I still haven't told anybody anything." They are free to leave us with a clear conscience.

We would like to truly believe that this was the opportunity we presented to Haut. By preparing a sealed statement to be released after his death, his true legacy pertaining to Roswell is now as complete as it can ever be. The verisimilitude known as the Roswell Incident has become all the clearer thanks to Walter Haut. And through his emotional evolution we would like to believe that he could look his old friend in the eye and say, "As long as I lived, I kept my word."

But as we should all profess, the truth is the truth, and the facts are the facts. And no government, no organization, and no one individual, whether advocate or debunker, has been given jurisdiction over defining what we are to accept as reality—a concept that would allow for those rare occasions when secrets do come from the grave.

Thank you for all the Christmas cards, Walter.

The following is the sealed affidavit of 1st. Lt. Walter G. Haut. It is presented here for the reader's consideration with the permission of his surviving family, unedited and without notes or editorial comment. It is provided for posthumous release for the sole purpose of being placed in the historic record by Mr. Haut, as was his final request with the sincerest of motives. Any assertions to the contrary are without merit. No reproduction of this statement can be granted without written request for permission from his surviving family.

SEALED AFFIDAVIT OF
WALTER G. HAUT

DATE: December 26, 2002

WITNESS: Chris Xxxxx

NOTARY: Beverlee Morgan

(1) My name is Walter G. Haut.

(2) I was born on June 2, 1922.

(3) My address is 1405 W. 7th Street, Roswell, NM 88203

(4) I am retired.

(5) In July, 1947, I was stationed at the Roswell Army Air Base in Roswell, New Mexico, serving as the base Public Information Officer. I had spent the 4th of July weekend (Saturday, the 5th, and Sunday, the 6th) at my private residence about 10 miles north of the base, which was located south of town.

(6) I was aware that someone had reported the remains of a downed vehicle by midmorning after my return to duty at the base on Monday, July 7. I was aware that Major Jesse A. Marcel, head of intelligence, was sent by the base commander, Col. William Blanchard, to investigate.

(7) By late in the afternoon that same day, I would learn that additional civilian reports came in regarding a second site just north of Roswell. I would spend the better part of the day attending to my regular duties hearing little if anything more.

(8) On Tuesday morning, July 8, I would attend the regularly scheduled staff meeting at 7:30 a.m. Besides Blanchard, Marcel; CIC Capt. Sheridan Cavitt; Col. James I. Hopkins, the operations officer; Major Patrick Saunders, the base adjutant; Major Isadore Brown, the personnel officer; Lt. Col. Ulysses S. Nero, the supply officer; and from Carswell AAF in Fort Worth, Texas, Blanchard's boss, Brig. Gen. Roger Ramey and his chief of staff, Col. Thomas J. DuBose were also in attendance. The

main topic of discussion was reported by Marcel and Cavitt regarding an extensive debris field in Lincoln County approx. 75 miles NW of Roswell. A preliminary briefing was provided by Blanchard about the second site approx. 40 miles north of town. Samples of wreckage were passed around the table. It was unlike any material I had or have ever seen in my life. Pieces, which resembled metal foil, paper thin yet extremely strong, and pieces with unusual markings along their length were handled from man to man, each voicing their opinion. No one was able to identify the crash debris.

(9)   One of the main concerns discussed at the meeting was whether we should go public or not with the discovery. Gen. Ramey proposed a plan, which I believe originated with his bosses at the Pentagon. Attention needed to be diverted from the more important site north of town by acknowledging the other location. Too many civilians were already involved and the press already was informed. I was not completely informed how this would be accomplished.

(10) At approximately 9:30 a.m. Col. Blanchard phoned my office and dictated the press release of having in our possession a flying disc, coming from a ranch northwest of Roswell, and Marcel flying the material to higher headquarters. I was to deliver the news release to radio stations KGFL and KSWS, and newspapers the *Daily Record* and the *Morning Dispatch*.

(11) By the time the news had hit the wire services, my office was inundated with phone calls from around the world. Messages stacked up on my desk, and rather than deal with the media concern, Col. Blanchard suggested that I go home and "hide out."

(12) Before leaving the base, Col. Blanchard took me personally to Building 84, a B-29 hangar located on the east side of the tarmac. Upon first approaching the building, I observed that it was under heavy guard both outside and inside. Once inside, I was permitted from a safe distance to first observe the object just recovered north of town. It was approx. 12 to 15 feet in length, not quite as wide, about 6 feet high, and more of an egg shape. Lighting was poor, but its surface did appear metallic. No windows, portholes, wings, tail section, or landing gear were visible.

(13) Also from a distance, I was able to see a couple of bodies under a canvas tarpaulin. Only the heads extended beyond the covering, and I was not able to make out any features. The heads did appear larger than normal and the contour of the canvas over the bodies suggested the size of a 10-year-old child. At a later date in Blanchard's office, he would extend his arm about 4 feet above the floor to indicate the height.

(14) I was informed of a temporary morgue set up to accommodate the recovered bodies.

(15) I was informed that the wreckage was not "hot" [radioactive].

(16) Upon his return from Fort Worth, Major Marcel described to me taking pieces of the wreckage to Gen. Ramey's office and after returning from a map room, finding the remains of a weather balloon and radar kite substituted while he was out of the room. Marcel was very upset over this situation. We would not discuss it again.

(17) I would be allowed to make at least one visit to one of the recovery sites during the military cleanup. I would return to the base with some of the wreckage which I would display in my office.

(18) I was aware two separate teams would return to each site months later for periodic searches for any remaining evidence.

(19) I am convinced that what I personally observed was some type of craft and its crew from outer space.

(20) I have not been paid nor given anything of value to make this statement, and it is the truth to the best of my recollection.

THIS STATEMENT IS TO REMAIN SEALED AND SECURED UNTIL THE TIME OF MY DEATH, AT WHICH TIME MY SURVIVING FAMILY WILL DETERMINE ITS DISPOSITION.

Signed: Walter G. Haut
Signature Witnessed by: Chris Xxxxxx
Dated: December 26, 2002

Afterword

Our investigation into the true nature of the events surrounding the apparent visitation of the planet Earth by extraterrestrial entities in 1947 continues apace. This volume has attempted to present to the reader, not a complete overview of the Roswell case or even our own investigation of it, but snapshots of some of the seminal events as they happened at the time, on a more personal level to the individuals involved. We hope that readers will appreciate the approach we have taken in this volume. The facts presented herein are as they have been described to us or as determined by our decades-encompassing investigation. The interpretations accorded these facts are solely those of the authors.

The authors may be contacted through the offices of the International UFO Museum & Research Center at:

114 North Main St.
Roswell, NM 88201
(800) 822-3545 or (505) 625-9495 [P]
(505) 625-1907 [F]
director@iufomrc.com

or directly at:

(267) 722-8121 [P]
(267) 722-8121 [F]
tcarey1947@aol.com
schmittdon47@aol.com
www.roswellinvestigator.com

Appendix I
Schematic Map of New Mexico

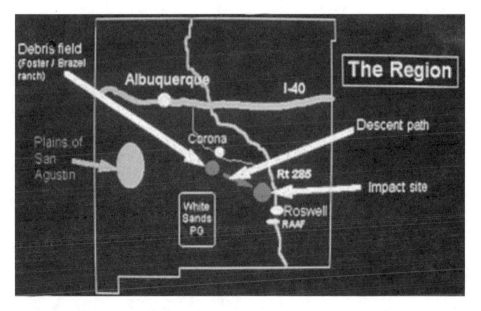

A schematic map of New Mexico showing the various crash locations, the Plains of San Agustin, White Sands Missile Range, Corona, Roswell, the RAAF, Albuquerque, and Santa Fe.

Photo printed with permission from John Kirby.

Appendix II
Crash Site Stone Marker

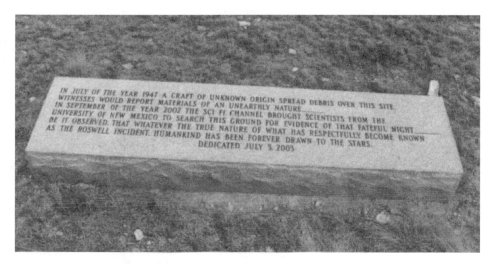

Image of the historical stone marker commissioned by the Sci Fi Channel, dedicated at the debris field site in 2003.

Photo courtesy of Tom Carey.

─────Appendix III─────
The Confession of Major Patrick Saunders

Shortly before his death in 1995, the former RAAF base adjutant in 1947, Maj. Patrick H. Saunders, purchased a number of copies of the then newly released paperback edition of *The Truth About the UFO Crash at Roswell* by Kevin Randle and Don Schmitt. Saunders then sent copies of the book around to close friends and family with a hand-written note on the flyleaf, as shown on the following page.

For years, we assumed that Saunders had written the note on that page out of convenience because it was the first page in the book. Years later, after the book's key witness, Frank Kaufmann, was shown to have been a fabricator of documents and therefore impeached as a reliable witness to the 1947 Roswell events, Randle and Carey independently reread the Saunders note, especially the passage it was atop, and came to the same epiphany—that the "truth" Saunders was referring to was *not* the entire book, but only the passage just under his hand-written note. In a January 2007 e-mail to Carey, Randle shared his revelation:

Major Patrick Saunders.

Photo printed with permission from the 1947 RAAF Yearbook

He [Saunders] didn't need to cram his words at the top of this page unless there was important information on it. Saunders confirmed, from his point of view, that this was the truth. He might not have agreed with everything in the book, but he did with this specific page....In a 1997 letter to me, one of Saunders' children wrote, "At one point, he bragged to me about how well he had covered the 'paper trail' associated with the clean-up!"....I skipped over this when I read the letter 10 years ago. When I saw it this time, it sent chills down my spine. Here for the first time was information that suggested a cover-up in place in Roswell...beyond what we can deduce from what others have said.

Here's the truth and I still haven't told anybody anything!

DAMAGE CONTROL

Files were altered. So were personal records, along with assignments and various codings and code words. Changing serial numbers ensured that those searching later would not be able to locate those who were involved in the recovery. Individuals were brought into Roswell from Alamogordo, Albuquerque, and Los Alamos. The MPs were a special unit constructed of military police elements from Kirtland, Alamogordo, and Roswell. If the men didn't know one another, or were separated after the event, they would be unable to compare notes, and that would make the secret easier to keep.

After the impact site was cleaned, the soldiers debriefed, and the bodies and the craft removed, silence fell. It would not be broken for almost forty-five years.

Page from *The Truth About the UFO Crash at Roswell*, by Kevin D. Randle and Donald R. Schmitt. New York: Avon Books, 1994. Image of Saunders' note courtesy of Kevin Randle.

Notes

Chapter 1

1. The term "Roswell Incident," used most often to describe the alleged crash, recovery, and cover-up of a UFO and its crew near the town of Roswell, N.M. in 1947, is derived from the title of first book ever published on the subject, *The Roswell Incident* by Charles Berlitz and William L. Moore, Grosset & Dunlap: New York [1980].

2. United States General Accounting Office, *Results of a Search for Records Concerning the 1947 Crash Near Roswell, New Mexico,* Pub. No. GAO/NSIAD-95-187, Washington, DC: GAO, July 1995.

3. The Air Force's *Project Mogul* balloon hypothesis is articulated in detail in its massive publication, *The Roswell Report: Fact versus Fiction in the New Mexico Desert*, by Richard Weaver, Washington, D.C.: U.S. Government Printing Office, 1995 (a 23-page Executive Summary was published in 1994); its time compression/dummies-from-the-sky hypothesis can be found in *The Roswell Report: Case Closed* by James McAndrew, Washington, D.C.: U.S. Government Printing Office/Barnes & Noble, Inc., 1997.

4. Broad, William J. "Wreckage of a 'Spaceship': Of This Earth (and U.S.)." *The New York Times*, page 1, 9/18/1994.

Chapter 2

1. Bullard, Thomas E. "Folklore Scholarship and UFO Reality." *International UFO Reporter* (IUR), Sept./Oct. 1988.

2. *The UFO Phenomenon—Seeing is Believing*, ABC—Feb. 24, 2005.

3. News release, U.S. Congressman Steven Schiff, July 28, 1995.

4. Personal letter to researcher Kent Jeffrey from Barry Goldwater, July 26, 1994.

Chapter 3

1. Bill Brazel, personal interviews, 1989–2003.

2. Loretta Proctor, personal interviews, 1989–1990, 1994–1995.

3. Sydney Wright, personal interview, 1998.

4. Hope Baldra, personal interview, 1998.

5. Budd Eppers, personal interview, 1999.

6. Truman Pierce, personal interview, 1999.

7. Glaze Sacra, personal interview, 1999.

8. Danny Boswell, personal interviews, 1999–2000.

9. Shirley Brazel, personal interview, 1990.

10. Bill Brazel, personal interviews, 1989–2003.

11. Ibid.

12. Charlie Schmid, personal interviews, 1991, 1993.

13. Paul Price, personal interview, 2006.

14. Robert Smith, personal interview, 1992.

15. Trini Chavez, personal interview, 2005.

16. Loretta Proctor, personal interview, 1994.

17. Budd Payne, personal interviews, 1990–1991.

18. Fawn Fritz, personal interviews, 2005–2006.

19. Jeff Wells, personal interviews, 1989–1990.

20. Robert Smith, personal interview, 1992.

21. L.D. Sparks, personal interview, 2000.

22. Jack Rodden, personal interview, 1990.

23. Leroy Lang, personal interview, 1998.

24. Hope Baldra, personal interview, 1998.

Chapter 4

1. Berlitz, Charles, and William L. Moore. *The Roswell Incident*. New York: Grosset & Dunlap, 1980.

2. In-person interviews conducted over the years with Mack Brazel's son, Bill Brazel, his daughter Bessie Brazel Schreiber, and his granddaughter Fawn Fritz.

3. Frank Joyce, personal interview, May 1998.

4. Jud Roberts, personal interviews, 1991, 1993.

5. Frank Joyce, personal interviews, 1989–2006. According to Joyce, the very next morning after the weather balloon press conference in Ft. Worth, MPs arrived at KGFL and went through every room, every desk drawer, searching for any reference contrary to the balloon explanation.

6. Gen. Michael Rexrold, personal interviews, 1990–1991. In 1947, Rexrold was the personal assistant to Senator Dennis Chavez. Rexrold told us that the senator never mentioned the Roswell Incident to him, but did make an unscheduled trip back to New Mexico after the holiday weekend.

7. Lydia Sleppy, personal interview, 1991.

8. Merle Tucker, personal interview, 1989. According to Tucker, he knew that Johnny McBoyle had tried to get out to the site just north of town and that he had been intercepted by the military. Once McBoyle returned to Roswell, the sheriff went to see him and warned him not to ever talk about it again. Tucker had no contact with either of the New Mexican senators or anyone else. He did hear that someone "official" had gone into his Roswell station and cleaned out all the paper about the event.

9. Lydia Sleppy, personal interview, 1991.

10. John McBoyle, telephone interview, 1990.

11. Frank Joyce, personal interviews, 1989–2006.

Chapter 5

1. Robin Adair, personal interview, 1993.

2. Ibid.

3. Ibid.

4. *Roswell Daily Record*

5. Ibid.

6. Ibid.

7. Randle and Schmitt, *UFO Crash at Roswell*.

Chapter 6

1. *Roswell*, Showtime/Viacom, 1994.
2. Jud Roberts, personal interview, 1991.
3. "Harassed Rancher Who Located 'Saucer' Sorry He Told About It," *Roswell Daily Record*, July 9, 1947.
4. Bill Brazel, personal interviews, 1989–2003.
5. Joe Brazel, personal interview, 2004.
6. Ibid.
7. Bill Brazel, personal interviews, 1989–2003.
8. Shirley Brazel, personal interviews, 1989–1991.
9. Bessie Brazel Schreiber, personal interviews, 1990–1991, 2000–2001.
10. Bill Brazel, personal interviews, 1989–2003.
11. Frank Joyce, personal interviews, 1989–2006.
12. Ernest Lueras, personal interview, 2000.
13. Fawn Fritz, personal interviews, 2005–2006.
14. Emerson Armstrong, personal interview, 1995. It was discovered that Armstrong was in charge of UFO investigations for the southwestern part of the United States out of Fort Bliss in El Paso, Texas in 1949. Even after providing him with documentation to that effect, he denied it was him and claimed he never heard of the Roswell Incident.
15. Bobby Wade, personal interviews, 1998, 2000.
16. Fawn Fritz, personal interviews, 2005–2006.
17. Howard Scoggin, telephone interview, 1999.
18. Bob Wolf, personal interviews, 1992, 1999.
19. Fawn Fritz, personal interviews, 2005–2006.

Chapter 7

1. Jesse Marcel Sr., transcript of personal interview conducted by Bob Pratt, Dec. 1979.
2. Robert Slusher, personal interviews, 1991, 2002.
3. Jesse Marcel Jr., personal interview, 1991.
4. Jesse Marcel Sr., transcript of personal interview conducted by Bob Pratt, Dec. 1979.
5. Lewis Rickett, personal interviews, 1991–1992.

6. Mary Cavitt, personal interview, 1991.

7. Ibid.

8. Herschel Grice, telephone interview, 2002.

9. Jesse Marcel Sr., transcript of personal interview conducted by Bob Pratt, Dec. 1979.

Chapter 8

1. We believe that the lack of a paper trail in the public record for Montoya's whereabouts on that day was done deliberately for political reasons to keep his name from being associated with the Roswell Incident, as well as for convenience in order to prevent the inundation of phone calls to his office that would surely follow.

2. There have been a number of witnesses who have testified that "one was alive." Alpha Edwards told our investigation in 1999 that her father had been a civilian working in the hangar area of the base when the "little men" arrived. He told her that "Everybody was running around, and a group of men carried one of them right past me and into the hangar. At first, I thought it was a small child because of its size. Then, after getting a quick look at it, I realized from the size and shape of its head and eyes that it wasn't from 'around here,' that it wasn't human. It was alive but appeared to be injured. I kept wondering why, if it was injured, they weren't taking it over to the hospital." This anecdotal account tracks with Joseph Montoya's claim of seeing one that was alive but injured inside the hangar lying on a table brought over from the mess hall.

3. Pete and Mary Anaya, personal interview, September 2002.

4. Headquartered at Wright-Patterson Air Force Base in Dayton, Ohio, Project Blue Book was the Air Force's official investigative unit for reports of UFOs. It was in existence from 1951 to 1969, during which it investigated in excess of 12,000 reported UFO cases, of which slightly more than 700 of these were designated as "unknown." Project Blue Book was shut down in 1969 at the conclusion of a three-year study of the UFO phenomenon by the University of Colorado. The Air Force no longer "officially" investigates UFOs.

Chapter 9

1. Thomas J. DuBose, personal interview, 1991.

2. Ibid.

3. Weisgall, Jonathan M. *Operation Crossroads: The atomic tests at Bikini Atoll.* Ramey retired from the Air Force as director of the Air Defense Command in 1957 as a three-star general. It remains curious that as a lt. general with a most impressive military history, including an Air Force base named after him, Ramey's biography is not included at the USAF Website, which does provide backgrounds on more than 2,000 other high-ranking officers.

Chapter 10

1. Patricia Rice, telephone interview, 6/3/2000 (and quoted in the *Dallas Morning News*, 7/6/1997).

2. Earl V. Fulford, telephone interviews, 2005–2006.

3. The wording of the press release strongly suggested that the 509th Bomb Group had in its possession the previous day, July 7, 1947 (even before Maj. Marcel had returned from the debris field on the Foster ranch in Lincoln County), enough evidence to conclude that the recovery then in progress involved an extraterrestrial event. It also suggests that the military was trying to divert the attention of the Roswell citizenry away from the crash site just north of town to a site farther away, nearer to Corona.

4. Richard Talbert, telephone interviews, 2003–2004.

5. May Rich (Rich's widow), telephone interview, 2004.

6. Paul McFerrin, telephone interview, 2003.

7. Jobie MacPherson, telephone interviews, 2001–2002.

8. Michael Menagh and Rolland Menagh, Jr., telephone interviews, 2005.

9. Earl Fulford, telephone interviews, 2005–2006.

10. Harvie L. Davis, telephone interview, 2005.

11. John Bunch, telephone interview, 2006.

12. Eugene C. Helnes, telephone interviews, 2005.

13. Earl Fulford, telephone interviews, 2005–2006.

14. George D. Houck, telephone interview, 2005.

15. Earl Fulford, telephone interviews, 2005–2006.

16. Ibid. There were in fact several courts-martial handed down at the time: Earl D. Downs was a PFC with the 390th ASS in charge of a detachment of airmen guarding the hangar containing the wreckage—he was court-martialed and thrown in the brig for several months along with the men of his detachment because one of them had, unknown to him, pocketed a small piece of wreckage from the hangar they were guarding.

17. Harry Girard, telephone interview, 2005.

18. Steve Whalen, Jr., telephone interview, 2005.

19. Earl Fulford, telephone interviews, 2005–2006. Fulford's account receives corroboration from the former S.Sgt. Milton C. Sprouse, who was a B-29 crew chief in the 830th Bomb Squadron in 1947. In a telephone interview in 2001, the 74-year-old Sprouse told our investigation that he and his crew had just returned to Roswell from Florida on *Dave's Dream* the evening of July 7. Sprouse said that the base was buzzing with talk about the crash. A week or so later, a few of Sprouse's buddies told him that they had been working late on one of the Silverplates the previous evening. They told Sprouse that they witnessed a C-54 transport pull up in front of the hangar (Hangar P-3), whereupon it was loaded with pieces of wreckage. They especially remembered one large piece that was loaded, but they couldn't get a closer look because of the guards posted around the hangar. "The rumor was that General Ramey was on the plane." In the morning, the plane was gone, and the hangar was empty.

Chapter 11

1. Thomas J. DuBose, personal interview, 1991.

2. Robert J. Barrowclough, personal interview, 2000.

3. Robert R. Porter, personal interview, 1991.

4. Walter G. Haut, personal interviews, 1989–2005.

5. James B. Johnson, personal interview, 1990.

6. Robert Porter, personal interview, 1991.

7. Robert B. Shirkey, personal interviews, 1990–2002.

8. Ibid.

9. Robert Porter, personal interview, 1991.

10. Ibid.

11. The famous images of Gen. Ramey's press conference on 7/8/49 have become temporarily misplaced between their original repository at the University of Texas, Arlington, and its successor proprietor, Corbis, Inc. Permission to include them here, therefore, could not be obtained.

Chapter 12

1. Rosemary McManus, personal interview, 1994.

2. *Atomic Blast*, February 21, 1947 (RAAF base newspaper).

3. Patricia Bush, personal interviews, 2004, 2006.

4. Glenn Dennis, personal interview, 1990.

5. E.M. Hall, personal interview, 1993.

6. George Bush, personal interview.

7. Ibid.

8. Ibid.

9. Ibid.

10. Jean Bush Overton, telephone interview, 1992.

11. Patricia Bush, personal interviews, 2004–2006.

12. Ibid.

13. Victor Golubic, quoted in *Roswell: Inconvenient Facts and the Will to Believe.*

Chapter 13

1. Berlitz, Charles, and William L. Moore. *The Roswell Incident.*

2. Randle, Kevin D. and Donald R. Schmitt, *UFO Crash At Roswell.*

3. Interview of the late Melvin Brown's daughter, Beverly Bean, in *Recollections of Roswell Part II*, Fund for UFO Research, Mt. Rainier, MD: 1992.

4. Interview of the late Pappy Henderson's wife, Sappho Henderson, in *Recollections of Roswell, Part II.*

5. Interview of Glenn Dennis, in *Recollections of Roswell, Part II.*

6. Randle and Schmitt, *The Truth About the UFO Crash at Roswell.*

7. The late Frank Kaufmann, a former personnel clerk at the Roswell base and later a 30-year member of the Roswell

Chamber of Commerce, claimed to have been a member of a super-secret ensemble, "The Nine." According to Kaufmann, the group was responsible for containing highly classified accidents and operations, such as that presented by the Roswell UFO recovery from the public. Before his death, Kaufmann admitted to us that he made up the Roswell crash site location. Asked why he didn't say anything previously when so much attention was being paid to it by the media, Kaufmann simply said, "It got out of control."

8. Loretta Proctor, personal interview, 1996. This site, known as the "Dee Proctor Body Site" is the *someplace else* where Mack Brazel told Frank Joyce that he had found bodies of "little people" during his first conversation with Joyce on July 6, 1947.

9. Edward Sain, telephone interview, 2005.

10. Steven Sain, telephone interview, 2005.

11. Mrs. Raymond Van Why, telephone interview, 2005. Mrs. Van Why's account of her husband's observation of a "disc" and Edward Sain's identification of Van Why as the one who guarded the bodies with him suggests that Van Why had been a guard at two sites: the impact site and the Dee Proctor Body Site.

12. Mrs. Wallace, in-person interview for our investigation, conducted by Dennis Balthaser, 1999.

13. From Frederick Benthal's notarized statement, signed May 5, 1993; see also Benthal's videotaped interview in *UFO Secret: the Roswell Crash 2000*, UFO Central Home Video, Inc., Venice, CA: 2001.

14. William J. Warnke, telephone interview, 2006.

15. Monte Dalton, telephone interview, 2005.

16. Pflock, Karl, *Roswell: Inconvenient Facts and the Will to Believe.* Dennis also confirmed this account to us several times since 1998.

17. Arthur Fluery's widow, telephone interview, 2005. Paul Camerato's widow confirmed her late husband's presence as an ambulance driver in Roswell at the time of the incident but could provide no additional information.

18. Mr. and Mrs. Eli Benjamin, personal interviews, 2003–2006.

Chapter 14

1. Leonard Stringfield, *The UFO Crash/Retrieval Syndrome*. Seguin, Texas: MUFON, 1980. Also, personal interviews, 1990–1992.

2. Ibid.

3. Ibid.

4. Ibid.

5. Beverly Bean, personal interview, 1991.

6. Leonard Stringfield, personal interviews, 1990–1992.

7. Son, (anonymity requested) of Dr. Foster's housekeeper (anonymity requested), personal interview, 1992.

8. Daughter, (anonymity requested), 1992.

Chapter 15

1. The witness list includes first-, second-, and third-hand witnesses. Legal proceedings consider anything other than first-hand, eyewitness testimony as "hearsay." However, if enough "hearsay" testimony is gathered that supports the case being presented, it can form the basis for a powerful corroboration of the case.

2. During WWII, Native Americans were often utilized in situations that required the implementation of extreme security, the thought being that Native Americans could be trusted to keep their mouths shut. At the RAAF in 1947, there was a small security detachment of Native Americans utilized in such highly sensitive situations.

3. Edward Harrison, personal interview, 2005.

4. The 393rd Bomb Squadron was the original bomb squadron of the 509th Composite Group when it was formed in 1944. It wasn't until after the war, when the 509th deployed to Roswell, that two additional bomb squadrons, the 715th and the 830th, joined the Bomb Group.

5. During the atomic bombing of Hiroshima, the *Necessary Evil* was responsible for photographing the event for posterity, while the *Straight Flush* was responsible for monitoring the weather over the target.

Chapter 17

1. Fawn Fritz, personal interview, 2006; Ardeth Vandercook, telephone interview, 2000.
2. Frank Joyce, personal interviews, 1998–2002.
3. Scroggins' widows, telephone interviews, 1999–2000.
4. Frankie Dwyer Rowe, personal interviews over many years.
5. AP wire story that ran in the *Albuquerque Journal* and *San Antonio Express*, unattributed but likely authored by Jason Kellahin. This information was given to us by Roswell researcher David Rudiak (see also *www.roswellproof.com*).
6. Randle and Schmitt. *The Truth About the UFO Crash at Roswell*.
7. Ibid.
8. Barbara Dugger, granddaughter of George and Inez Wilcox, videotaped interview in *Recollections of Roswell Part II*.

Chapter 18

1. Arthur Exon, personal and telephone interviews over many years.
2. When trying to recall a 60-year-old event, this defense is not outside the realm of believability.
3. Horatio held off the entire Etruscan army from advancing on Rome by single-handedly controlling their access to the city via a small bridge over the Tiber River.
4. Tommy Thompson, personal interviews, 1998, 2001.
5. Edwin Easley, telephone interview conducted by Kevin Randle; Nancy Easley Johnson (Edwin's daughter), personal interviews, 2002.
6. Sheridan and Mary Cavitt, personal interviews, 1990s.
7. Lewis S. "Bill" Rickett, personal interviews, 1989–1992.
8. Ibid. The son of Sheridan Cavitt, Joe, a practicing attorney, passed on to our investigation an interesting story about the time the entire family was sitting down to Thanksgiving dinner in the mid-1980's. Joe made the mistake of asking his father, "Well dad, whatever became of that "black box" you guys found at Roswell?" According to Joe, the remark caught his father completely by surprise. "He just sat there for a moment, turned red, gritted his teeth, got up from his chair and stormed from the room. I never brought it up again."

9. Lewis Rickett, personal interviews, 1989–1992.

10. Ibid.

11. Ibid.

12. Lewis Rickett, Mrs. Lewis Rickett, Sheridan Cavitt, Mrs. Sheridan Cavitt, personal interviews.

Chapter 19

1. McBoyle's son and daughter-in-law, telephone interview, 1999; Berlitz and Moore, *The Roswell Incident*.

2. Tommy Thompson, personal interviews, 1998, 2000.

3. Berlitz and Moore, *The Roswell Incident*.

4. *The Roswell Report: Fact vs. Fiction in the New Mexico Desert*, by Col. Richard L. Weaver, United States Air Force, 1995.

5. Lewis Ricket, personal interviews, 1989–1992; videotaped interview of Rickett in *Recollections of Roswell Part II*, 1992.

6. Sheridan and Mrs. Cavitt, personal interviews conducted by Kevin Randle and Donald Schmitt, 1990s.

7. Mrs. Mary Cavitt, personal interviews, 1990s; "Will the Real Sheridan Cavitt Please Stand Up?" by Thomas J. Carey in the *International UFO Reporter*.

Chapter 20

1. Gen. William H. Blanchard's daughter, Dale, quoted in "Did a UFO Really Crash in Roswell?" by Jill H. Lawrence in *Paradigm*, September 1996.

2. Marion Brimberry, telephone interview, 2000.

3. Lewis "Bill" Rickett, personal interviews, 1989–1992.

4. Ibid.

5. Ibid.

6. Ibid.

Chapter 21

1. U.S. Intelligence Community: Organization, Operations and Management.

2. FBI Dallas Bureau Transmission, July 8, 1947.

3. Arthur Exon, personal interviews, 1990–1991, 1994, 2000.

4. Ibid.
5. Ibid.
6. Ibid.
7. Ibid.
8. Joseph Briley, personal interviews, 1992, 2000, 2006.
9. Arthur Exon, personal interviews, 1990–1991, 1994, 2000.
10. Ibid.
11. El Paso radio interview of Gen. Roger Ramey in which it was stated that "...only people in Kansas didn't report any flying saucers because it was a dry state." Prior to the Roswell Incident, Ramey is quoted as referring to such reports as "Buck Rogers stuff." Ramey said, "People were probably seeing heat waves or misidentifying distant jet planes." Associated Press/United Press International.
12. U.S. Intelligence Community: Organization, Operations and Management.

Chapter 22

1. Edwin Easley, telephone interview, 1990.
2. Nancy Strickland, personal interviews, 1990, 1992, 2002.
3. Dr. Harold Granek, personal interviews, 1991, 2002.
4. Family of Patrick Saunders, personal interviews, 1991, 1995.
5. Sarah Mounce, telephone interview, 2000.
6. Wanda Lida, telephone interview, 2000.
7. Larry Rowlette, personal interview, 2005.
8. Carlene Rowlette Green, personal interview, 2005.
9. Beverly Bean, personal interview, 1991.
10. Elaine Vegh, personal interview, 1990.
11. Mary Ann Gardner, personal interview, 1990.
12. Barbara Dugger, personal interview, 1991.
13. Blanche Wahnee, Wanda Wahnee Priddy, and Meyers Wahnee, Jr. (Meyers Wahnee's children), telephone interviews, 2005.
14. Sheridan Cavitt, personal interviews, 1990–1994.
15. Mary Cavitt, personal interviews, 1990–2000.
16. Joseph Cavitt, personal interview, 1998.
17. Cavitt personal physician (anonymity requested), personal interview, 2001.

Chapter 23

1. The quote is attributed to an unnamed former military officer by the late Karl Pflock in his 2001 book *Roswell: Inconvenient Facts and the Will to Believe.*

2. Proof of this came from an interview that we conducted in 2002 with the 74-year-old Lloyd E. Nelson, a former PFC who clerked for Walter Haut in the RAAF base Public Information Office in 1947. According to Nelson, he remembers Walter Haut coming into the office at the time of the incident with Maj. Marcel. He had assumed that his boss and Marcel had just come back from the crash site, because each was holding and showing around the office small pieces of wreckage debris. "I was shown an I-beam or two by Marcel and Walter that were very short and had reddish writing on them that I did not recognize. I handled these myself. I also handled a very hard ceramic-type material like flint that appeared to have been broken off something. It was darker on one side and lighter on the other. It really wasn't metal. I also was shown and handled three pieces of very thin, aluminum-like metal, which was very hard. Marcel told me that they had been testing the metal and that all of it was very light and very hard, and that it was unlike anything that anyone had ever seen. Before they left the office, Marcel and Walter told everyone present not to say anything about what they had just seen. I believe that this meeting took place on Friday, July 11, because I remember that I didn't work the next day." In 2000 or 2001, Lloyd Nelson called Walter Haut to try to find out what Walter knew and why he had been so quiet about it over the ensuing years, considering what he knew to be true about Walter. "To my dismay," Nelson told us, "Walter would not confirm anything to me. I know that he was there, but he wouldn't admit it, even to me."

3. Walter Haut, personal interviews, 1989–2002.

Bibliography

Anderson, Jack, and Michael Binstein. "Air Force Tried to Lead Everyone Astray on Roswell Incident." *Albuquerque Journal.* June 1, 1995.

Berlitz, Charles, and William L. Moore. *The Roswell Incident.* New York: Grosset & Dunlap, 1980.

Broad, William J. "Wreckage of a 'Spaceship': Of This Earth (and U.S.)." *The New York Times.* Sept. 18, 1994.

Brokaw, Tom. *The Greatest Generation.* New York: Random House, 1998.

Bullard, Thomas E. "Folklore Scholarship and UFO Reality." *International UFO Reporter.* Sept./Oct., 1988.

Campbell, John W., Jr. "Who goes there?" *Astounding Science Fiction.* New York: Street & Smith. August, 1938.

Carey, Thomas J. "Will the real Sheridan Cavitt, please stand up?" *International UFO Reporter.* Vol. 23, No. 3. Fall, 1998.

Carey, Tom, and Don Schmitt. *Witness to Roswell* [Magazine]. Roswell, N.M.: Triton, 2003.

Dennis, Glenn. *1947 Roswell Incident.* Roswell, N.M.: Alpha-Omega, 1991.

Fuhrman, Mark. *Murder in Greenwich: Who Killed Martha Moxley?* New York: HarperCollins, 1998.

"Gen. Ramey Empties Roswell Saucer." *Roswell Daily Record.* July 9, 1947.

"Harassed Rancher Who Located 'Saucer' Sorry He Told About It." *Roswell Daily Record.* July 9, 1947.

Headquarters United States Air Force. Capt. James McAndrew. *The Roswell Report: Case Closed.* Washington, D.C.: Barnes & Noble by arrangement with the U.S. Government Printing Office, 1997.

Headquarters United States Air Force. Col. Richard L. Weaver. *Report of Air Force Research Regarding the 'Roswell Incident.'* Washington, D.C.: U.S. Government Printing Office, 1994.

Headquarters United States Air Force. Col. Richard L. Weaver and 1st Lt. James McAndrew. *The Roswell Report: Fact vs. Fiction in the New Mexico Desert.* Washington, D.C.: U.S. Government Printing Office, 1995.

Lawrence, Jill H. "Did a UFO Really Crash at Roswell?" *Paradigm.* September, 1996.

McAvennie, Mike, ed., with contributions from William H. Doleman, Ph.D., Thomas J. Carey, and Donald R. Schmitt. *A Sci Fi Channel Book: The Roswell Dig Diaries.* New York: Pocket Books, 2004.

"New Base Surgeon Assigned to Sqdn. M." *The Atomic Blast.* Public Information Office of the 509th Bomb Group, RAAF. Feb. 21, 1947.

Pflock, Karl T. *Roswell: Inconvenient Facts and the Will to Believe.* Amherst, N.Y.: Prometheus Books, 2001.

"RAAF Captures Flying Saucer On Ranch in Roswell Region." *Roswell Daily Record.* July 8, 1947.

RAAF Roswell, New Mexico [509th Bomb Group/Roswell Army Air Field Yearbook]. Roswell, N.M.: RAAF, 1947.

Randle, Kevin D., and Donald R. Schmitt. *The Truth About the UFO Crash at Roswell.* New York: Avon Books, 1994.

───────. *UFO Crash at Roswell.* New York: Avon Books, 1991.

Recollections of Roswell, Part II. Mount Rainier, Md.: Fund for UFO Research, 1992.

Research Division, College of Engineering, NYU. *Technical Report No. 93.02: Constant Level Balloons.* Jan. 31, 1949.

Rice, Patricia D. "Roswell Aliens: Air Force Deception." Letter to the *Dallas Morning News.* July 6, 1997.

Richelson, Jeffrey. *The U.S. Intelligence Community: Organization, Operations and Management, 1947–1989, 3rd Edition.* Boulder, Colo.: Westview Press, 1995.

The Roswell Crash: Startling New Evidence. The Sci Fi Channel, 2002.

Roswell Remembered: A City on the Edge of History. Crystal Sky Productions, 1995.

Roswell: The UFO Cover-Up. Showtime/Viacom, 1994.

Ruppelt, Edward J. *The Report on Unidentified Objects*. Garden City, N.Y.: Doubleday, 1956.

Schiff, Steven. "News Release." Release of GAO report detailing results of records search related to events surrounding alleged 1947 UFO crash near Roswell, N.M. July 28, 1995.

Shawcross, Tim. *The Roswell File*. Osceola, Wisc.: Motorbooks, 1997.

Shirkey, Robert J. *Roswell 1947: 'I Was There'*. Roswell, N.M.: Movin' On, 1999.

Stowers, Carlton. "A half century later, witnesses insist little green—or maybe brown—men crashed in New Mexico." From *www.dallasobserver.com*. Originally published by the *Dallas Observer*. April 3, 2003.

Stringfield, Leonard H. "Roswell & The X-15: UFO Basics." *Mufon UFO Journal*. No. 259, November, 1989.

————. "We Are Now A Part Of History." *UFO Crash/Retrievals Status Report VI: The Inner Sanctum*. Cincinnati, Ohio: Leonard H. Stringfield, 1991.

UFO Secret: the Roswell Crash 2000. Venice, Calif.: UFO Central Home Video, 2001.

"UFOs: Seeing is Believing." *Peter Jennings Reporting*. ABC News. Feb. 24, 2005.

United States General Accounting Office. *Results of a Search for Records Concerning the 1947 Crash Near Roswell, New Mexico*. Pub. No. GAO/NSIAD-95-187. Washington, D.C.: GAO, 1995.

Vigil, Maurilio, and Roy Lujan. "Parallels in the Careers of Two Hispanic U.S. Senators." *New Mexico Historical Review*. No. 47. October, 1972.

Weisgall, Jonathan M. *Operation Crossroads: the Atomic Tests at Bikini Atoll*. Annapolis, M.D.: Naval Institute Press. April, 1994.

Index

About the Authors

Thomas J. Carey, a native Philadelphian, resides in Huntingdon Valley, Pennsylvania. He holds degrees from Temple University (B.S.) and California State University, Sacramento (M.A.), and also attended the University of Toronto for its Ph.D. program in anthropology. An Air Force veteran who held a Top Secret/Crypto clearance, Tom is now a Philadelphia area businessman. He has also been a Mutual UFO Network (MUFON) state section sirector in Southeastern Pennsylvania from 1986 to 2002, a special investigator for the J. Allen Hynek Center for UFO Studies from 1991 to 2001, and a member of the CUFOS board of directors from 1997 to 2001. Tom began investigating aspects of the Roswell Incident in 1991 for the Roswell investigative team of Kevin Randle and Don Schmitt, and since 1998 has teamed exclusively with Don Schmitt to continue a proactive investigation of the case. Tom has authored or coauthored more than 30 published articles about the Roswell events of 1947, and has contributed to a number of books on the subject as well. He has appeared as a guest on many radio and TV shows throughout the country and has contributed to a number of Roswell-related documentaries on-screen and behind the scenes. Most recently, Tom was a consultant and interviewee (with Don Schmitt) on the highly acclaimed and rated Sci Fi Channel documentary, *The Roswell Crash: Startling New Evidence*, the History Channel's *Conspiracy Theory—Roswell*, the Travel Channel's *Weird Travels—Roswell*, and the Sci Fi Channel's *Sci Fi Investigates—Roswell*. Tom and his wife Doreen have two grown children.

Donald R. Schmitt resides in his native Wisconsin on a 45-acre ranch located just outside of Milwaukee in a little hamlet called Hubertus. Don possesses a Bachelors degree from Concordia University and has taken graduate courses in criminal justice at St. John's University. He has worked for the U.S. Postal Service for the past 23 years. A talented artist, he has also freelanced as a medical and commercial illustrator. Possessing a fine baritone voice, Don also sings publicly for special occasions in the Milwaukee area. Don is the former director of special investigations and codirector of the J. Allen Hynek Center for UFO Studies (CUFOS). He teamed with Kevin Randle in 1988 to investigate the Roswell Incident, a collaboration that resulted in many published articles and two best-selling books, *UFO Crash at Roswell* and *The Truth About the UFO Crash at Roswell*. The critically acclaimed movie, *Roswell*, to which Don was a consultant, was based on the first book. Teaming with Tom Carey in 1998, Don has vowed to continue a proactive Roswell investigation until the ultimate truth is learned. Don and his wife Marie are relative newlyweds, having been married for just more than two years.